America's Commitment to Culture

America's Commitment to Culture

Government and the Arts

EDITED BY
Kevin V. Mulcahy and Margaret Jane Wyszomirski

Routledge
Taylor & Francis Group
NEW YORK AND LONDON

First published 1995 by Westview Press, Inc.

Published 2021 by Routledge
605 Third Avenue, New York, NY 10017
2 Park Square, Milton Park, Abingdon, Oxon OX14 4RN

Routledge is an imprint of the Taylor & Francis Group, an informa business

Copyright © 1995 by Taylor & Francis

All rights reserved. No part of this book may be reprinted or reproduced or utilised in any form or by any electronic, mechanical, or other means, now known or hereafter invented, including photocopying and recording, or in any information storage or retrieval system, without permission in writing from the publishers.

Notice:
Product or corporate names may be trademarks or registered trademarks, and are used only for identification and explanation without intent to infringe.

**A CIP catalog record for this book is available from the Library of Congress.
ISBN 0-8133-0692-2**

ISBN 13: 978-0-3670-0710-2 (hbk)
ISBN 13: 978-0-3671-5697-8 (pbk)

For

Emily D. Mulcahy, again

and

Dorothea Wyszomirski Bower

Contents

Acknowledgments   xi
About the Editors and Contributors   xiii

1 **From Accord to Discord: Arts Policy During and After the Culture Wars**, Margaret Jane Wyszomirski   1

    The Controversy of 1989-1990, 2
    Continuing Skirmishes: 1991 and 1992, 10
    Myths and Misconceptions, 19
    Changes and Challenges in the Arts Policy Context, 32
    From Accord to Discord and Beyond, 39

2 **The Politics of Arts Policy: Subgovernment to Issue Network**, Margaret Jane Wyszomirski   47

    Policy and Policy Systems, 48
    Prelude: Establishing the Arts on the Federal Agenda, 50
    The Development of an Arts Subgovernment, 53
    A Mature Arts Subgovernment in Action, 56
    Counterpoint in the 1980's: Conflict and Erosion, 60
    A Changed Policy Politics, 66

3 **Federal Arts Patronage in the New Deal**, Lawrence D. Mankin   77

    New Deal Programs: The Support, 77
    WPA Art Programs: The Attack, 83
    Accomplishments of WPA Arts Projects, 88
    Conclusion, 91

4 **To Change a Nation's Cultural Policy: The Kennedy Administration and the Arts in the United States, 1961-1963**, *Milton C. Cummings, Jr.*   95

    Prologue, 95
    The Beginning, 98
    Groping for a Policy, 99
    Defeat in the House of Representatives, 102
    A Special Consultant to the President for the Arts, 103
    The Job of the Special Consultant, 106
    The Advisory Council on the Arts, 108
    The Role of the Arts Constituency, 109
    The Final Months, 111
    Epilogue, 112
    John F. Kennedy and the Arts -- An Assessment, 114

5 **The Organization of Public Support for the Arts**, *Margaret Jane Wyszomirski and Kevin V. Mulcahy*   121

    A Range of Federal Arts Activity, 122
    The National Endowment for the Arts, 125
    The Intergovernmental System of Support for the Arts, 132
    Public Support for the Arts: The Record and Future Challenges, 137

6 **Leadership and the NEA: The Roles of the Chairperson and the National Council on the Arts**, *David B. Pankratz and Carla Hanzal*   144

    The NEA Chairperson and the National Council: Authorizing Language, 144
    Council Roles and Procedures, 146
    The Roles and Records of the NEA Chairman, 149
    The Stevens Years (1966-69), 150
    The Hanks Years (1969-77), 152
    The Biddle Years (1977-81), 155
    The Hodsoll Years (1981-89), 157
    The Frohnmayer Years (1989-92), 161
    Leadership and the NEA, 164

7   **The NEA and the Reauthorization Process: Congress
    and Arts Policy Issues**, *Kevin V. Mulcahy*   169

   Do Advisory Panels Provide an Impartial System for
      Awarding Grants? 172
   Is the Geographic Distribution of Grants Equitable? 174
   Who Should Receive Public Support? 176
   What is the Government's Responsibility to Promote
      Good Art? 177
   Should Public Arts Policy Be Populist or Elitist? 180
   What is the Record of the Arts Agency? 181
   Concluding Observations, 183

8   **The Process of Commissioning Public Sculpture:
    "Due" or "Duel,"** *Judith Huggins Balfe*   189

   Public Arts Commissioning During the New Deal, 191
   Alternative Contemporary Models: the NEA and GSA, 193
   "Tilted Arc" and the Vietnam Memorial, 196
   Art in Transit, 200
   The Future of Public Art Commissions, 202

9   **The Public Interest and Arts Policy**,
    Kevin V. Mulcahy   205

   The "Kulturkampf" in Political Perspective, 205
   Public Culture and Private Culture, 209
   Reorganizing the NEA by Goal, 212
   Institutional Support, 215
   Arts Development, 215
   Arts Education, 216
   Individual Artist Support, 217
   Panels, Representativeness, and Public Support for
      the Arts, 217
   Arts Policy and Public Accountability, 220
   Toward a Latitudinarian Arts Policy, 223

Index   229
About the Book   235

Acknowledgments

The preparation of this book would not have been possible without the indefatigable labor provided by the students at Louisiana State University in the Chancellor's Undergraduate Assistant Scholarship Programs. These student workers included: Kerry Miller, Rodd Naquin, Veronica Haynes, Bryan Pourciau, John Archambeault, Niki Woodson, Nalini Raghavan and Katherine Signorelli. Besides word processing, photocopying, citation checking, and other office duties, these students demonstrated unstinting good cheer and patience. Special thanks is also due to Eric Johnson, Morris Garner, Tonia Chiesa, and Kell Mercer, who as undergraduate research assistants at LSU provided invaluable help in the realization of this project.

Special thanks also go to Mindy Berry and Nancy Farley for their able and timely research assistance and to the Georgetown University Graduate Public Policy Program for its support and assistance while this project was being finished. We are also grateful to various colleagues, particularly Judith H. Balfe of CUNY-Staten Island, Arch Dotson of Cornell University, and Roberta Dunn in Washington, D.C., who read and commented on early drafts of various chapters.

Kevin V. Mulcahy
Margaret Jane Wyszomirski

About the Editors and Contributors

Kevin V. Mulcahy (Ph.D., Brown, 1976) is a professor of Political Science at Louisiana State University. Among other works, he is the coeditor of *Public Policy and the Arts* and *The Challenge to Reform Arts Education*. He is a former cultural adviser to the Speaker of the Louisiana house of Representatives and testified as an expert witness before congressionally-mandated Independent Commission on the National Endowment for the Arts. Currently he is doing research on cultural policy making in France and Quebec.

Margaret Jane Wyszomirski (Ph.D., Cornell, 1979) is a professor of Political Science and Director of the Arts Management Program at Case Western Reserve University. From 1985 to 1988, she directed the Georgetown University Graduate Public Policy Program. In 1990, she was the Staff Director of the Independent Commission on the National Endowment for the Arts and from 1991 through 1993 was Director of Policy, Planning, Research and Budget at the National Endowment for the Arts. She has written extensively on art and cultural policy and the presidency and served on the editorial boards of three scholarly journals and on the advisory committees of various national research projects.

Judith Huggins Balfe (Ph.D., Rutgers, 1979) is associate professor of sociology at the City University of New York. She has chaired three of the Annual Conferences on Social Theory, Politics and the Arts and is the executive editor of *The Journal of Arts Management, Law and Society*. She is co-editor of *Art, Ideology and Politics*; *Arts Education Beyond the Classroom;* and editor of *Paying the Piper: Causes and Consequences of Art Patronage*.

Milton C. Cummings, Jr. (Ph.D., Harvard, 1960) is a professor of political science at Johns Hopkins University. In addition to many works on american government and politics, he is the coeditor of *The Patron State: Government and the Arts in Industrialized Democracies*.

Carla Hanzal (M.A., American University,1992) is an artist and arts manager in Washington, D.C. In 1990 she served as Research Associate for the Independent Commission on the National Endowment for the Arts. Currently, she is Exhibitions Director at the International Sculpture Center, Washington, D.C.

Lawrence D. Mankin (Ph.D., University of Illinois, 1976) is professor of Public Affairs and Special Assistant to the President of Arizona State University. He has published articles on public personnel management and public policy and the arts. He has also served on the Government Relations Committee of the Phoenix Symphony.

David B. Pankratz (Ph.D., Ohio State, 1992) is an arts consultant based in Alexandria, Virginia. Among other writings, he is the author of *Multiculturalism and the Arts* and coeditor of *The Challenge to Reform Arts Education.* Formerly the Director of Program Development at Urban Gateways: The Center for Arts in Education, he also served as associate director of the 1990 Independent Commission on the National Endowment for the Arts.

1

From Accord to Discord: Arts Policy During and After the Culture Wars

Margaret Jane Wyszomirski

Indirect, sporadic, narrow and tentative. Historically, this has characterized the commitment to culture and the arts of the United States government. Only in 1965, amidst lofty sentiments, worthy intentions and some trepidation, did the federal government begin a very modest program of ongoing support for arts and humanities activities with the establishment of the National Endowments for the Arts and for the Humanities. During the subsequent three decades, over three billion dollars were appropriated to the National Endowment for the Arts (NEA) to foster the nonprofit arts in America and to expand arts participation opportunities for citizens across the nation. In turn, these federal funds have been a catalyst and an example for increased state, corporate, and foundation support for the arts.

For many years, the agency gained political support and artsworld applause while generating little controversy or criticism. Yet despite a largely positive record, the principle of federal support for the arts continues to be contested: sometimes by artists who fear the possible heavy hand of government control; other times by those who see it as an instance of government waste or overreach. In 1989, the NEA began to confront the most serious political challenge of its administrative life. The controversy revealed many inherent ambiguities of principle, purpose, and priority in federal arts policy. It also demonstrated how much the political dynamics and environment of arts policy had changed. By the late 1980's, the world had become fundamentally different from what it had been in the mid-1960's.

The Controversy of 1989-1990

Each Spring, Congress considers an annual appropriations bill to that will fund the National Endowment for the Arts. Generally, this process is focussed in the Interior Appropriations subcommittee of the U.S. House of Representatives where Congressman Sidney Yates (D-IL) conducts a friendly inquiry into the recent activities and pending requests of the NEA. Typically, NEA program directors provide illustrations of how far the agency's money has stretched in support of worthy arts activities. Only in the earliest years of the Reagan Administration was the budget of the NEA threatened with significant cuts as part of an overall critique of "Big Government." In response, both the arts community and congressional supporters effectively mobilized to protect the agency's funds from serious and exceptional reduction. More commonly, the testimony of both agency and public witnesses presented a contrapunctual litany: one part stressing the benefits additional funds could engender, while another part bemoans the inadequacy of current funds and the lack of real growth since the late 1970's. Congressional supporters would sympathize with the funding complaints, perhaps add a little to the proposed budget, and compliment the agency for its good work.

This congenial pattern of action changed abruptly in 1989, as a storm of criticism and controversy began to gather around the NEA. At first, it focussed on Andres Serrano's photograph of a crucifix immersed in urine and entitled "Piss Christ." The NEA had awarded a grant of $75,000 to the Southeast Center for Contemporary Art (SECCA) to support a program called "Awards in the Visual Arts" -- a program that had been winning NEA support since 1981. Serrano was one of ten artists selected by a SECCA panel of five jurors to receive a $15,000 fellowship. Part of the award also sponsored a travelling exhibit that included works by all the fellowship artists; that show included the photograph "Piss Christ." When an NEA Visual Arts panel had reviewed SECCA's application in March 1987, specific artists or artworks were not identified. The final stop of the travelling exhibit was Richmond, Virginia, where it attracted the attention and provoked a letter-writing campaign by the Reverend Donald Wildmon's American Family Association. This criticism was soon taken up by televangelist Pat Robertson, who condemned the work and the exhibit on his Christian Broadcasting Network as "blasphemy paid for by the government." Senator Alphonse D'Amato (R-NY) denounced the Serrano photograph as a "...piece of filth..." which was "...a deplorable, despicable display of vulgarity."[1] Senator Helms (R-NC) was concerned that ...the National Endowment's procedures for selecting artists and works of art deserving of taxpayer support are badly, badly flawed if this is an example of the kind of programs they fund with taxpayers' money."[2] Reacting to the Serrano grant, a letter co-signed by twenty-five Senators was sent to acting NEA Chairman, Hugh Southern, asking the Endowment to review and reform its grant-making procedures.

During June 1989, art figured prominently in two other controversies. In one instance, another NEA grant attracted congressional protest as Representative Richard Armey (R-TX) and more than one hundred members of Congress wrote the NEA in protest of its funding for the museum exhibit, "Robert Mapplethorpe: The Perfect Moment" which included portraits, flower studies, nudes of children, and homoerotic works, including the now notorious photos of one man urinating into the mouth of another and the picture of the artist with a bullwhip sticking out of his rectum. The travelling exhibit, organized by the Institute of Contemporary Art at the University of Pennsylvania, had been recommended for its $30,000 NEA grant by a peer panel that, it was later learned, had been rife with conflicts of interest. Also that month, the United States Supreme Court ruled that desecration of the flag was protected speech. The decision invalidated anti-desecration laws in forty-eight states, including those of Illinois that had been enacted the previous year in response to a student exhibit at the School of the Art Institute of Chicago. The exhibit included Scott Tyler's work entitled, "What is the Proper Way to Display a U.S. Flag?" Tyler's work included an actual U.S. flag placed on the gallery floor, inviting viewer comments and responses to the question posed; in order to comment, viewers had to step on the flag to reach the ledger. Throughout the Summer, public funding for the arts and flag desecration became the twin peaks of a symbolic politics of values and standards.

In July, the Mapplethorpe exhibit was scheduled to appear at the Corcoran Gallery in Washington, D.C. Aware that the show was attracting unusual public criticism and concerned that some of the nudes of children might run afoul of District of Columbia regulations concerning child pornography, the Corcoran canceled the show. In doing so, the museum stated that it felt its action to be "prudent" because, in the circumstances, the show might "be so inflammatory and provocative as to invite consequences" negative to the museum and to the NEA.[3] Members of the artistic community decried the Corcoran action as "capitulation" to political pressure that could cost the institution its professional credibility.[4] Jock Reynolds, Director of the Washington Project for the Arts called the Corcoran cancellation "an insult to [the] public's intelligence" that exhibited "bad faith toward the public [and] toward the artist."[5] Eventually, to protest the museum's action, more than a dozen artists withdrew from two exhibits designed to survey trends in contemporary art at the Corcoran.[6] By the end of the year, Corcoran director, Christina Orr-Cahall resigned as director of the museum. Thus, the clamor from the right was joined by outrage from the left in a battle over community standards vs. professional standards, of obscenity and blasphemy vs. artistic freedom.

On one side, conservatives and religious groups contended that both the NEA and its artistic constituency seemed to regard expressions of the aesthetic taste (or distaste) of taxpayers as unwarranted interference and potential censorship while treating the tastes and opinions of arts professionals and peer panelists as incontrovertible.[7] On the other side, artists and their civil libertarian allies asserted that "those who receive public funds deserve the freedom to create...regardless of its possible interpretation by some as disagreeable or offensive."[8] Congressman Dana Rohrabacher (R-CA) argued that "the answer is getting the government out of the arts," while Representative Charles Stenholm (D-TX) suggested a cut in the NEA's budget as "a shot across the bow...sending the appropriate message" of Congressional concern.[9] Even the NEA's staunchest supporters, such as Senator Claiborne Pell (D-RI) offered that "...serious errors in judgment were made when such works were recommended for funding by their respective peer panels" and Senator Ted Kennedy called the controversial grants "aberrations."[10] The NEA's appropriations subcommittee chairman Representative Sidney Yates (D-IL) proposed changes in the agency's subgranting procedures that would make the Endowment more responsive and accountable for the work it supported.

Meanwhile, the NEA, headed by an acting chairman and awaiting the appointment of a new chairman by the Bush Administration, was alternatively thunderstruck by the intensity of the uproar and naively hopeful that the controversy would blow over. Instead, the agency's annual budget review stretched through the summer and into the autumn of 1989, expanding beyond the normal confines of the Interior Appropriations subcommittee onto floor debate in both Houses as it attracted extensive media coverage. While Congress considered an array of amendments to the NEA's appropriation bill, it rejected the more drastic proposals. Although Congress approved a ban on Endowment funds for works that might be "considered obscene, and that do not have serious literary, artistic, political or scientific value,"[11] it rejected a more far-reaching and restrictive amendment sponsored by Senator Jesse Helms. The Helms Amendment would have prohibited the use of federal funds for promoting, disseminating, or producing:

1. obscene or indecent materials, including but not limited to, depictions of sadomasochism, homoeroticism, the exploitation of children, or individuals engaged in sex acts; or

2. material which denigrates the objects or beliefs of the adherents of a particular religion or non-religion; or

3. material which denigrates, debases, or reviles a person, group or class of citizens on the basis of race, creed, sex, handicap, age, or national origin.[12]

Similarly, following a July House vote of 361 to 65,[13] Congress reduced the NEA's appropriation by $45,000 -- a sum equal to the amount of the two grants awarded to Serrano by SECCA and to the Institute for Contemporary Art for the Mapplethorpe exhibit. In doing so, Congress rejected three other proposals -- to eliminate the NEA, to cut it by 10 percent, or to cut it by 5 percent.

These were not easy, routine, or unnoticed legislative decisions. For example, the National Republican Congressional Committee (NRCC) targeted 21 House Democrats who voted against cutting any of the NEA's fund. The NRCC sent press releases to these members' districts accusing them of supporting "sexually explicit and anti-religious works of art that are offensive to millions of Americans."[14] Thus, as the first round of the NEA controversy ended, the political stakes of this policy issue had escalated. In an effort to channel the partisan, ideological and political debate away from the legislative forum, the FY 1990 appropriations bill also established a bipartisan Independent Commission to examine the NEA's grant-making procedures and standards and report its findings and recommendations to the Congress within the year.

Seeking to comply with the anti-obscenity prohibition in the FY 1990 appropriation, the newly confirmed NEA chairman, John Frohnmayer, instituted a requirement that all grantees sign a pledge of compliance that they would not use federal monies for projects that were obscene. Artists objected and some, rather than sign the pledge, turned down grants which they had been awarded. Others initiated legal suits against the agency for infringing on their constitutional right of freedom of expression. Meanwhile, the politically untested NEA Chairman withdrew a grant to Artists Space in New York City for a show, "Witnesses: Against Our Vanishing", about AIDS that included images of homosexuality and whose catalog criticized public figures such as Senator Jesse Helms, John Cardinal O'Connor and Representative William Dannemeyer. Chairman

Frohnmayer's explanation was that the show's political purpose detracted from its artistic merits, and that "political discourse ought to be in the political arena and not in a show sponsored by the Endowment."[15]

This was broadly regarded as an overreaction. Congressman Pat Williams (D-MT) called Chairman Frohnmayer's decision "a further bruising of freedom of artistic expression," while constitutional lawyer Floyd Abrams called it "an appalling surrender of First Amendment principle."[16] Leonard Bernstein refused to accept the National Medal of Arts in protest of the NEA action, while another Medal recipient, painter Robert Motherwell, accepted the award but offered to give his prize of $10,000 to Artists Space to replace the canceled grant.[17] Although Frohnmayer quickly reinstated the grant, his decisional fumble left agency critics, supporters, and arts constituents equally unsure of his principles and dissatisfied with his judgment.

In March of 1990, the NEA's periodic reauthorization review provided an occasion to renew the controversy over standards and content restrictions. Conservative groups like the Eagle Forum and the Traditional Values Coalition announced their opposition to reauthorization for the NEA unless restrictions were enacted. Simultaneously, under fire from many of the same groups, commercial recording companies agreed to institute a system of uniform warning labels concerning sexually explicit lyrics. Congressmen E. Thomas Coleman (R-MO) and Paul B. Henry (R-MI), the ranking Republican members of the NEA's House authorizing subcommittee, warned "...that resistance to any restriction on funding could threaten the NEA's existence."[18] Concurrently, the liberal advocacy group, People for the American Way, issued a report stating that "Far Right" demagogues had launched "...a coordinated campaign of distortion" and that "...for the sake of the First Amendment, the Far Right's effort to defund the NEA must be defeated."[19]

The Bush Administration sent up a straight reauthorization bill for congressional consideration, with President Bush himself declaring that he was against content restrictions and against censorship. While expressing "full confidence in John Frohnmayer, the President also noted that he was "deeply offended by some of the filth...to which federal money has gone. And [to] some of the sacrilegious, blasphemous depictions...."[20] A National Campaign for Freedom of Expression (NCFE) was organized by artistic activists and targeted the reelection campaigns of NEA critics Senator Jesse Helms and Representative Dana Rohrabacher. Thus, the arts and the NEA had become negative ammunition in electoral campaigns against the foes of the agency as well as against its friends.

Increasingly, the debate was cast as a choice between "artistic freedom" and "government accountability." In this debate, both sides claimed constitutional grounds, pointing either to the First Amendment or to the inherent principle of popular sovereignty. With the April 1990 indictment of the Contemporary Arts Center of Cincinnati and its director, Dennis Barrie,[21] on obscenity charges stemming from the exhibit of the Mapplethorpe show, possible legal consequences of the policy debate became apparent.

Under the continuing stress, the arts community fractured, finding it extremely difficult to bring a united reauthorization proposal to House Post-secondary Education Subcommittee Chairman Pat Williams (D-MT). In an effort to deflect the issues of obscenity and content restrictions, House members, Tom Coleman (R-MO) and Steve Gunderson (R-WI), introduced a proposal to restructure the agency by transferring greater grant-making authority and resources to the states. The proposal was made with the apparent concurrence of the leadership of the National Assembly of State Arts Agencies (NASAA), as well as, it was rumored, with the agreement of NEA Chairman Frohnmayer. Reaction from other elements of the arts community was swift and negative as NASAA was denounced for crass political opportunism. Representative Williams observed that "the two very worst things that could happen are apparently about to happen...one is that the Republicans are going to come up with legislation different than President Bush has requested. And the second is that the arts groups themselves are moving toward disagreement and disarray...."[22] Meanwhile, Rep. Sidney Yates (D-IL), one of the NEA's prime defenders, noted that "Nobody wants to be branded as being in favor of obscenity," particularly in an election year.[23]

New fuel was added to the dispute when syndicated columnists, Evans and Novak, broke a story just before the May 1990 meeting of the National Council for the Arts, concerning pending grant awards to four performance artists. These were Holly Hughes, Karen Finley, Tim Miller, and John Fleck, whose works involved homosexuality, feminism AIDS, nudity, and urination. The story eventually provoked Chairman Frohnmayer to fire his Deputy Chairman, Al Feltzenberg, and to table and later reject the applications in question. Charging political motivation, outraged artists contested the rejection in the courts.

In June, the congressionally-mandated Independent Commission finally convened. Former Democratic Congressman John Brademas and former Nixon White House advisor Leonard Garment -- both proponents of federal support for the arts -- were elected its co-chairmen. Under their politically astute and administratively experienced leadership, the Commission held extensive hearings and deliberations during the next two months, as it searched for a reasonable position that would moderate the conflict and attract a winning coalition for reauthorizing the NEA. Congress deferred action on the NEA's reauthorization bill in the hope that the Commission could forge a compromise that would help defuse the conflict.

As the Summer progressed, obscenity charges were brought against the rap group "2 Live Crew" in Florida, while in New York and in California the New School for Social Research and the Bella Lewitsky Dance Company filed separate suits against the NEA challenging the constitutionality of its new anti-obscenity pledge. In addition, extremists of both stripes were busy: in August, AIDS activists disrupted the quarterly meeting of the National Council on the Arts, while conservative and religious groups inundated Congress with mail opposing the NEA and various of its grant supported projects.

Contrary to previous experience, an extraordinary number of amendments to the NEA's reauthorization bill were offered, presenting further evidence that the breadth of the debate had spilled over its customary subcommittee boundaries. In all, twenty-six amendments were proposed. Some amendments proposed to abolish the agency; to direct federal support for the protection of culturally significant landscapes; to establish new programs for arts in the inner cities, rural areas and for other underserved groups; or to encourage grantees to purchase American-made equipment and products. Other amendments involved calls to require a variety of procedural changes and requirements; to prohibit awards for works that were offensive or denigrating in various ways; to expand the agency's educational mandate; and to require grant review panel meetings to be open to the public.

On September 11, the Independent Commission issued a unanimous report recommending against legislating specific content restrictions, and called for the NEA to rescind their requirement that grantees certify that the projects they propose to produce with public support would not be obscene. In calling for extensive procedural changes, the report emphasized the accountability and authority of the Chairman. Furthermore, the Commission articulated what it felt was the necessary middle ground for a public policy consensus. While supporting the standard of artistic excellence, it also called for other public standards; to serve the purposes which Congress had determined for the agency, to use a process that was accountable and free of conflicts of interest; to make awards with an awareness of the geographic and cultural diversity of the nation and with respect for the differing beliefs and values of the American people. It characterized the Endowment's task as one of offering artists a "spacious sense of freedom" while maintaining "public confidence in its stewardship of public funds."[24] Finally, as a statement of principle, the Commission reminded everyone of basic Congressional assumptions in creating the agency. Namely, that the NEA was "a public agency established to serve the purposes the public expresses through its elected representatives" and that "the arts belong to all the American people and not only to those who benefit directly from the agency."[25]

In the short-run, the report of the Independent Commission demonstrated that it was possible to find a position that adherents of many points of view in the debate could accede to. In that way, the Commission helped to generate momentum toward a resolution of the reauthorization imbroglio. In the mid-term, the Commission identified a number of procedural and organizational changes that might strengthen the NEA. While some of these were adopted in 1990, others have not, to date, been followed and are likely to resurface for consideration at the next reauthorization. Implicit to many of these procedural recommendations of the Commission and to the administrative changes and requirements mandated by the 1990 reauthorization was a concern that too often the agency simply did not know exactly what activities it was supporting. Thus calls for greater involvement by the Chairperson and the National Council, for project descriptions and interim reports, and for more choice among grant recommendations from panels pointed to a political concern that the agency was structurally hindered in trying to make responsible and accountable decisions. Finally, in the long term, although few would disagree with the principles articulated by the Commission, many would fail to appreciate the administrative and programmatic ramifications of the call to serve both the general public and the arts constituency.

During October, positive momentum continued to grow. First, Cincinnati museum director Dennis Barrie was acquitted of obscenity charges stemming from the Mapplethorpe exhibit. The NEA succeeded in securing a reauthorization from Congress that called for many significant legislative and operational changes. A shortened reauthorization term -- from three to five years -- indicated a weakening of legislative trust and a concomitant desire for closer congressional oversight. Other provisions increased the proportion of funds allocated to state programs (from 20 percent to 27.5 percent) and set aside another proportion of funds (7.5 percent) for programs designed to reach underserved communities particularly in rural and inner city areas. The net effect of these changes was to decrease the funds available to the discipline programs -- which some viewed as the source of controversial grant awards -- but which certainly supported many of the largest and best organized segments of the professional arts community.

While the 1990 reauthorization did not impose explicit content restrictions, it did create penalties and procedures concerning any NEA-financed artwork that was found obscene by the courts. It also called for the agency to take into consideration "general standards of decency and respect for the diverse beliefs and values of the American public." Finally, the reauthorization mandated a number of procedural changes, including more stringent conflict-of-interest regulations, the addition of a layperson to grant review panels, requirements for project descriptions and interim reports, and a more explicit statement of the Chairman's grant authority.

Clearly, the immediate arts policy crisis had been weathered. It was equally clear, however, that this was no simple restoration of the status quo ante.

Continuing Skirmishes: 1991 and 1992

As events subsequently demonstrated, the reauthorization of the NEA in 1990 did not end the debate over federal arts policy nor the controversy surrounding the agency. Neither was public dispute over values such as freedom of expression or decency resolved. Fears of censorship and expectations of accountability continued. Indeed, during 1991 and 1992, continuing conflict was triggered by judicial decisions as well as grant decisions, by legislative, policy, and electoral politics.

During the first year after the NEA reauthorization fight, judicial decisions helped keep the issues of freedom of expression and decency regulations alive. A federal district court in California found the NEA's anti-obscenity pledge to be unconstitutional.[26] In March, a federal appeals court in Washington heard arguments against FCC regulations concerning indecent programming and in May found such rules to be unconstitutional.[27] In May, the Supreme Court ruled in *Rust v. Sullivan* that government could impose conditions on those receiving money (in this case, physicians in federally funded clinics). This decision gave rise to anxious speculation as to its possible application to the NEA and arts funding.[28] Meanwhile, the pending lawsuit of the "NEA Four" -- the four performance artists who were suing the agency for improper denial of grants -- was expanded. Now the American Civil Liberties Union (ACLU) and the National Campaign for Freedom of Expression joined the plaintiffs in also challenging the "decency" language of the 1990 reauthorization.[29] In the Summer, both the ACLU and People for the American Way announced anti-censorship projects to help protect artists' rights.[30]

Even as the NEA implemented extensive procedural changes, it had to defend its actions in approximately two dozen other art grant controversies.[31] In many of these instances, NEA funds were involved; in others, the agency was wrongly criticized for projects it had not supported. None of these reached the fever pitch and sensationalism of the Mapplethorpe and Serrano cases. However, as this succession of cases continued to attract legislative and public attention, Congressional trust in the NEA was further undermined and White House faith in Chairman Frohnmayer continued to erode. Meanwhile, the Smithsonian and the National Endowment for the Humanities (NEH), came under fire for espousing political agendas through particular exhibits or appointments.[32]

In 1991, the legislative decisions concerning arts appropriations were disappointing and demoralizing. While other federal cultural agencies such as the NEH, the Smithsonian and the National Gallery each received budget increases, the NEA's funding level remained static. Concurrently, aggregate state funding for the arts experienced a precipitous decline of 22 percent for FY 1992. As the NEA's FY 1992 appropriation bill progressed through Congress, many of the arguments about content standards resurfaced. While statutorily, Congress refrained from imposing content restrictions, there was an ominous reversal of congressional sentiment as well as a growing disaffection from Chairman Frohnmayer. In September 1991, the Senate voted 68 to 28 in favor of a Helms amendment, in contrast to its 1989 vote of 62 to 35 against a similar proposal. The October vote in the House tallied 286 to 135 in favor in 1991, compared to 264 to 53 against in 1989. Only deft negotiation at the conference committee derailed the attempt to insert content restrictions into the FY 1992 appropriation.[33] In a deal that was characterized as "corn for porn", support for an unrestricted NEA was traded for opposition to raising grazing fees on public lands -- a truly creative example of legislative logrolling.

During the floor debate in the House, proponents of the NEA began to develop a line of argument that shifted criticism from the agency to the Chairman, suggesting that the resignation of Chairman Frohnmayer might be a solution.[34] Congressional discontent with the chairman increased when, shortly after the FY 1992 appropriations was approved, Mr. Frohnmayer announced that he had approved grants to two of the controversial performance artists who were suing the NEA -- Holly Hughes and Tim Miller. Because the issue of offensive material had been so critical to the appropriations debate, key members of Congress and their staffs were appalled with the Chairman's decisions. Many felt that the awards were insensitive to the political climate and that the timing of the grants gave at least the appearance that pertinent information had been withheld during the legislative process.

In short, during the year following reauthorization, the NEA was buffeted administratively, legislatively, financially, and judicially. As a consequence, the agency could do little to restabilize its political position, restore its public image, or re-energize internal morale and operations. Yet 1992 proved to be even more unsettled.

The new year of 1992 began with new crises, more stress, and escalating conflict. For a second, disappointing year in a row, the Bush Administration requested a static budget for the NEA while proposing increases for NEH, the Smithsonian Institute, and the National Gallery. The financial state of the arts seemed increasingly precarious as orchestras, theaters, and dance groups confronted growing deficits amidst a continuing recession.[35] The Corporation for Public Broadcasting (CPB) faced bitter political opposition to its reauthorization, with some legislators and analysts arguing that the system had "outlived its usefulness." Others criticized CPB's programming: some charging that it lacked balance and betrayed a "liberal tilt," while others were concerned about indecency. In addition, some congressmen complained about a lack of accountability in certain of CPB's operating practices.[36] The president of PBS, Bruce Christensen, asserted that "PBS had become a new scapegoat for right-wing organizations that previously attacked the National Endowment for the Arts...."[37] Clearly, cultural issues remained volatile.

Early in 1992, Congress and the White House were inundated with letters and calls from evangelical pro-family groups protesting NEA funding for two publications of a literary magazine called Portable Lower East Side. The two issues were entitled "Queer City" and "Live Sex Acts" which included prose, poetry and photographs that showed or described live sex acts as well as a "rap-style poem, laced with vulgarities, depicting Christ as a pedophile and celebrating violence against a white female jogger."[38] Such incidents indicated that new grant controversies were continuing to dog the agency.

At a tense February meeting of the National Council for the Arts, Chairman Frohnmayer pushed the Council to meet its "obligation to exercise artistic judgment" and urged it to reject the recommendation of peer review panels on two grant applications.[39] Lengthy debate followed a public review of a sexually explicit video tape of performance artist Scarlet O which was submitted with the application of Franklin Furnace (a New York performance space that had received NEA grants for 16 years). Also viewed and discussed were slides (which included homoerotic photographs) as part of the application of Highways (a small Los Angeles gallery and performance space). While some Council members worried about respecting the panel review process, others decried the quality of the work before them and felt the Endowment might have been set up by provocative applicants operating in an "in your face" style.[40] By a vote of 17 to 1, the National Council refused to recommend these two applications to the Chairman and, under stipulations of the 1990 reauthorization, the Chairman then had no choice but to reject funding for these applications. In this case, the Chairman had not only elicited the backing of the Council, he had insisted that they publicly apply standards of artistic excellence and articulate how (and if) public support was justified.

Electorally, Republican conservative candidate Patrick Buchanan mounted a strong campaign against President Bush in the New Hampshire primary. One of Buchanan's strategies was to attack the Administration for "subsidizing both filthy and blasphemous art."[41] Thus, the primary elections brought the NEA and its grant controversies into the high stakes and high visibility arena of presidential politics, where they were cast as a liability for the incumbent president and, potentially, for various legislative supporters in their own campaigns.

On February 22, NEA Chairman Frohnmayer announced his resignation. Thus, following years of public conflict, months of eroding support in Congress and the White House, and increasing friction with the National Council, the Chairman bowed to the inevitable fact that he himself had become a contentious issue, a hamstrung administrator, and a political liability.

Yet even Frohnmayer's resignation did not dampen the campaign fervor. Calling the NEA the "upholstered playpen" of the "Eastern liberal establishment," Pat Buchanan proclaimed that if he were president, he would "clean house at the NEA...the place would be shut down, padlocked and fumigated."[42] In late February, Buchanan televised an attack advertisement as part of his Southern primary campaign in anticipation of Super Tuesday. The 30-second spot featured slow-motion segments of a public television film, "Tongues Untied" that had been awarded support both by the NEA and by PBS. As images of gay black men in chains and leather harnesses moved across the television screen, a voice said

> In the last three years, the Bush Administration has wasted our tax dollars on pornographic and blasphemous art too shocking to show. This so-called art has glorified homosexuality, exploited children and perverted the image of Jesus Christ. Even after good people protested. Bush continued to fund this kind of art. Send Bush a message. We need a leader who will fight for what we believe in.[43]

Even though the Buchanan candidacy waned by Summer, a fear of the negative politics of controversial art remained. Indeed, some legislative supporters, such as Senator Dale Bumpers (D-AR), faced conservative religious criticism. Others such as Representative Tom Coleman (R-MO), found that his supportive role in the reauthorization of the NEA contributed to defeat at the polls in November. Representative Pat Williams (D-MT), the subcommittee leader for NEA reauthorization, successfully fought a close election in which he was attacked as "Porno Pat" by his opponent for a redistricted single seat in Montana.

In May, the Senior Deputy Chairman of the NEA, Anne-Imelda Radice, assumed the role of acting Chairman. Her primary concern was to arrest the decline of Congressional support for the agency -- both by seeking to defuse conservative criticism and by reestablishing legislative trust in the judgment and responsibility of the agency. In testimony to the House Subcommittee on Interior Appropriations on May 5th, she assured legislators that "the concerns of the taxpayers, the concerns of the Congress...have as much weight" as artistic concerns, and that the new chairman was prepared to make difficult decisions when necessary.[44] Republican subcommittee member Ralph Regula (R-OH), praised her position, while subcommittee Chairman and Democrat, Sidney Yates (D-IL) admitted that her stance "...might be necessary in view of the temper of the times."[45]

One indication of Acting Chairman Radice's effectiveness with Congress could be seen in the relatively easy passage of the NEA's annual appropriation for the first time since 1989. Meanwhile religious conservatives muted their criticism since they found the new chairman to be "sensitive to [their] concerns," there was less "perceived need for more drastic action." Concurrently, Melanne Verveer, executive vice president of the liberal advocacy group, People for the American Way, acknowledged that "...The members [of Congress] feel that [she] will proceed in ways that won't cause controversy. So they don't have to do anything legislatively" with regard to possible content restrictions.[46]

However, even as the thunder on the right and the harsh attentions of Congress were contained, ire from the arts community was sparked. Exercising her executive decision-making authority over two applications that had received divided panel support, acting Chairman Radice rejected two grants for museum exhibits that focussed on images and sculptures of human body parts, including genitalia. Both applications had been endorsed by the National Council for the Arts.[47] In her decision, she stated that she found these applications were "...unlikely to have the long-term artistic significance necessary to merit Endowment funding."[48]

Howls of outrage arose from parts of the arts and civil liberties communities, including composer Stephen Sondheim (and, later, author Wallace Stegner) who turned down the National Medal of Arts award protesting that the NEA was becoming "...a symbol of censorship and repression rather than encouragement and support."[49] Applicants such as Beacon Press and the Artist Trust of Seattle refused their awards to protest the decision.

Others in the arts community saw the grant rejections not so much as censorship but as challenges to the power of the peer panels -- and through them, the ability of the artists to control the grant decisions of the agency. Thus, after deliberating for four days, a sculpture review panel suspended operations without making any grant recommendations, arguing that the "...process of peer panel review had been severely compromised and placed in great jeopardy."[50] Shortly thereafter a second panel -- the theater panel reviewing applications in the solo theater artist category -- presented the Chairman with a list of demands and walked away without conducting the application evaluation process when these demands were not met.[51] As a consequence, funds originally earmarked for sculpture and solo theater fellowships were either shifted to regional arts organizations for award or were reallocated to other categories within the Endowment.

Other segments of the arts community were more reasonable in their reactions. Twenty-five other panels reviewing applications in other programs at the Endowment completed their work.[52] Various national arts service organizations took the following measured positions:[53]

From the National Assembly of Local Arts Agencies (NALAA):

NALAA is urging caution, deliberation, discussion and pragmatism for all parties at this time. It is time to recognize and understand the political nature of the current situation, the political context of all current decisions, the political background of the genesis of NEA money, and the political ramifications of actions taken today on future federal support for the arts in America. People in the arts must not fool themselves into thinking that the workings of the NEA...occur or have ever occurred outside this context.

...it is unproductive and destructive to the NEA to focus attention on the decisions of the Acting Chair. It is equally unproductive and damaging to artists and to federal funding for the arts, for panels to disband or not finish their work in protest. It is damaging to the arts, artists, arts organizations and public funding for the arts to focus blame or hostility on the agency, the NEA in this case, for carrying out the will of its boss, the Congress of the United States.

From the American Arts Alliance (AAA):

In recent times, members of Congress and the American public have been misled by the extreme views of a limited number of individuals to undervalue the significant contributions of the National Endowment for the Arts to life in the United States.

The decision of Anne-Imelda Radice, Acting Chairman..., to reject grants that had been recommended for approval by both a peer review panel and the Presidentially-nominated National Council for the Arts is one of the many consequences of the fundamental misunderstanding of the value of the Endowment and its procedures. The arts community, working together must correct the record by heightening the awareness of the general public as to the value of the arts to our national life....

From the American Association of Museums (AAM):

We regret that the Acting Chair of the National Endowment for the Arts found it necessary to reject [these] grants...However, it is important to focus our concern and attention on the source of this problem, not the symptom. It seems clear that the Acting Chair is attempting to carry out the letter of the law and the intent of Congress. Therefore, efforts to resolve this issue should be more appropriately directed to the Congress -- and not the NEA. The Congress is reacting to a perceived opinion of the general public regarding the NEA and its activities. It is our opinion that through inaccurate and misleading information provided that public, a vocal minority has misled the Congress in their perception.

> The entire cultural community has a responsibility to use all its effort to insure that the American public has complete and accurate information about the NEA and the degree to which it has benefitted the broadest public...In no segment of the Federal government has there been greater benefit to all the people of this country for the dollars invested.

As these comments illustrate, some leaders of the arts community saw the NEA as being whip-sawed in trying to be responsive to two discordant masters. On one hand, Congress was urging decency and common sense in grant awards. On the other hand, artists were demanding autonomy and freedom from political considerations or administrative controls. For arts leaders seeking to maintain the political viability of the NEA, the new political strategy was to work at changing legislative perceptions of the agency, its record, and its value, rather than attacking the agency for trying to walk a figurative political tightrope. Such a strategy was intended to allow the NEA to avoid the tragic dilemma of choosing sides among its constituencies.

This balancing act was made even more challenging by the June decision of Federal District Court Judge A. Wallace Tashima that found the 1990 reauthorization language regarding "decency" to be unconstitutionally vague and overbroad. The ruling also opened the way for a trial in which the NEA-Four would have a chance to prove that their grant rejections were procedurally improper.[54] A year later, in June of 1993, the NEA and the artistic plaintiffs agreed to an out-of-court settlement totalling $252,000 over the rejected grants; $50,000 went to the plaintiffs to compensate for the grants and as compensation for their claims under the Privacy Act, the rest went to pay for legal costs.[55]

While artists and civil libertarians celebrated the Tashima decision and the settlement, they were shocked when the new Clinton Administration appealed the decision with regard to the decency clause, arguing that although the arts enjoy First Amendment protection, this did "...not mean that any restriction on government funding of that activity is facially invalid."[56]

During Radice's tenure as acting Chairman of the NEA, the Congressional pressure eased even as political attention turned to the presidential election campaign of 1992. With the election of Bill Clinton, many anticipated a White House that was more engaged and supportive of the arts and of the NEA. Although a new Chairman was not in place until October of 1993, the arts community was pleased that it was one of their own -- actress Jane Alexander. There was also relief that Congress sought to extend the NEA's reauthorization for two more years in order to give the new Administration an opportunity to set its course and to prove itself. Nonetheless, the arts were not high on the Clinton Administration's policy agenda, which was crowded with big issues such as the budget deficit, health care and welfare reform, economic and job stimulation, and foreign affairs from Bosnia and Haiti to the Soviet Union and trade issues.

Cultural policy issues, however, continued to attract public attention. Concern about the content of cultural products was a prominent feature of debates throughout 1993 and into 1994 concerning violence on television and in the movies. Violence, sex and profanity were factors in calls for instituting a rating system for video games and in protests against rap lyrics. The Twentieth Century Fund issued a report on public television, calling for changes in funding practices premised on the principle that "...contributions by all taxpayers should benefit all taxpayers."[57] In August 1993 in Cobb County, Georgia, the County Commission voted to abolish funding for the arts all together when a dispute over public support for arts activities that included references to homosexuality clashed with support for community, family-oriented values. The President was criticized for being star-struck and allowing Hollywood too much entree to policy matters.[58] Negotiations for the new GATT treaty nearly broke down over a dispute concerning film, music and other artistic products.

The conservative Christian Action Network renewed its criticism of the NEA over the reinstatement of grants to three gay and lesbian film festivals, while Pat Buchanan urged a Christian Coalition conference audience of 2000 activists to continue to be vigilant in the "culture war" because "...Culture is the Ho Chi Minh trail of power; you surrender that province and you lose America."[59] In 1993, the NEA became the only federal cultural agency to experience a significant decrease in its funding -- losing $4.7 million during an appropriation process that was characterized by growing concern over the federal budget deficit, an unsuccessful attempt to abolish individual fellowship grants, and complaints over a new set of offensive grants.[60]

Similarly, in 1994, the House voted for a 2 percent reduction in the NEA's appropriations for FY 1995, while the Senate cut the budget by 5 percent, specifically slicing the programs for theater, visual arts, and presenting and commissioning. The action followed a new controversy over a performance by Ron Athey that was sponsored by the Walker Art Center and supported, in part, by Endowment money. The HIV-positive artist carved ritual patterns on the back of a fellow artist, blotted the blood with paper towels and hung these over the audience on a clothesline. At the same time that the NEA was being criticized for lack of control over its grants, Congress was passing legislation giving the Kennedy Center more control over its business operations. In other words, in 1993 and 1994 the volume and intensity of policy attention to arts policy issues decreased from the roar of the previous four years, but the debate was neither resolved nor abandoned, merely muted.

Myths and Misconceptions

The discord and conflict of the late 1980's and early 1990's over cultural issues in general and about arts policy in particular were facilitated and exacerbated by certain myths and misconceptions that reigned among the arts policy community. Some of these were explicitly proclaimed, others went unstated. Together, these myths and misconceptions were key elements in the paradigm that implicitly guided general policy strategy as well as specific grant decisions.

Myths

Myth #1: the norm for federal arts policy was set in the 1970's. Perhaps the most pervasive myth of arts policy holds that the rapid and relatively untroubled expansion of public support for the arts was normal and sustainable. The subsequent NEA budgetary pattern that went from slowed growth in the late 1970's, through threat to stasis in the 1980's, to persistent incremental decline in the 1990's was therefore regarded as abnormal. As a result, the arts community focussed great energy and attention on the fight to regain funding momentum for the NEA and paid scant attention to the fate of other programs throughout government that supported artists (such as CETA or federal design policies) or affected arts activities (such as tax reforms or education policy). Realistically, when compared to other federal agencies and programs, the NEA's budgetary growth of the 1970's was quite anomalous and could not be sustained indefinitely. The double-digit inflation of the late 1970's, the Reagan Revolution attack on Big Government and domestic spending in the 1980's, and the growing size of and concern over the federal deficit, all helped cloud such rosy expectations. Yet throughout the 1980's as well as during the controversy of 1989-92, the arts community persisted in basing its advocacy strategy on the assumption that the aberrational arrest in public funding growth was only temporary and that the fate of the NEA's budget was their paramount, indeed virtually their sole, concern.

Similarly, an entire and key generation of arts administrators and policy leaders shared the formative experiences of the booming 1970's. To many of these, the temporary circumstances of the 1970's acquired the aura of permanency. Thus, growing public interest and financial support for arts activities, increasingly positive political regard although low policy visibility, reliance on a star system for leadership, and dependence on federal validation and legitimation of artworld trends came to be standing expectations.

Another manifestation of the 1970's mythic norm regarded art disciplines as the primary organizing principle for federal grant programs. Yet in reality, half the programs and slightly more than half the NEA's grant money is awarded through programs that are interdisciplinary or functional. In addition, many state and local arts agencies were organized on functional or recipient bases. Furthermore, in the 1990's, Congressional policy mandates were all functional -- do more in arts education, reach underserved communities better, support international projects.

Yet another premise that flowed from the 1970's norm considered the NEA to be the dominant public arts agency
-- both among federal agencies who administered programs to support the arts and between the federal government and state and local arts agencies. Yet by 1985, the combined amount of state support for the arts had surpassed that of the NEA, and local/municipal support was approximately twice the state level. At the federal level, while the NEA sometimes acted as the spokesman for the interests of the arts community to other agencies and often advised other agencies, more federal money reached artists and arts activities through the combination of other programs (such as the GSA Art in Architecture Program, USIA, the Smithsonian Institution, public broadcasting, CETA, UDAG grants and even military bands) than through NEA grants. Yet many of this generation of arts administrators and policy leaders, experiencing a mythic myopia, find it difficult to adjust their political strategy, policy assumptions, or principles of administrative organization to the changed world of the 1990's.

Turning the normative assumptions of the 1970's into operating systems often lent an unintentional elitist cast to arts programs, priorities and leadership styles. For example, considerable attention has been drawn recently to how the 1970's gave rise to the fallacious expectation of continuing growth and the standard that bigger was better.[61] This assumption helped fuel an expansion among established arts organizations and a growth quest among small, new, or culturally specific institutions. In the process, some organizations over-expanded, others overloaded and burned-out artistic and administrative personnel, and yet others distorted their missions in the attempt to attain unrealistic ambitions. Thus, the standards of organizational "success" seemed elitist in emphasizing the large and established institutions. As the financial resources necessary to sustain this elitist growth model failed to keep up with field expectations, smaller and newer groups grew increasingly frustrated as their ambitions eluded them, while larger organizations received less money for which they had to satisfy more requirements.

The growth of arts audiences, particularly in size and in geographic dispersion, seemed to cultivate a "field of dreams" presumption that if quality, professional arts were made available, the citizenry would patronize them (in all senses of the words "patronize" -- through attendance, through financial contributions and through political approval). The arts policy community had come to expect that public opinion was either positive or was inconsequentially apathetic. Thus, in the virtual absence of organized, political opposition, it was all too easy to believe that the opinion and taste of the arts community were the only views that counted and that others were either uninformed, unimportant or philistine. Yet with art education in the schools considered inconsistent, sporadic and expendable, generations of citizens were coming of age with little knowledge or appreciation of the arts even as media and technological advances were bringing more kinds of art and entertainment into the home.

The success of a Nancy Hanks, the effectiveness of a Senator Pell or Congressman Brademas, the early efforts of select foundation and corporate sponsors, the reliance on arts service organization spokesmen, all cultivated a star system of arts policy leadership that resonated with artworld experience with conductors, choreographers, museum directors, theatrical directors and presenting impresarios. Such a system relies on individuals who guard their preeminence -- a fact that figured in restiveness and ambiguity about their proper role among some National Council members, particularly as interim and weak NEA Chairmen seemed to leave a leadership vacuum at the agency as the crisis stretched from 1989 into 1992. Reliance on policy leadership "stars", however, seemed to release the rank and file of the arts community from responsibility for monitoring and managing the national political environment, for cultivating more extensive leadership capacity, or for building committed and diversified publics. From this perspective, policy leadership was, by definition, supportive. At worst, some public officials in key positions (particularly, the President) might be disinterested. The paradigm did not allow for the possibility of opposition leadership and perseverance. As a result, the arts policy system is particularly vulnerable to disruptions following the loss of key individuals, to anguish at anything less than full and unconditional commitment from public proponents, to sniping at and scapegoating its own leaders when troubles continued, and to charges that its spokesmen were unrepresentative of the general public.

Furthermore, the budgetary successes of the 1970's and the persistence of this generation of arts leadership fostered a belief that if the NEA continued doing what had been successful in the 1970's, it would still be effective and appropriate in the 1980's and 1990's. Yet initial successes helped generate new problems. For example, the successful institution-expanding style of the 1970's is no longer appropriate for the environment and resources of the 1990's. Yet, NEA grant program guidelines, eligibility requirements and evaluation criteria continue, in large part, to be premised in earlier practices and assumptions. Similarly, the success of the agency and its public partners in redistributing artistic opportunities across the nation led some to argue that the NEA had accomplished its goal (and was therefore obsolete). Conversely, others argued that while inequity as a matter of national geography might have been reduced, now priority should be given to inequity based on cultural diversity and intra-regional geography (e.g., rural and inner city disadvantages).

As the mythic norm of the 1970's exerted its hold, the NEA and many of its constituents and supporters chose to hunker down during the 1980's to preserve programs, categories, and expectations amidst declining or static budgets. During the last 15 years, numerous opportunities for revision and adaptation have arisen but the agency has sidestepped most of these. Challenges were either repelled (as with the 1979 Congressional investigative report) or coopted (as was the 1981 Presidential Task Force on the Arts and Humanities). Serious questions were finessed (as in the Peer Panel Study reported to Congress in 1987). In extreme distress, reformist recommendations might be adopted, but only in part and with little appreciation for the political logic or the administrative principles upon which they were based (as with the Independent Commission of 1990). Only rarely, as in the case of arts education (and the NEAs *Toward Civilization report*) were serious policy and programmatic assessment undertaken, leading to constructive policy change. For the most past, waiting for better times to return, the agency and much of the arts policy community neglected opportunities to rethink priorities and capabilities that might have, in the long term, strengthened their political position, improved their administrative effectiveness, expanded their financial options, or accommodated a changing policy environment.

Myth #2: federal arts policy and administration is non-political. In all likelihood, this myth evolved from the quest of the arts policy community to avoid partisanship and political patronage in grant awards. These efforts were certainly in tune with the intentions of the legislative creators of the Endowment who believed that the arts should enjoy bipartisan support as a general public benefit since they were a measure of national pride and civilization as well as constitutionally protected as a matter of freedom of expression. However, it was naive to believe that political considerations could be divorced from the purposes, procedures and actions of a federal agency which is subject to annual appropriations and periodic reauthorization and that is headed by a politically accountable executive.

Indeed, each of the first four chairmen of the Endowment demonstrated considerable political astuteness, often masquerading as apoliticalness while embracing bipartisanship. The political financier Roger Stevens used concurrent positions on the White House staff and as head of the developing Kennedy Center to bolster his political capital as the first chairman of the Endowment. Nancy Hanks propagated the myth of non-politicalness even as she practiced an adept political and bipartisan entrepreneurship. Although Livingston Biddle's appointment was criticized as being "too political", his close ties to Congress and his long experience in legislative politics were assets in piloting the Endowment through philosophical and partisan controversies. Frank Hodsoll's experience in bureaucratic politics and close ties to key White House staff served him well in protecting the agency even though his policy agenda was limited. Such political skills were essential to the survival and development of the NEA. In contrast, John Frohnmayer, mistaking myth for reality, never appreciated the political character of his job[62] and acted as though the Endowment was a private foundation insulated from its political environment.

The myth of non-politicalness supported other misconceptions. On the one hand, it allowed a subtle transformation in the agency's purpose by drawing its attention away from the necessities of maintaining general public legitimacy. Instead of focussing on stabilizing and increasing the capacity of the nonprofit arts in order to expand public access to artistic opportunities of high quality, a belief arose that the NEA's mission was to insulate artists from the forces of the marketplace, fill the income-earnings gap of arts organizations, and publicly legitimize the tastes and judgments of the arts community.[63] This, in turn, supported a romantic notion of aesthetic independence, that, at times, allowed artistic freedom to drift into private license, unmindful of social responsibility or the necessity to engage with a public wider than the arts community.[64]

Such autonomy was institutionalized in the panel system which staunchly protects its prerogatives to assess artistic excellence and determine merit. Recently, the panels have found these prerogatives challenged both internally and externally. Within the arts community, demographic change has spurred a growing restiveness among multicultural artists and arts organizations who voice a sense of inequitable treatment under this paradigm.[65] Philosophically, after 20 years of post-modernist debunking of all standards, some in the arts community have repudiated the very term "quality" as a "symbol of exclusion" and " a pretext for preserving the authority of the heterosexual white male."[66] Thus, while panel practices may be insulated from partisan interference, they can also become isolated from general public opinion and the public interest.[67] As a consequence of this insulation, the representativeness of the panels is a persistent concern and the judgment of the panels can be subject to challenge.

The myth of non-politicalness also leads to the perception that debate, disagreement and differences of opinion are either ill-willed or unnecessary. In turn, this led either to a quest for political unanimity before action or to a reciprocal deference to discipline specialization. The first alternative leaves a false impression that there is little difference of opinion, policy assumptions or programmatic preferences among the various components of the arts community. Concomitantly, the expectation of unanimity breeds an intolerance of differences and stifles more general debate in the policy process. The second alternative evokes logrolling among the constituent elements of the arts community and does little to engender a spirit of compromise or accommodation useful in the larger political arena. The fact that both NEA chairmen and the Presidents they served during the Johnson, Nixon and Carter administrations fostered a bipartisan support system for the arts led many to misinterpret this to mean that the arts are non-political.

A belief in the intrinsic value of the arts led to the assumption that the arts enjoy positive public support and therefore that criticism and opposition are aberrations provoked by opportunists with suspect motives. Indeed, while the arts community has become more adept at mobilizing information and presenting positive evidence, it seems to regard its own public relations representations as indisputable fact, rather than recognizing their interpretative and often incomplete character. For example, a number of surveys and studies have sought to proclaim and demonstrate a positive public regard for the arts. These may take the form of periodic public opinion polls indicating that Americans want more arts for their children and are willing to pay more in taxes to support the arts, or of national surveys indicating that people want more opportunities to participate in more arts activities,[68] or of economic impact studies that aim to demonstrate the financial and development value of the arts in particular communities. While useful in advocacy, none of this evidence actually demonstrates the relative strength of such positive sentiments. That is, what priority do parents give to more art in the schools compared to better math, science, computer training, or sports? Similarly, given a choice between more arts activities, more sports events, more exercise, more outdoor activities, more movies, or more family time, then how many people would actually participate in more arts activities? Likewise, how valuable is the economic impact of the arts in a community compared to the economic impact of the local university, sports franchise, manufacturing plant, or computer company? What is the net economic impact of the arts rather than the apparent gross figures? Is economic impact a full measure of the societal value of the arts? And what is government's role with regard to the cultural industries, both nonprofit and commercial?

In contrast, a recent survey commissioned by the National Cultural Alliance found that while 81 percent of their respondents felt the arts were essential for well-rounded communities and individuals, a preponderance (68 percent) also noted that the arts played little to no role in their lives.[69] In other words, while the American public may indicate positive attitudes towards the arts, these are seldom translated into active participation in the arts or firm support for governmental arts agencies. Rather these studies indicate a weak and malleable public opinion that has proven to be quite susceptible to circumstantial variability. Indeed, as art critic Robert Hughes has observed, there has "never been a consensus for national cultural endowments."[70]

Myth #3: there is no national arts policy. Throughout its history, the Arts Endowment has sought to obscure (if not abjure) its policy-making role. Chairmen have typically argued that they have no art policy, only a policy to support the arts; that they respond and react to the needs of the field rather than articulate policy goals or priorities that can serve as a guide to action. Nevertheless, the agency is expected to exercise leadership of the field, serve as the spokesman for the arts in the halls of governmental power, and at times, has been regarded as the embodiment of the public interest in the arts.

Federal arts policy tends to be implicit, indirect and segmented, rather than explicitly articulated by the leadership of the NEA or to be the subject of coherent public discussion. However, the fact that there is no single statement of arts policy or clear identification of policy goals does not mean that there has been no policy.[71] Policy generally emanates from the panels of the NEA (with an occasional initiative of the Chairman or a National Council member). It is articulated through grant application guidelines and awards -- a fragmented practice that distracts attention from both the existence and the character of policy. Conversely, Congress, through recent reauthorization language, has been quite clear in setting policy priorities for the Endowment that include furthering arts education, expanding rural and inner city opportunities, and promoting greater decentralization to the states.

Paradoxically, although the existence of policy is denied, the impact of the NEA has been claimed as one of its greatest successes. An NEA grant has acquired the status of a "good housekeeping seal of approval," an imprimatur influencing the patronage decisions of private and other public supporters. The purpose of a federal arts agency is not simply to assess artists, arts organizations, and arts projects to certify their professional excellence. In other fields, such certification is a matter of professional self-governance (often through credential requirements, rating systems, or licensing procedures). Nor does it require the award of federal grant money. Rather, a public agency determines excellence in order to assure the funds that it expends in pursuit of its policy purposes are a responsible expenditure of the public's money. Thus, the myth that there is no arts policy leaves grant funding decisions and the application of standards of excellence devoid of policy purpose.

Alternatively, the federal government has more cultural policies than are administered by the NEA. This is not always readily apparent given the fragmented character of these programs, which are found in other cultural institutions such as the NEH, IMS, CPB/PBS, the National Gallery, and Smithsonian Institution as well as in other governmental organizations such as GSA, USIA, or the Departments of Treasury, Labor or Education. Operating on the myth that there is no arts policy, the arts community tends to focus primarily on the arts agency, to the neglect of the programs and actions of other agencies that may affect the arts. Presuming that there is no arts policy makes it difficult to conceive of possibilities for policy linkage and coordination among agencies. Thus, opportunities both to advance the arts and to improve the social impact of the arts are missed because of a constricted policy conceptualization.

Maintaining that there is no arts policy, the arts community has developed little capacity or interest in establishing policy definitions; refining political rationales; developing program options; engaging in programmatic; structural or administrative evaluation; or gathering reliable and policy-relevant information. As a consequence, the arts community is frequently forced to react to how others have posed policy issues, finds itself without counter-proposals in the face of criticism, and lacks sufficient information for even defensive (much less for pro-active) effectiveness. This situation also leads the NEA into an untenable position of having to defend every grant decision on its own merits and in its own terms rather than as part of a general policy that enjoys a public consensus.

It may be particularly difficult for the arts community and the NEA to dispel the myth of no policy for at least two reasons. First, in their eyes, policy-making is tainted as being political. Therefore an explicit discussion of policy would seem to violate both the myth of no policy and the myth of non-politicalness. Secondly, the concept of policy is essentially modern and the process of policy-making is integrative and consensual. In contrast, axioms of the contemporary post-modern artsworld are deconstructive and individualistic, sometimes to the point of aggressiveness, alienation or separatism. Thus, some fundamental assumptions and perspectives of the arts and the policy worlds diverge; reconciliation or even accommodation between the two is fraught with difficulties.

The foregoing myths and their consequences have framed the conduct and controversies of arts policy for the past twenty years and continue to exert a strong influence on public debate. While all myths possess an essential truth, myths are not facts. In part, myths exert an influence because they are so inbred that they are unrecognized and therefore go unexamined, unquestioned, and unchanged.

Misconceptions

In addition to the three arts policy myths discussed above, three virtually unnoticed misconceptions have also developed and are likely to perpetuate the recurrence of controversy, impede creative policy innovation, and hinder political success in the future.

The first misconception: the audience is the public. In policy terms, this reasoning by analogy has proven to be a nearly fatal fallacy. While the audience is part of the public, it is only the interested, supportive segment of the general public. Thinking that the audience is the entire public, allows the arts community to suppose that public opinion and the public interest are positively addressed through the normal activities of artists and arts organizations. It believes that those not actively in the audience are either uninformed or unreached, and that those who are uninterested or negative can, in large part, be ignored. In public policy, the presumption is that the plurality of interests will include both supporters and opponents, that supporters may be involved for a variety of reasons, and that a broad contingent of the apathetic are potentially mobilizable to either support or opposition.

The misperception that the audience was the public was one factor in the surprise that stunned the arts community into initial inaction and the belief that things would "blow over" during the early months of the controversy of 1989-1990. It also tends to lead the arts constituency to miscalculations about the relations between public officials and the public. Public officials may educate and lead their constituents, but must also be responsive and accountable to them. Arts organizations and artists market to their audiences, and some act as trustees of the artistic resources with which they are entrusted. However, to market to an audience is not the same relationship as to be accountable to a public.

The second misconception: the decision-making standard of artistic excellence is mistaken for a policy goal. Generally stated, this tautology holds that the goal of federal arts policy is to encourage artistic excellence simply because it is excellent and we know it is excellent because professional artists who are regarded by their peers as proficient practitioners and craftsmen say so. This is to erroneously presume that the general public regards art, specifically that certified by arts professionals, is a public good and therefore, that excellent art for art's sake is in the public interest. While artists and some patrons tend to believe this, there are many in the polity who would dispute this view. Indeed, art for art's sake has never been a sufficient rationale for public support of the arts in the United States.

More accurately, excellence is a pre-condition, not the goal, of public support. Meeting this expectation is a way of justifying that public funds are being spent wisely and well to realize other legitimate policy goals. The NEA's authorizing legislation advances many goals that artistic excellence can serve.[72] It can help recognize and preserve artistic and cultural significance and authenticity. It can promote and help to maintain professionalism. It can encourage and develop the appreciation and enjoyment of the arts by the citizenry. It can help assure that valuable art opportunities will be available to those who for reasons of financial means, location, or other disadvantage might not otherwise have access. It can contribute to the nation's international leadership or be a compliment (and antidote) to science and technology.

The distinction was clear at the creation of the NEA when the Report of the Senate Labor and Public Welfare Committee noted that the "standard" [of artistic excellence] was "to serve the broad purpose of the act."[73] Clearly, the standard was neither public purpose nor policy goal. More recently, the 1990 Independent Commission on the NEA reiterated the same point in answering one of its major Congressional queries. Congress's question was "...whether the standard for publicly funded art should be different than the standard for privately funded art..." The Independent Commission's finding stated that

> "The Commission agrees that when measured solely in terms of aesthetic or artistic qualities, there should be no differences in the standard for publicly funded art from the standard for privately funded art -- that standard should be artistic excellence.
>
> But to support art from public funds entails considerations that go beyond artistic excellence. Publicly funded art must take into account the conditions that traditionally govern the use of public money. In addition, publicly funded art must, of course, serve the purposes which Congress has defined for the National Endowment for the Arts."[74]

The Commission went on to elaborate that "...the National Endowment for the Arts, as a public agency, has a responsibility to serve the public interest and promote the general welfare...." Several public purposes are articulated in Section (5)(c) of the Agency's authorizing statute. Of these public purposes, only one involves encouraging and assisting artists "...to achieve standards of professional excellence..." as well as to "...achieve wider distribution of their works...or...to work in residence at an educational or cultural institution...." The other policy goals all address the public or public purposes -- the citizenry's access to and diversity of artistic opportunities or encouraging the public's knowledge, understanding, appreciation and enjoyment of the arts.

Clearly, the bipartisan Independent Commission sought to emphasize the public benefits to be derived from federal funding for the arts rather than an "art for art's sake" philosophy. To further make that point, the

Independent Commission recommended, and Congress subsequently enacted, a change in the preamble of the NEA's authorizing legislation to read that "...the arts and the humanities belong to all the people of the United States." Nevertheless, peer panelists -- whose task is to apply the standard of artistic excellence -- persist in asserting that meeting their excellence standard constitutes sufficient reason for awarding public support. Meanwhile, NEA Chairman have failed to clearly articulate the public purposes to be served through funding decisions. And both Chairman and the National Council have seldom reached beyond the standard of excellence to consider public purposes or conditions as further criteria to guide their own judgments in the grant decision-making process.

The third misconception: the recent controversy was an aberration and the problems that provoked debate have faded. At best, this represents wishful thinking that the problem has been "solved" (either by the reforms following the 1990 reauthorization or by the change of administration). This conclusion can be arrived at only if one defines the policy problem of 1989-1992 very narrowly, as a dispute over a handful of specific grant decisions. Yet the wide swath of public debate that ensued indicates that bigger and more important issues were involved. These ranged from what is national arts policy and what might be the legitimate procedures, standards, and goals of that policy; to a belated recognition that the arts can be powerful transmitters of social values and carriers of identity; to a debate about general governmental priorities in an age of fiscal constraints; to questions of political power and who makes public decisions and what are the basis for their authority to do so. Although the concepts of accountability, censorship, freedom of expression, sponsorship, decency, obscenity, and public interest were hurled as epithets from conflicting sides of the debate, such significant public policy issues were scarcely addressed in the emotional and sensationalized conflict of 1989-1992.

Alternatively, the problem has been redefined as a failure of public relations. According to this definition, either the NEA (and its constituency) has been remiss in cultivating a strong, positive public image or the agency and its grantees have been the innocent victims of misleading and inaccurate information propagated by right-wing zealots, religious fanatics and intolerant homophobes. This misconception embodies a common strategy of a public agency or official in trouble. They attempt to define the problem as faulty public relations -- either they aren't getting their record or position out convincingly, or else the media is not treating them fairly, or opponents have engaged in a misinformation campaign. In other words, the idea is to convince the public that there is not a problem -- only the mistaken perception of a problem or an inadequate appreciation for the achievements that counter-balance the small number of problematic agency actions. This strategy was prominent throughout the controversy of 1989-92, was inherent in the NEA's increased publication and self promotion activities, including a nine minute video narrated by Walter Cronkite. It can be seen in the lobbying thrust of arts service organizations in the past few years, and is the keystone of Chairman Jane Alexander's extensive public relations efforts.

The relative quiescence of Congress and the press during 1993 and early 1994 is taken as evidence of a successful solution. However, it could just as readily indicate a breathing spell needed after the political exhaustion induced by the debate of 1989-92. Similarly, the current lull might reflect a preoccupation with other policy issues, such as health care reform, military downsizing, the budget deficit, or economic and employment stimulation. Or, it might derive from both proponents and opponents biding their time, allowing a new administration to establish its own stamp on the agency. In each of these possible scenarios, the issues that were focal points of the previous controversy have not been resolved but simply put on hold, awaiting a triggering event or a new opportunity to resurface. With comprehensive reauthorization hearings scheduled for 1995, an occasion for debate is certain. As new grant controversies or staffing questions arise, there will be other incidents as well.

While public relations failures have indeed been an important contributing factor to the recent controversies, they are not its source. Conversely, although a well-designed public relations strategy can be helpful, it cannot substitute for informed policy debate nor fully relegitimize the political position of the NEA. Indeed, given the myths and misconceptions that are inherent in current arts policy as well as the significant societal and political changes in the agency's environment, a reliance on image repair is quite inadequate to the task at hand.

Surely there were also myths and misconceptions among the NEA's critics during the period of 1989 to 1992. Prominent among these was a tendency to hold the agency to standards of public accountability that were exceptionally stringent. Even though the Agency never acknowledged that any of even its most controversial grants were failures or errors, an agency that is generally credited with a 95 to 99 percent rate of successful grants has a margin of error lower than widely regarded public opinion polls and higher than the batting average of stellar baseball players. Certainly it is unreasonable to allow public agencies or officials no margin of error, or expect all their actions or decisions to find full and ready endorsement by the public. Yet this seemed to be the standard to which many of its critics tried to hold the NEA.

Similarly, critics of arts policy propagated the fallacy that specific grants were representative of the actions of the agency as a whole. Yet, for every grant for a controversial museum exhibit like the Robert Mapplethorpe retrospective, there were scores more that would be regarded as informative, thoughtful, and enjoyable. For each of the fellowships awarded to the four controversial performance artists that sued the agency, there were hundreds of other fellowships that went unquestioned. Indeed, most of the grants that generated controversy were not typical of the kinds of projects generally supported by the agency, since they involved contemporary work, often work considered to be on the cutting edge, rather than the work of well-established artists, companies, or traditions that comprise the bulk of NEA grants.

It was also unfair that the NEA was sometimes held accountable for projects and artists that it did not support, such as Annie Sprinkle or the "Death Masks" exhibit in New York City. Similarly, it was a misrepresentation to try to hold the agency accountable for everything that a grantee did just because the agency had supported a project of a specific artist or arts institution. Nor was it fair to continue to flog the NEA over the Mapplethorpe and Serrano projects years after the fact.

Certainly it was a myth to believe that a federal agency could exert control over the viewpoints expressed by each of its grantees, whether these concerned expressions of sexuality, commentary on public issues, or assertions of racial, ethnic or gender identity. Indeed, outside prohibitions against funding lobbying and expectations that grantees would be in compliance with other federal laws, the NEA is enjoined against interfering in the internal affairs of its grantees.

The myths and misconceptions of the critics of federal arts policy played an essential role in the controversies of 1989-1992. Such fallacies are beyond the control of the arts community which can only seek to dispute and dispel them. On the other hand, the arts policy community is responsible for the consequences of its own myths and misconceptions.

Changes and Challenges in the Arts Policy Context

Much has changed in the arts, in politics, and in society since the Arts Endowment was established. Some of these changes have all ready influenced the context and issues of federal arts policy. Others have affected the way in which the arts policy system functions. And yet others present challenges that the arts policy system must confront. Certainly, demographic changes -- from the changing racial and ethnic composition of the population, to the aging and suburbanization of Americans -- as well as the rapid advance and impact of technological change will effect each of us and a range of policies in many ways. To do justice to any of these changes would require more detail and space than is available here. However, dimensions of change in the arts and in politics that affect arts policy can be identified and briefly discussed.

The Arts

First, the arts themselves have changed since the 1960's. Certainly the artsworld has grown and diversified, thus expanding the network of professionals while also increasing competition among them. The cultivation of a complex and interdependent system of public and private funding for the arts has been one of the historic successes of national arts policy; but maintaining balance, vitality, and independence among each of these funding sources is a continuous challenge, particularly in a changing economy and a more pluralistic artsworld.

With regard to grant review at the NEA, greater cultural pluralism makes the peer review process more difficult even as economic conditions raise the stakes involved in securing an NEA grant. More artists creating more kinds of art implies the need for a more competitive and complex assessment process in making awards. Simultaneously, culturally diverse artists and arts groups question the authority and standards of those affecting government decisions and demand a fairer share of public resources and attention. In addition, as cultural issues assume a larger role in public policy, the arts community must meet the challenge of rethinking the distinctions and interrelationships of art and culture, art and entertainment, professional and amateur, cultural democracy and cultural diversity as well as clarify key concepts and their public value such as excellence, experimentation, and accessibility.

Second, art, particularly visual art, has become less abstract and minimal and more content driven, politically and socially engaged, and emotionally charged. Until recently, the content or viewpoint of most of the art that came to the NEA was seldom an issue, in part because style and form were usually paramount over content. Now, in the politicized and socially conscious artsworld of the 1990's, political message, social meaning, and ideological content are more prevalent, particularly in contemporary, cutting edge art. It follows, that since contemporary art is more likely to take on controversial issues, political controversy is more likely to be provoked by contemporary art.[75] Indeed, while the artsworld and grant review panels are adamant about avoiding outside political pressure and politicization, they sometimes fail to recognize that to support or defend an artwork primarily on its political content or viewpoint is to be equally politicized. In both cases, the problem is that political preferences are substituted for aesthetic assessments. Conversely, some cultural commentators see a recent tendency for debate on social issues to occur in cultural forums and to take place through cultural proxies. Such an aestheticization of politics seldom resolves the basic political or social differences, rather it simply deflects conflict into another realm using another set of symbols and language.[76]

In short, by its sheer scope, distribution, and evolution, art has acquired more public attention and also become more politically engaged. Furthermore, as art moves from being perceived as a trivial, marginal, leisure activity to being recognized as a conduit for social values and a manifestation of personal as well as community identity, the significance of arts policy has risen. Thus, a critical challenge is threading a policy course that respects artistic freedom as well as recognizes the limits of public tolerance -- a challenge heightened by a society that is acutely conscious of its divisions rather than its commonalities.

Third, the political visibility of arts policy has risen. No longer is arts policy a low-cost, publicly invisible preserve of the arts community and its administrative and legislative allies. Instead, arts and cultural policy issues have moved off the style pages and onto the front pages. It has moved out of the concert halls and the museum galleries and into the homes of millions of Americans through network news stories, public and cable television, and direct mail campaigns. For the first time, arts policy finds that it has organized political opposition, rather than just individual critics. After four years of controversy, the political environment has changed from mildly supportive and somewhat apathetic to highly sensitized and somewhat critical of the actions of the NEA. Dealing with this increased political attention is likely to continue to challenge the arts community in the 1990's.

Partly as a defensive tactic, the arts have sought to expand their rationale from an emphasis on the intrinsic value of the arts to an intrinsic-plus-social-utility set of arguments. Hence the arts community has begun to argue that the arts invigorate education and advance complex thinking skills; can help reclaim at-risk youth; can foster economic and community development; are a mechanism for international understanding; a generator of jobs; and a tool for various other social programs. In other words, public arts advocates have begun to move away from an emphasis on art for art's sake to articulating various ways in which the arts can be linked to and serve other policies.

Fourth, the arts find themselves in heightened competition for scarce resources, particularly for money and time. Increased media options have presented the arts with greater competition for the time and attention of audiences. Technological advances seem only to increase this competition as well as the costs of being competitive. As the federal budget deficit has become the backdrop against which all federal programs are viewed, the arts find themselves in fiercer competition to maintain the public dollars that they currently receive. As corporations grapple with international competition, global ownership and organizational downsizing amidst a society confronting serious social and educational problems, the competition for corporate philanthropy is intense. Thus, the arts are challenged to make a more persuasive case for their significance and support than ever before.

Finally, the arts community has changed politically in significant ways. Today, there is a fully developed inter-governmental system of public arts agencies as well as a truly national distribution of artists and arts organizations. Building this national arts infrastructure is another policy success of the past thirty years; maintaining and fully engaging it is a challenge for the future. The organization and political experience of arts service organizations now provides the backbone of an influential and mobilizable political constituency. But this network of organizations is fragmented and difficult to coordinate and less effective than it might be, particularly when it comes to dealing with a changing political environment and an expanding set of cultural policy issues.

Thus, in many important ways, the state of the arts in 1965 when the NEA was established is quite different from the artsworld that currently exists.

The Political Environment

Politics and political processes have also changed significantly since the NEA was created. Partisan identification among the citizenry has weakened even as public officials operating through decades of divided government seemed to exhibit greater partisanship in policy debate.

Governance has often seemed to vacillate between gridlock and bipartisanship. Interest groups, particularly single interest groups, proliferated. Special interests are seen as fragmenting the policy process even as the interrelationships among policies became more apparent. The personnel of public institutions experienced substantial turnover and also became more representative of the populace. Elections became more participatory and more expensive. The Cold War ended, redirecting ideological and philosophical dispute from the international plane to domestic affairs. A growing federal deficit and unstable economic conditions increased social spending demands on government as its resources became more limited. A renewed focus on the effectiveness of government programs arose fueling a call for more accountability in government including the current efforts to reinvent and simplify government and to set performance standards for government programs.

Such systemic changes can have ramifications for arts politics and policy. The extraordinary turnover in Congress has meant that the arts, like other policy communities, have periodically lost key legislative supporters. This certainly happened in the elections of 1980 and will occur again in the foreseeable future with the inevitable retirement of Representative Sidney Yates and Senator Claiborne Pell. Furthermore, over 100 new members of Congress were elected in 1992 and additional change is imminent as announced retirements continue at an all-time high going into the 1994 campaigns. Thus, arts advocates face the challenge of a legislature of strangers -- a significant number of whom have little or no experience with arts policy issues or interests. Reaching these new members and wooing as many of them as possible to the arts coalition is crucial for the future viability of the arts policy system.

Similarly, turnover among administrators at cultural agencies and among arts service organizations has been significant and often destabilizing, particularly when there are protracted periods of interim leadership and extended vacancies. This creates uncertainty as to who the spokesmen are for arts policy; it also expands the task of the arts community in establishing effective political communications. Furthermore, as the arts community adjusts to the need to interact with more agencies and more officials rather than just the NEA, rapid turnover complicates communication and coordination problems.

Likewise the proliferation of organized interest groups requires greater consultative efforts among arts service organizations, a broader search for political allies, and increased awareness of the actions of opponent groups. This proliferation has been fueled by at least three factors: the successful growth of the arts community, the recognition of related interests and groups, and the tendency toward ideological polarization in domestic and social concerns. Indeed, some saw the controversy that the NEA confronted between 1989-1992 as part of an ideological "culture war." A casualty of that war was the carefully cultivated bipartisan support coalition for the arts. If arts policy is to avoid the worst of ideological and partisan polarization, then the arts policy community faces a crucial challenge in rebuilding and carefully nurturing bipartisan support. Like other institutions that have experienced an erosion of public trust, the NEA has lost its luster as a popular agency. Consequently, Congress has passed increasingly specific legislative directives concerning the NEA. These include earmarking appropriations for specific purposes that Congress endorses, such as education or rural and inner-city projects as well as trying to target cuts in programs that have been controversial. Recently, it has also authorized more funds for arts education, but has put them under the administration of the Department of Education, not the NEA. Certainly, Congress is likely to require a full report on what the agency has done to implement the various procedural revisions mandated by the 1990 reauthorization. Evidence that the agency has intentionally practiced bad faith or allowed lax implementation is unlikely to help it regain legislative trust.

At the same time, various administrative structures and procedures have become redundant or outmoded so that the grant review and administrative processes of the NEA are now so convoluted and complex that they resemble Rube Goldberg contraptions. Hence, a reexamination and simplification of the overall procedures and requirements of the grant-making process might be in order.

Furthermore, a number of government agencies are increasingly concerned with demonstrating success both programmatically and politically. Members of the arts policy community tend to regard these two goals as nearly reciprocal -- that is, programmatic success will generate political success.[77] Consequently, the arts community and the NEA have focussed on demonstrating and arguing that the programs and grants of the NEA over the past twenty-odd years have produced positive artistic results. However, the relationship is not so simple, particularly since political success or failure is likely to be significantly affected by circumstances, forces, and philosophies beyond public arts programs themselves. These factors can include basic philosophies of government (limited or expansive); religious/moral debate; elements of social, educational, and communications policy; conditions of partisan control of the various institutions of government; and judgments about the roles and capabilities of various levels of government. All of these can be seen in the controversy of 1989-1992, indicating flaws in the political success of the NEA. Even while there was general acknowledgement of the positive programmatic record of the NEA, there was evidence of political failure. Certainly a challenge for the remainder of the century will be for the arts policy community to prevent political failure while achieving programmatic success.

Finally, general political and policy trends are likely to have spillover effects on arts and cultural policy. Establishing standards in an effort to improve the effectiveness of public policy implementation as well as to reduce its size and cost have become general concerns. For example, two administrations have spent five years developing educational standards. The general governmental concern with standards is likely to affect how the NEA defines and operationalizes the standards and criteria it uses in grant award decisions as well as the determination of policy priorities. Furthermore, the Agency will also be expected to devise performance review standards that are outcomes (or impact)-oriented rather than input-focussed (such as budget or personnel levels) or process-oriented (such as panel diversity).

The Clinton Administration's emphasis on domestic investment as a policy priority has challenged the arts to think of themselves in new ways -- as educational and social investments -- rather than as artistic subsidies. Other policy initiatives must be recognized for the possible indirect effects they might have on the cultural sectors. For example, as federal interest in the development of the information super-highway advances, the arts and humanities must forge new political linkages and assert their interests and needs in this policy forum.

Similarly, other cultural or grant-making agencies may have spillover effects on the NEA. For example, the debate has been opened over reinventing public television, with suggestions for change in funding practices, for reasserting its educational mission, for emphasizing its activities in children's television, and for accommodating technological advances and the consequent increased competition from commercial cable television. Many of these issues resonate with questions about the NEA and arts policy; others, such as the impact of technology, are just beginning to appear on the policy screens of the arts community. For another example, the scientific community has spent the last few years in extended debate about establishing priorities in federal science policy, recommending changes in how the institutions of government deal with science issues, recognizing the inter-agency linkages involved in science and technology policy, and in "selling science to the public."[78] Again, these concerns have similarities to issues confronting arts policy.

As even this brief discussion of changes and challenges demonstrates, art, politics and society are each dynamic. Since arts policy is shaped by each of these forces, it too must be dynamic if it is to meet current needs, conditions, and opportunities.

From Accord to Discord and Beyond

When the arts first appeared on the national agenda, the policy problem was essentially defined as the economic incapacity of nonprofit cultural institutions to provide quality artistic opportunities to citizens throughout the nation. The creation of the National Endowment for the Arts and the establishment of on-going public funding for the arts were intended to provide a policy solution to this public problem.

In the early 1960's, a citizen's artistic opportunities depended, in large part, on where they lived, while education, income, gender, race and ethnicity also exerted an effect. In other words, the arts confronted a fundamental distribution problem leading to inequitable public access to cultural opportunities. In their 1966 report from the Twentieth Century Fund, economists Baumol and Bowen argued that nonprofit arts organizations could not solve this distribution problem themselves because they faced an economic dilemma. An "income-earnings gap" placed a systemic constraint on nonprofit arts organizations which threatened their solvency and impeded their ability to reach broader audiences. Hence, public action was necessary if cultural equity were to be promoted and the nation's artistic resources maintained.

A decade of efforts by a few, private foundations suggested that, with the help of outside patronage, communities could support the development of more arts organizations and reach broader audiences. Other nations as well as a few states (notably New York) provided models for a government patronage role. Various societal conditions -- rising educational levels, proliferating media technology, international political and cultural competition, domestic economic prosperity, urban vitality -- seemed hospitable to an activist state expanding into new social policy topics, including the arts.

Thus, the arts were seen as both a problem for which public solutions seemed possible, as well as an attractive and low-cost programmatic solution for other policy issues such as education, public diplomacy, or public television. In other words, the articulation of an arts policy problem converged with the availability of feasible programmatic options as well as with receptive political and economic conditions. The decisions that flowed from these circumstances established patterns of program implementation, institutional structure, policy influence and political action that persisted and prospered for the next fifteen years.[79]

In the 1980's, this stable and positive convergence of policy, program and political circumstances changed. The Reagan Revolution was critical of the expansionist, welfare state and sought to constrict its reach. Big government and policy topics perceived to be at the fringes of the state's authority -- including federal arts policy -- were redefined as part of the problem that led to budget deficits, excessive government spending and intrusive government. Defense, foreign affairs, and national security policy matters displaced social programs as spending priorities.

Many of the societal conditions that had been hospitable to arts policy in the 1960's and 1970's became less supportive in the 1980's. Instead of economic prosperity, there was intense international economic competition. Rather than rising educational levels, the deficiencies of the educational system were a growing concern. People were increasingly aware of the problems and costs of technological and media advances. Cities were beset by problems and the population had become predominantly suburban. The apparent social consensus and optimism of the 1950's into the early 1960's had transformed into dissension and pessimism about long-term prosperity. The prospect of increasing leisure time gave way to the perception of no leisure time. Confidence in America's international leadership has been replaced with the ambiguity of the post-Cold War world. In other words, most of the conditions that seemed hospitable to government's initial involvement in arts policy have changed, resulting in a less supportive environment.

Conversely during the 1980's, as the NEA and its constituency fought to preserve federal funding levels, arts policy seemed to narrow to the single goal of getting as much public money to the professional nonprofit arts as possible. Thus, as the public benefits derived from arts funding and the public purposes served by arts policy became less manifest, the political feasibility of federal arts programs became more questionable.

Given such shifts as well as changes in the arts, it is little wonder that arts policy has moved from accord to discord. On the one hand, continuation of the recent discord will only threaten the NEA and federal arts policy with political failure. On the other hand, the previous arts policy accord cannot simply be resurrected.

Clearly, any new policy paradigm is more likely to encompass a set of cultural policies rather than to focus exclusively on arts policy. The challenges, resources and context of arts policy for the 21st century are very different from those of thirty years ago. Consequently, arts and cultural programs and priorities will require rethinking and recasting if they are to transform the "culture wars" of recent years into a productive policy accord for the new century.

Notes

1. Comments of Senator Alphonse D'Amato in Senate debate, May 18, 1989, quoted in Richard Bolton,ed., *Culture Wars* (New York: The New Press, 1992) p.28-9.

2. Jesse Helms comments, quoted in *Culture Wars*, p. 31; for a similar comment from Senator D'Amato see p 29.

3. Freeborn G. Jewett and David Lloyd Kreeger, "The Corcoran: We Did the Right Thing," *The Washington Post*, 29 June 1989. The statement's authors are the former president and the former chairman of the board of the Corcoran Gallery of Art.

4. Joshua P. Smith, "Why the Corcoran Made A Big Mistake," *The Washington Post*, 18 June 1989.

5. Jock Reynolds as quoted by Grace Glueck in "Art on the Firing Line," *The New York Times*, 9 July 1989

6. Paul Richard, "Artists Cancel Exhibitions at Corcoran," *The Washington Post*, 30 August 1989

7. See for example, *The Washington Times*, 28 June 1989; Samuel Lipman, "Say No to Trash," *The New York Times*, 23 June 1989; or Senator Slade Gorton's statement to the Senate on 31 May 1989 (reprinted in *Culture Wars*), pp. 33-37. Congressman Richard Armey (R-TX) accused the NEA of being "arrogant, standoffish, totally uncooperative and even belligerent..." and that the NEA seems to "want freedom without responsibility." Armey as quoted in Frank Kuznik, "NEA Under Siege," *Museum and Arts Washington*, Nov/Dec 1989, p.55

8. Statement from the National Association of Artists' Organizations, 16 July 1989 as quoted in *Culture Wars*, p. 63.

9. Quoted in George Hager, "House Rejects Attack on NEA, Passes FY'90 Interior Bill," *Congressional Quarterly Weekly*, July 15, 1989, p. 1763.

10. In excerpts of Senate debate July 26, 1989, pp. 83 and 80 respectively of Bolton, *Culture Wars*.

11. See *Congressional Quarterly Weekly*, 30 September 1989, p. 2550. Also see 9 December 1989, p. 3345. For press accounts, see *The Washington Post*, 30 September 1989 and *The New York Times*, 30 September 1989.

12. *Congressional Record*, July 26, 1989, p. S8806. Also see Michael Oreskes, "Senate Votes to Bar US Support of 'Obscene or Indecent' Artwork," *The New York Times*, 27 July 1989 and Elizabeth Kastor, "Senate Votes to Expand NEA Grant Ban," *The Washington Post*, 27 July 1989.

13. See Robin Toner, "House Sends Arts Endowment Message on Taxpayers' Taste," *The New York Times*, 13 July 1989.

14. Tom Kenworthy, "GOP Tries to Turn 2 Votes Against Democrats," *The Washington Post*, 19 July 1989.

15. Quoted in William H. Honan, "Arts Endowment Pulls Its Grant Show on AIDS," *The New York Times*, 9 November 1989.

16. Williams is quoted by Elizabeth Kastor, "Arts Supporters Decry NEA Grant Denial," *The Washington Post*, 10 November 1989. Abrams is quoted by William H. Honan, "The Endowment vs. the Arts: Anger and Concern," *The New York Times*, 10 November 1989.

17. Elizabeth Kastor, "Bernstein Rejects Medal in Arts Controversy," *The Washington Post*, 16 November 1989.

18. *Congressional Quarterly Weekly*, 24 March 1990, p. 922.

19. Statements included in the press release by People For the American Way, "The Far Right's Latest Target: Freedom in the Arts," (Washington, D.C.: 20 March 1990.

20. Text of the President's statement as quoted in *The Chronicle of Higher Education*, 4 April 1990.

21. *The Washington Post*, 28 March 1990, p. D1 & D3; *The New York Times*, 29 March 1990, p. A1 & 21.

22. Williams quoted in *The Washington Post*, 14 May 1990, p. C1. For a summary account of the NEA controversy leading into the 1990 reauthorization debate, see Marie Tessier, "Tying Down Federal Funds for the Arts," *Editorial Research Reports*, 25 May 1990, pp. 302-315.

23. *Ibid.*, p. 312.

24. Independent Commission, *Report to Congress on the National Endowment for the Arts*, (Washington, D.C., September 1990), p. 2-3. (Hereafter referred to as *Report on the NEA*).

25. *Ibid.*, p. 59.

26. A Federal District court in Los Angeles found that the NEA's certification requirement "...place[d] an obstacle in the grant of the recipient's path to exercise of his constitutional speech rights." See report in *The New York Times*, 10 January 1991. By late February 1991, the NEA announced that it was dropping the anti-obscenity pledge requirement. See, *The Washington Post*, 21 February 1991.

27. On the January hearing, see *The Washington Post*, 28 January 1991. On the May decision, see *The Washington Post* and *The New York Times*, 18 May 1991.

28. *The Washington Post*, 3 June 1991 and John Hammer, "On the Potential Impact of *Rust v. Sullivan* as a Model for Content-Based Restrictions on Federal Arts and Humanities Funding," *The Journal of Arts Management, Law and Society*, Vol. 22, No. 3 (Fall 1992), pp. 277-280.

29. *The Washington Post*, 19 March 1991.

30. The ACLU launched its Arts Censorship Project that included such activities as fighting record labelling bills in state legislatures, investigating Justice Department methods in anti-obscenity raids, serving as co-counsel on the NEA Four case, and representing actress Vanessa Redgrave concerning alleged reprisals against her for statements opposing the Persian Gulf War. The project of People For the American Way was Artsave, which was to provide technical assistance as well as research cataloging and publicizing of artists' claims of instances of attempted censorship. See *The Washington Post*, 17 June 1991.

31. In April 1992, in response to a Congressional request, the NEA's Office of Congressional Affairs prepared a document that listed and provided information about all controversial grants that had elicited legislative and/or media inquiries. That document listed 55 grants and subgrants for the period between 1989 and April of 1992.

32. Republican Senators Ted Stevens (Alaska) and Slade Gorton (Washington), members of the Senate Appropriations Committee, accused the Smithsonian Institution of "advancing a left-leaning political agenda" and hinted at possible funding cuts if their concerns were not addressed. *The Washington Post* 16 May 1991. The NEH was embroiled in debate over the Carole Iannone nomination to the National Council on the Humanities during the Spring of 1991.

33. *The Washington Post*, 17 October 1991.

34. 137 *Congressional Record*, H7989.

35. Bernard Holland, "U.S. Orchestras Face Up to Trouble And the Bottom Line," *The New York Times*, 15 June 1992. Also, National Endowment for the Arts, *The Arts in America, 1992*, (Washington, D.C.: National Endowment for the Arts, November 1992), pp. II-7-10.

36. For details of the congressional debate over public television, see Mike Mills, "Senate Tunes Out Critics, Boosts Public TV, Radio," *Congressional Quarterly Weekly*, 6 June 1992, pp. 1598-99. Also *Congressional Record-Senate*, 2 June 1992, pp. S7304-7473.

37. Bill Carter, "Conservatives Call for PBS to Go Private or Go Dark," *The New York Times*, 30 April 1992, p. A1 and C15.

38. *The Washington Times*, 22 February 1992; also *The Washington Post*, 10 February 1992.

39. The Chairman was quoted in *The Washington Post*, 10 February 1992.

40. On the Council discussion see, National Endowment for the Arts, "Minutes of the 111th Meeting of the National Council on the Arts," January 31 and February 1, 1992, pp. 21-22. Also see Chapter 8 of *Arts in Crisis: The National Endowment for the Arts Versus America*, by Joseph Wesley Zeigler, (Chicago: A Cappella Press, 1994).

41. *The Philadelphia Inquirer*, 22 February 1991.

42. *The Washington Post*, 28 February 1992.

43. Ibid.

44. Kim Masters, "Acting Arts Chief Vows to Keep It Clean," *The Washington Post*, 6 May 1992, p. A1.

45. Ibid., p. A6.

46. Bruce D. Brown, "NEA Funds: Smooth Sailing in House," *The Washington Post*, 24 July 1992. An NEA staff member reported that in the Summer of 1992,

conservative critics of the agency had not raised questions about controversial grants that year and that "staff members of at least 10 to 15 liberal members of the House and Senate ..called to say 'you're doing exactly what we want you to do.'" As reported in *The New York Times*, 1 August 1992. p. 18.

47. The two applications in question concerned an exhibit proposed by the List Visual Arts Center at the Massachusetts Institute of Technology entitled "Corporal Politics" and a photographic show on "Anonymity and Identity" proposed by the Anderson Gallery at Virginia Commonwealth University.

48. Anne-Imelda Radice," Decision on Declining to Fund Applications from the List Center and the Anderson Gallery," (National Endowment for the Arts, press release, May 12, 1992).

49. *The New York Times*, 13 May 1992, p. D26.

50. As stated in a letter from the sculpture review panel to the NEA Chairman as reported in *The Washington Post*, 16 May 1992.

51. Mary Ann French, "2nd Arts Panel Walks Out," *The Washington Post*, 21 May 1992, p. D1 and 4.

52. See *The Washington Post*, 22 May 1992 and *The New York Times*, 1 August 1992.

53. All of the following statements were issued in press releases, dated 22 May 1992.

54. For reports of the District Court decision in *Finley v. The National Endowment for the Arts*, see *The New York Times* and *The Washington Post*, 10 June 1992.

55. *The Washington Post*, 5 June 1993, D1 and 9.

56. *The Washington Post*, 22 June 1993; also see *The New York Times*, 6 April 1993.

57. Twentieth Century Fund, *Quality Time? The Report of the Task Force on Public Television*, (New York: Twentieth Century Fund Press, 1993). The quote is from task force member Lawrence K. Grossman, former president of PBS and NBC News, as reported in *The Washington Post*, 14 July 1993.

58. For example, see Maureen Dowd, "Washington Is Star Struck As Hollywood Gets Serious," *The New York Times*, 9 May 1993 and Richard Cohen, "Star Struck," *The Washington Post*, 13 May 1993.

59. *The Washington Post*, 12 September 1993.

60. In the Summer, the House voted to reduce the NEA's FY 1994 budget by 5 percent, or approximately $9 million, *The Washington Post*, 16 July 1993. In September, the Senate appropriations committee restored half of the funds, *The Washington Post*, 16 September 1993. Among the arts projects that aroused legislative concern were NEA grants to three gay and lesbian film festivals that included films that were called graphic and obscene; the "Abject Art" exhibit of the Whitney Museum that included a three-foot mound of plastic excrement, films by Annie Sprinkle and Suzie Silver, and works by Andres Serrano and Robert Mapplethorpe. See, *The Washington Post*, 12 July 1993. A project in the San Diego area also drew considerable comment; it involved a group of three experimental artists who gave away $5,000 in ten dollar bills as "a work of art and a political statement about the interaction of physical space with intellectual space and civic space." See *The New York Times*, 12 August 1993.

61. Nello McDaniel and George Thorn, *Rethinking and Restructuring the Arts Organization*, (New York: FEDAPT, 1990).

62. William H. Honan, in his article "Why Frohnmayer Lost U.S. Arts Post," reports that many observers of Federal cultural patronage found that the Chairman's "fatal mistake" was "his failure to grasp who his true constituency was..." For example, Leonard Garment, former co-chairman of the Independent Commission on the NEA, observed that he "had tried to explain to Frohnmayer that his real constituency was not the artists but the President, Congress and the public..." *The New York Times*, 27 February 1992.

63. Adrian M.S. Piper, "Government Support for Unconventional Works of Art," in *Culture and Democracy* edited by Andrew Buchwalter, (Boulder: Westview Press, 1992), pp. 217-222. Piper notes that without some form of public support, artists would be disinclined to produce anything but the uncontroversial and popularly marketable works favored by corporate sponsors and the entertainment industry. Piper considers "unconventional" to be "works of art that offer critical alternatives to prevailing power relations" and sees private patronage practices as tantamount to "passive censorship."

64. Carol Becker, "The Social Responsibility of Artists," in Buchwalter, ed., *Culture and Democracy*, pp. 239-248.

65. For example, see Robert Garfias, "Cultural Equity: Cultural Diversity and the Arts in America," and Gerald D. Yoshitomi, "Cultural Equity: Cultural Democracy," in *Public Money and the Muse*, (New York: W.W. Norton, 1991), pp. 182-194 and 195-215.

66. Michael Brenson, "Is 'Quality' an Idea Whose Time Has Gone?" *The New York Times*, Section II, 22 July 1990.

67. Such concerns affect not only the advisory panels of the NEA but those used by other governmental agencies. For example, Bruce L.R. Smith in *The Advisers, Scientists in the Advisory Process*, (Washington, D.C.: The Brookings Institution, 1992) sees a similar concern about scientific advisory panels. Smith notes that "the challenge that the nation faces is to make the advisory system contribute to the larger ends of effective government rather than merely to constitute a layer of bureaucratic clutter or to prolong and complicate political controversies." For critics, the major problem is "that a narrow group of citizens, reflecting only partial interests, gets privileged access to decisionmakers under the guise of neutral expertise." Thus, the fundamental issue in a democracy is "the continuing struggle to understand how knowledge and power interrelate and coexist." See pp. 191-192.

68. On the willingness of Americans to pay more in taxes if it were used to support arts and cultural activities and facilities as well as on support for the importance of art to the education of school-age children, see *Americans and the Arts VI* conducted by LH Research/Louis Harris, (New York: American Council for the Arts, 1992). A recent National Endowment for the Arts report, *Arts Participation in America: 1982-1992* prepared by Jack Faucett Associates and John P. Robinson, (Washington, D.C.: NEA, October 1993), found that 71 percent of survey respondents expressed an interest in attending more arts performances or displays. See p. 57.

69. The survey commissioned by the National Cultural Alliance was titled "The Importance of the Arts and Humanities to American Society." See *The Washington Post*, 5 February 1993.

70. Comments from Robert Hughes at the June 1993 conference on arts policy at the Massachusetts Institute of Technology.

71. This myth is increasingly challenged by commentators of both the left and of the right. For example, Gerald D. Yoshitomi in "Cultural Equity: Cultural Democracy" in Benedict, *Public Money and the Muse*, pp. 195-215, calls for a broader articulation of "cultural policy" and argues that current policy is structurally inappropriate for an increasingly heterogenous society. On the other hand, Samuel Lipman argues that national cultural policy has been three-pronged: dedication to affirmative action, promotion of multiculturalism, and public sponsorship for cutting edge art. See "The State of National Cultural Policy," in Buchwalter, ed., *Culture and Democracy*, pp. 47-57.

72. See Public Law 89-209, Sections 2 and 5(c); also Independent Commission, *Report on the NEA*, pp. 11-15.

73. Quoted in Independent Commission, *Report on the NEA*, p. 15.

74 *Report on the NEA*, pp. 57-60, particularly p. 57.

75. Joy Sperling in "The Right to Offend and the Power to Provoke: The Role of Controversy in American Art," discusses the activist art of the 1990's as being essentially "transgressive" rather than avant garde and as being committed to specific and highly charged issues such as the rights of women and gays, the environment, or certain kinds of medical research. See pps. 229-235 in Buchwalter, *Culture and Democracy*. Other prominent critics and commentators discuss this phenomenon under a variety of names. For example, Robert Hughes calls this a "culture of complaint," while Arthur Danto calls it "disturbatory art."

76. See Russell A. Berman, "Popular Culture, Political Culture, Public Culture," in Buchwalter, *Culture and Democracy*, pp. 261-276.

77. For an insightful case study of programmatic success and political failure, see Gary Mucciaroni, *The Political Failure of Employment Policy, 1945-1982*, (Pittsburgh: University of Pittsburgh Press, 1990).

78. On "selling science to the public," see Colleen Cordes, "National Science Foundations New Chief Aims to Market Science." *Chronicle of Higher Education*, 12 January 1994, p. A27. A major effort to discuss science policy goals and recommendations for change in the science policy system, see the series of reports of the Carnegie Commission on Science, Technology and Government issued between 1991 and 1994.

79. On the institutionalization of structure-induced equilibrium within policy subsystems, see Frank R. Baumgartner and Bryan Jones, *Agendas and Instability in American Politics* (Chicago: University of Chicago Press, 1993), especially pg.238.

2

The Politics of Arts Policy: Subgovernment to Issue Network

Margaret Jane Wyszomirski

In the nearly three decades since the establishment of the National Endowment for the Arts, the political dynamics and focal issues of federal arts policy have changed considerably. Initially, arts policy developed as a relatively simple distributive policy subgovernment focussed on increasing financial resources for the NEA and, through it, to the arts constituency. During the 1970's, this distributive subgovernment matured into a stable system, characterized by low visibility issues and cooperative relations among its triple alliance partners -- the arts community, the NEA and its authorizing and appropriations subcommittees in Congress. Together this alliance secured resources and distributed subsidies to artists, arts organizations, and arts agencies on the premise that the arts were desirable and of public benefit to society as a whole. During the 1980's, however, the mutuality of interest within the subgovernment triad began to show signs of divergence, even as the number and type of issues affecting the arts increased and diversified, often engaging political players from outside the original policy subgovernment. Not only did Congress increase reporting requirements on the NEA, but the decade began with a special Task Force and ended with an Independent Commission both convened to consider the NEA's purposes and procedures.

Beginning in 1985 and emphatically since 1989, regulatory policy issues concerning grants supporting allegedly offensive, pornographic, obscene, indecent, and/or blasphemous activities have gained considerable prominence. The emergence of this regulatory element challenged heretofore prevailing public benefit assumptions and prompted different policy politics. In this new environment, policy actors other than those with direct artistic interests provoked visible and heated debate that destabilized the interrelations of the arts policy triangle and often deflected issue resolution into a broader congressional arena, such as conference committees or floor action in the House and/or Senate. As is common to other regulatory issues, the proposed regulations concerning the content of arts to be funded with public money provoked considerable conflict and invoked repeated debate between 1989 and 1992. The attendant constitutional issues only intensified the political conflict.

As the conflictual politics of regulatory policy continued unresolved, Congress sought to redefine the matter by mandating new procedures and by authorizing different distributive priorities for the Endowment. As new procedural mandates were met, administrative and staff costs of convening larger, more diverse and conflict-of-interest-free panels mounted, eroding the resources and attention available for artistic support and policy leadership. Agency attempts to administer, first, anti-obscenity and, later, decency provisions could find no consensus, but instead drew criticism from the left (and the arts community) for being censorious and from the right (and fundamentalist opponents) for being too permissive.

The new priorities included an increased emphasis on decentralized public access through the states, a focus on reaching under-served communities, and a greater emphasis on arts education. As these new priorities were implemented within a static agency budget level, the net result was to redistribute funding allocations with less money available for direct award to artists and arts organizations through discipline-based programs. This shift further disrupted the distributive policy subgovernment system. Furthermore, to effectively address its expanded educational mandate, the Arts Endowment was thrust into another policy arena, scrambling to link into the education reform agenda that had great momentum and its own network of political players. Thus, by the 1990's, the arts policy system had evolved into a complex and unpredictable issue network simultaneously concerned with distributive, regulatory, and redistributive issues.

Policy and Policy Systems

Analysts of American public policy have long recognized that all policy is not of a kind. Rather, policies can vary by subject matter (e.g., education, transportation, arts, etc.); by the kind and/or source of financial resources involved (e.g., tax, entitlement, discretionary, etc.); by the beneficiary or target group(s) affected; by the societal impact of the public outcome; by the policy-making process followed; and by the set of political relationships engaged.[1]

One fundamental subject matter grouping distinguishes domestic policy from national security policy. Sometimes a third set of policies is discerned -- "constituent issues" -- that involve the rules of political action including constitutional issues. Among domestic policies, three types of policy can be distinguished according to the set of political relationships involved. These three types are distributive, regulatory and redistributive policy.

Each of these types is characterized by a different political process and a different set of relationships among principal actors. The first domestic policy type, distributive policy, is perceived by policy participants as a "win-win" situation. That is, issues are generally resolved in a manner that is perceived favorably by the three major policy actors involved -- the concerned constituency group, the relevant congressional subcommittee and the lead administrative agency. The interactions among these actors remain relatively stable over time and are marked by relatively low public visibility and a high degree of cooperation and logrolling. Together, the three political actors constitute a subgovernment system capable of making distributive decisions in a decentralized manner, with little reference to their impact on other fields or policies. Thus, distributive policies provide subsidies to groups, organizations or individuals for private activities that are deemed desirable to society as a whole and that, at least in theory, might not otherwise be undertaken.

The second domestic policy type is regulatory policy. It aims to limit the provision of specific resources to one or a few groups chosen from a larger number of potential competitors or else it aims to protect the public by setting conditions for certain kinds of private activity. The former is competitive regulation and the latter protective regulation. Because those entities vulnerable to regulation generally would prefer to avoid such restrictions, regulatory policy debate tends to be visible and participants have a clear sense of what is at stake. While subgovernments may be a feature of the regulatory policy landscape, they are not as controlling as in distributive policy arenas. Instead, coalitions of interested groups tend to be unstable, depending upon what is at stake and how highly it is valued. Similarly, although Congressional subcommittees are involved in regulatory decisions, their actions are frequently altered either in the full House or Senate or in conference committee. Finally, the lead administrative agency generally has less autonomy of action and is subject to more extensive Congressional guidance and oversight. Because many regulatory issues recur, the policy process tends to be extended with continuing controversy, bargaining and compromise efforts.

The third domestic policy type is redistributive, or a "win-lose" situation. Redistributive policies are intended to reallocate resources (e.g., political, financial, legal) or some other valued item among significant social groupings such as classes, ethnic or racial groups, or between geographic regions. Because resources or privileges seem to shift to one group at the expense of another, these policies generate visible and prolonged political controversy that is often highly ideological. Unlike the relatively small circles of participants that are characteristic of distributive and regulatory politics, many groups and individuals get involved in redistributive policy debates even if they do not have a direct interest at stake. Similarly, a broad segment of Congress is generally involved in the redistributive policy politics, including full committees, party leaders, full Floor action and conference committees. Executive actors are likely to include not only a lead agency or bureau, but other agencies or bureaus, as well as the president, his top advisors and appointees. In other words, issue networks rather than subgovernment systems are characteristic of redistributive policy.

In contrast to a subgovernment, an issue network is diffuse, fluid and volatile. As Hugo Heclo has noted, an issue network contains many changing participants with variable degrees of mutual commitment.[2] Rather than being united in control over an issue area, the members of an issue network vie with each other for policy influence. Rather than basing their policy positions on direct, tangible and (generally) economic interests, members of an issue network bring an intellectual or emotional commitment to specific issues which, in turn, determines their interests. Whereas a subgovernment may be a shared interest group, an issue network is an interested knowledge group. If specific issues arise that energize an issue network, this may overlay an existing subgovernment policy system, thereby complicating and destabilizing the policy politics involved.

These analytical concepts of subgovernment and issue network and of different types of policy and their attendant political configurations are useful in understanding the pattern of arts policy and politics over the past thirty years and in assessing the current situation.

Prelude: Establishing the Arts on the Federal Agenda

The New Deal experiment with employment programs for artists was followed by decades of political controversy and Congressional investigations concerning allegedly subversive activities and beliefs of some artists. As a consequence, artists and politicians regarded each other with mutual distrust. Although a small group of Congressional arts advocates nurtured the idea of political support for the arts during the 1950's and early 1960's, their efforts to exert arts policy leadership were insufficient to establish a federal arts policy. Nonetheless, they helped incubate the issue as well as developed a set of supportive arguments.

Tenuous presidential attention to the arts began to emerge late in the Eisenhower presidency with conditional support for a National Cultural Center project in Washington and as a subject of concern to the 1960 report of the President's Commission on National Goals.[3] Active, albeit largely symbolic, presidential policy leadership efforts acquired momentum during the Kennedy Administration. The Democratic Party platform of 1960 was the first major party arts plank;[4] it called for the establishment of a federal advisory agency to be concerned with the cultural resources of the nation. Presidential gestures towards artists, including inaugural invitations and White House cultural soirees, set a new tone for relations between government and artists.

During the Kennedy Administration, the concept of a patronage partnership involving business, private philanthropy and government began to develop. The three primary elements of this approach held that: (1) the federal government had a responsibility to foster conditions in which the arts could thrive; (2) existing cultural institutions were being threatened by a financial crisis unlikely to be resolved without public subsidy; and (3) the federal government should be even-handed in its support for intellectual creativity, with the arts and humanities meriting public support as well as the sciences.

Although President Kennedy's arts policy leadership initiatives were tragically cut short, his successor Lyndon Johnson carried the effort to fruition with the help of congressional cultural policy advocates. The largely moribund effort to raise funds for the construction of a National Cultural Center in Washington was reinvigorated and redirected toward creating a living memorial to the assassinated president -- the John F. Kennedy Center for the Performing Arts. Similarly, the repeatedly frustrated efforts to establish a Federal Advisory Council on the Arts finally succeeded in May of 1964.

President Johnson made federal support for the arts and humanities a part of the educational policy agenda of the Great Society. With this strong presidential endorsement and support from the academically-based humanities community as well as from a few artist unions, a bill to establish a National Foundation for the Arts and Humanities, comprised of separate Endowments for the Arts and for the Humanities, quickly moved through Congress to enactment.[5]

The National Endowment for the Arts (NEA), established by PL 89-209 in September of 1965, is the first federal agency to have as its primary mission the administration of a federal arts policy. Although historically, various agencies and policies have had significant indirect effects on the arts (e.g., tax and copyright laws and labor programs), there was no organized, direct and on-going Federal support for the arts until the establishment of the Arts Endowment. The NEA was to award grants of financial support to artists and arts organizations for projects undertaken in partnership with private and non-federal resources.

Thus, after two decades of tentative and contested legislative and executive efforts, a post-New Deal federal commitment to the arts was finally realized with creation of the National Foundation for the Arts and Humanities in September of 1965. This accomplishment had been possible only through a presidential-congressional alliance in pursuit of a broad-gauged educational policy agenda. The policy goals of much of LBJ's Great Society educational agenda including the arts were inherently redistributive -- intended to expand and change the pattern of public access to, and benefit from, educational (and cultural) opportunities. However, the implementation strategy of the consequent federal programs was essentially distributive -- that is, through the award of both financial and symbolic incentives.[6] In this way, the Johnson Administration used a familiar strategy for defusing a potentially conflictual redistributive policy issue -- it redefined it as a set of distributive benefits.

But the conditions that produced this window of policy opportunity were short lived. The new arts agency had few resources. After receiving a start-up FY 1966 appropriation of $2.5 million, the NEA's annual budget rose to approximately $7 million in FY 1967 and then stalled at that level for the next three years. During that time, as the President grew increasingly preoccupied with the Vietnam War, much of the momentum for his domestic programs as well as his ability to effectively champion initiatives such as the NEA dissipated both legislatively and publicly.

Indeed, by 1968, concern over the ability to fund both "guns and butter" programs bred circumstances in which congressional opponents of federal arts support sought to make the NEA's reauthorization and appropriation a test vote about fiscal responsibility. Concurrently, other congressional critics sought to revoke the agency's authority to make grants to individuals, citing concern for both fiscal responsibility and quality control accountability.[7] With weakened presidential support and lacking strong organized arts support, congressional proponents could only preserve a basic federal commitment to support for the arts; budgetary resources for the Endowment were essentially frozen at a minimal and inadequate level. In retrospect, however, this low funding level may have had a longer-term positive effect since it further muted the potential redistributive aspects of federal arts support while allowing constituency demand for distributive benefits to build up.

Thus, at the advent of the Nixon presidency, a tenuous federal policy of support for the arts had positioned the NEA as the administrator of future federal support if advocates in the arts as well as in Congress could secure the necessary resources. To realize this possibility, each component of the nascent policy subgovernment needed to overcome its own weakness -- shallow and dispersed congressional support, a fragmented and under-organized arts constituency, and the meager administrative and financial capacity of the agency.

The Development of an Arts Subgovernment

During the tenure of Nancy Hanks as Chairman of the National Endowment for the Arts (1969-1977), as each component of the arts policy system matured, an "iron triangle" of interrelationships developed between the agency, its congressional oversight and appropriations committees, and the organized arts constituency. During this stage both presidential leadership and congressional support were vital to the subgovernment's development.

Recognizing the initial weaknesses of the arts policy system, Hanks first secured presidential support for the agency and its programs, thereby providing political "cover" while she worked to cultivate broad congressional support, to mobilize the arts constituency, and to develop agency capacity.[8] Hanks reinforced this presidential linkage through an alliance with White House Special Consultant Leonard Garment, through the development of friendly working relations with OMB (particularly Deputy Director Caspar Weinberger), and through personal service to the president and members of his family.[9]

Under Hanks, the NEA became a "patron of political action," helping to mobilize its constituency from the top down by encouraging groups that would "promote new legislative agendas and social values."[10] In the process, three objectives were addressed. First, grant support to arts institutions helped to increase the compensation of artists (thus providing a direct benefit in return for the early political support of unions).[11] Second, the financial needs of artistic institutions were addressed. And lastly, the potential for direct and tangible benefits (i.e. grant support) provided the arts community with an incentive to mobilize into a political constituency.

Sequentially, Hanks identified elements of the arts community in economic need and encouraged them to lobby for increased appropriations in return for the promise of increased federal grant assistance. First orchestras and museums were approached. These had numerous, widely distributed, and well organized associations, and could mount extensive and effective lobbying efforts. In turn, dance, theater, literature, film, architecture and the growing complement of state arts agencies were enlisted in the common interest.

Beyond evoking group action, Hanks took concrete steps to develop the weak and divided arts community into a coordinated and politically effective constituency. Starting in 1970, the NEA annually awarded between 5 and 9 percent of its program funds to support and develop arts service organizations[12] which were also capable of undertaking political advocacy. Indeed, the agency not only supported established service organizations, but also promoted the creation of completely new ones, such as OPERA America and the National Assembly of State Arts Agencies. Thus, "the NEA patronized the political action of a constituency which, in turn, supported the agency's quest for more resources that could be channeled back into the very constituency the agency had helped to expand and organize."[13]

Concurrently, the agency convened peer review panels to provide expert assessments and funding recommendations concerning grant applications. Through this advisory practice, the arts constituency was given a stake in the agency itself. In the advisory panels, the arts community assumed a major, indeed generally a decisive, role with regard to individual grant awards as well as an important role in the development of policy for each program and, cumulatively, for the agency as a whole. Similarly, as different components of the arts community were enlisted into the agency's political support group, they were also drawn into NEA decision-making and became the beneficiaries of the distribution of federal grants.

During Hanks's tenure, the NEA budget increased from $8.2 million (FY 1970) to $123.5 million (FY 1978). Meanwhile, the staff grew by nearly 600 percent to process a 900 percent increase in grant applications and a 600 percent rise in grant awards. The NEA's internal organization expanded from 8 programs to 12 fully articulated ones. Within the umbrella of the National Foundation for the Arts and the Humanities, the agency's administrative structure also began to specialize and diversify. In short, the agency became institutionalized.

Under Chairman Hanks, the NEA and the arts constituency also embarked on a campaign to make the agency, its work, and America's artistic resources better known to members of Congress and to demonstrate that cultural benefits and opportunities were reaching constituents in individual congressional districts and the nation at large. The agency itself employed a number of tactics. Both Chairman Hanks and Deputy Chairman Michael Straight made courtesy calls to congressional offices. The Deputy Chairman also extended a series of concert and theater invitations at the Kennedy Center to members of Congress. The agency mounted an extensive publicity campaign pointing out the positive effects of grants throughout the country.[14]

To emphasize its broad distributive reach, the NEA sought to encourage and subsidize the establishment of an arts council in every state and territory. By FY 1975, all 50 states and six special jurisdictions had an arts agency and the NEA was distributing 20 percent of its program funds as block grants to the states. As Dick Netzer has argued, "The political price of large-scale federal support for the arts in the United States [was] an overriding emphasis on wider availability."[15] Indeed, the breadth of geographic distribution of NEA awards and funds has been a recurrent concern of both authorizing and appropriating committees.

Growing congressional support of the NEA and the arts community was reflected in the development of the congressional component of the arts subgovernment during the 1970's. While at the start of the decade, there was little legislative consensus concerning arts policy or the NEA, by 1977 House Majority Whip John Brademas (D-IN) could declare the arts to be "politically saleable."[16] During this period, the arts were championed by three strategically positioned subcommittee chairmen. In the Senate, Claiborne Pell (D-RI) headed the special, then Subcommittee on Education, Arts and Humanities. In the House, Representative John Brademas (D-IN) chaired the equivalent authorizing subcommittee (variously concerned with postsecondary or select education)[17] while Representative Julia Butler Hansen (D-WA) chaired the House

Appropriations Subcommittee that considered the NEA's annual budget. Typical of the politics of distributive policy, these Congressional subcommittee members generally made the final decisions on policy after receiving input from expert administrators and representatives of the grantees. The legislative leadership of Senator Pell and Representative Brademas was a central force in defining the character of a public arts policy, securing a place for the arts on the national policy agenda, and articulating the federal government's role in maintaining the vitality of American arts.

One sign of growing congressional acceptance could be found in the lengthening of the NEA's reauthorization cycle from a 2-year reauthorization in the 1960's, to a 3-year term beginning in 1970, to a 4 year period in 1976, and eventually to a 5-year term in 1980. Similarly, with presidential support, the agency's financial resources grew through the 1970's -- the NEA budget grew from $8 million in FY 1970 to $123 million in FY 1978. This underwrote an unusually conflict-free redistributive policy goal via popular distributive means that reached broad geographic and discipline communities. It also supported staff expansion, programmatic diversification and administrative specialization as the agency became institutionalized. Thus the NEA developed its own organizational ability as well as a mutually reinforcing relationship with its constituency which had, in turn, become an effective interest group capable of advocating its interests both with the agency and with a more receptive Congress.

A Mature Arts Subgovernment in Action

During the early 1970's, federal arts policy had gained a bipartisan support base as well as a positive legislative-executive coalition despite conditions of divided government. This facilitated the evolution of a federal arts policy subgovernment that fit the classic distributive policy pattern (stable relations among the proponents, low visibility, and mutual cooperation under Congressional subcommittee guidance) and that was quite successful in securing additional resources to benefit its mutual interests. Thus, with an effective subgovernment in place, as later presidents proved less supportive, the arts subgovernment demonstrated its capacity for independent political viability.[18]

The shift in policy leadership to Congress can be seen in the appointment of the third NEA Chairman, Livingston Biddle. Whereas the first two Chairmen -- Roger Stevens and Nancy Hanks -- had clearly been presidential preferences, Biddle was obviously the congressional candidate, specifically of oversight subcommittee chairman Senator Pell. As such, Biddle "embodied the concerns of the agency's friendly congressional critics, sharing with them a different program orientation for the Endowment."[19]

Consequently, Biddle sought to foster greater policy decision-making participation for the state arts agencies as well as for the National Council. He also diversified review panel composition and increased the rotation of program directors. A new emphasis on "access" and "availability" was manifest in increased support for folk arts, art festivals, and "popular" artforms (such as musical theater) and mediums (such as public television and film). In general, Biddle sought to shift additional support to new and minority-based arts activities and reduce the emphasis on established "elite" institutions. Furthermore, the heretofore neglected Federal Council for the Arts and Humanities (FCAH) was activated. In seeking to develop connections, often through inter-agency agreements, between the arts and other policy areas (such as labor, education, energy, international exchanges, transportation, and community development), the FCAH extended the arts policy system in a search for new allies and additional resources.

While these changes were amenable to President Carter, it was clear that the impetus for redirection was coming from Congress, specifically from congressional arts supporters within the arts subgovernment. It, therefore, required a different strategy from that used to counter opposition or criticism from outside the policy triad. Consequently, the NEA was drawn more (and more directly) into advocacy, rather than relying upon its arts constituency. Indeed, as a result of a Federal-State Reassessment Task Force in 1977, the NEA professed that "advocacy is of such importance that it should not be the sole responsibility of any program or office but should be a major component within the Endowment and of the highest priority."[20] In its 1978 Annual Report, the NEA defined its leadership role as being responsive to field needs and undertaking

> "...to provide leadership on behalf of the arts (a) through advocacy and cooperation with government agencies on all matters relating to the arts; and (b) through advocacy with private institutions to stimulate increasing support for the arts from the private sector."[21]

Another indication of congressional assertiveness in arts policy could be found in the emergence of Representative Sidney Yates as the new House leader on arts policy. Yates succeeded to the chairmanship of the

House Appropriations Subcommittee on Interior and Related Agencies in 1975. In 1979, he asserted his claim to the arts policy leadership role with the request that the Appropriations Committee's investigative staff conduct a study of the NEA's application review process. The subsequent report launched a barrage of criticism against the agency.[22] Encompassing not only the application review process but many aspects of agency operation and policy-making, the scope of this staff report clearly exceeded its initial charge and raised a number of issues more appropriate for an authorization (rather than an appropriations) committee. Although NEA Chairman Biddle succeeded in refuting and deflecting the charges, some of its concerns were either administratively addressed (such as panel diversity) or resurfaced in later years.

Just as the Agency and the congressional elements of the arts subgovernment were experiencing change and adjustment during the late 1970's, the character of the arts constituency also evolved during these years. As a consequence of the slowed pace of NEA budgetary growth after 1976, various elements of the arts constituency found themselves in competition with one another for resources. The sense of unity and common purpose that had prevailed earlier in the decade became strained.

Furthermore, as various arts interests became better organized, they came to expect a greater and more equal role in policy formation at the NEA. This was particularly true of the state arts agencies, which formed their own service organization in 1976 and sought a partnership with the NEA rather than simply patronage from it.[23] Various arts service organizations developed membership information and data collection systems, thus beginning to build a capacity to provide information to support their cause and demonstrate their needs to both Congress and to the NEA.

In addition, the arts constituency, with support and leadership from the Arts Endowment, developed new rationales for public support, most notably the "economic impact" argument which was highly persuasive with both federal and state legislators by demonstrating the positive economic externalities generated by arts activities.[24] Finally, in 1977, service organizations representing museum directors; dance, opera and theater companies, and symphony orchestras joined together to form an explicit advocacy agency -- the American Arts Alliance (AAA) -- to advance their interests through lobbying.[25]

By the end of the 1970's it could be said that each element of the arts policy triangle had achieved a level of political influence and/or organizational development such that the arts policy subgovernment was capable not only of action independent of presidential support but potentially of acting as a triple alliance against a president if he threatened its common interests.

Despite this apparent strength, the arts subgovernment harbored subtle weaknesses. On the congressional side, while support was strategically located institutionally, strongly committed supporters were few in number while broader legislative support was shallow and malleable. Additionally, while the arts constituency was committed to the agency, their capacity for supporting congressional allies was underdeveloped.

In strong subgovernments, the interest group component can provide its congressional partners with three essential political resources -- votes, campaign money, and policy information.[26] The arts constituency was notably deficient on the first two of these and weak on the third. It had made little effort to mobilize voter support for elected officials who were arts advocates. Despite the major reforms transforming campaign financing during the late seventies, the arts community avoided campaign politics, preferring to maintain a non-political, non-partisan stance apparently both as a matter of philosophy and of legality.

As a matter of philosophy, the arts conception of themselves as a merit good operating in the general public interest led them to believe that they were above partisan politics. Therefore, election activity was not only distasteful to most of the arts constituency, but viewed as an activity that might expose them to the changing winds of political fortune. As a matter of legality, the most organized and active segments of the arts constituency were associations of nonprofit arts institutions such as museums, symphonies, and theatrical, operatic and dance production companies. As nonprofit entities, these organizations are enjoined from electioneering by provisions of the federal tax code.[27] Because of these legal prohibitions, arts organizations avoided campaign involvement; implicitly, the extension of these norms seemed to constrain political activities by artists and arts administrators as well.

Finally, the arts constituency, through its service organizations and with Endowment funding, developed some ability to provide policy-makers with policy-relevant data. However, this information was often anecdotal; and even when empirical, it was usually fragmented by discipline and/or function. Conversely, the Agency had undertaken little research, planning or program evaluation capacity. Out of an apparently misguided sense of self-protection, the Endowment never made a serious, ongoing commitment to present or analyze data on its applications or grants.[28] Nor did it articulate a set of clear priorities with time-measurable objectives that might serve as policy statements to orient future programs or to guide research and analysis. Instead the agency relied on specialized but idiosyncratic dialogue among staff, panels, and the National Council to provide information and evaluation. The agency had no interest in supporting research or policy development outside the agency in universities or think tanks.[29] Nor did it take up the research and agenda-setting function that private foundations had exercised so effectively when they had helped put the arts on the national policy agenda in the 1960's.[30] Thus, the policy information and analysis capabilities of the arts subgovernment failed to match the growing scale and reach of the agency's operations.

A fundamental weakness of the arts subgovernment was its insufficiency of political capital in the primary forms of political currency -- political allies, policy information, and electoral influence. Indeed, the arts subgovernment had essentially been trading on its political assets and had done little in the way of building reserves to deal with potential emergencies, to weather transitions, or to create new opportunities.

Counterpoint in the 1980's: Conflict and Erosion

The election of 1980 changed both the presidential and congressional environment for the arts. On the congressional side, significant changes occurred in both the Senate and the House. The switch in majority party control of the Senate (from Democrats to Republicans) resulted in the replacement of Senator Claiborne Pell (D-RI) with Republican Senator Robert Stafford (R-VT) as Chairman of the NEA's oversight committee. Although Stafford proved to be a friend of the arts, he was not the champion that Pell had been.

In the House, the arts policy network lost two long-term, active supporters when Democratic Majority Whip John Brademas (D-IN) and Post-secondary Education Subcommittee member Frank Thompson (D-NJ) failed to win reelection. Other House arts advocates -- taking note of the partisan shift in the Senate and of losses among supporters in the House, as well as expecting to face an unsupportive administration -- recognized a need to organize to "guide more arts legislation through Congress and to protect arts agencies from anticipated budget cuts."[31] Under the leadership of Representative Fred Richmond (D-NY), a Congressional Arts Caucus (CAC) was formed. Founded with 50 members in January of 1981, the Caucus tripled in size within a year to become one of the larger House service organizations.[32] Thus, the emergence of a Congressional Arts Caucus expanded the legislative support network for the arts just as it was preparing to face its most serious presidential challenge.

Meanwhile the election of Ronald Reagan as president brought to office the first executive since the establishment of the NEA who recommended a substantial cut in its budget -- a proposed cut of 50 percent for FY 1982 as well as an immediate $32 million rescission of FY 1981 funds that would have left the agency virtually penniless for the remainder of the year and which threatened to defund some of its largest (orchestras), most numerous (visual arts) and most prestigious (challenge grants) programs.[33] Damaging in themselves, these reductions were even more ominous since widely viewed in the arts community as but the first step toward the eventual elimination of federal patronage.

In the face of this common distributive policy threat the arts constituency rallied to protect its direct economic interests by supporting the NEA and its resources. In this effort, it was aided not only by the newly-mobilized congressional support represented in the Arts Caucus, but also by the hold-over chairman of the Endowment, Livingston Biddle. Eventually, the arts subgovernment alliance of congressional supporters, the arts constituency, and agency administrators succeeded in deflecting President Reagan's proposed reductions, defeating the rescission and limiting FY 1982 budget allocation to approximately a 10 percent cut -- a rate common among many discretionary domestic programs in the first year of the Reagan Administration. In addition, the arts subgovernment also succeeded in co-opting and persuading a Presidential Task Force on the Arts and Humanities to endorse heartily the structure of the NEA and to praise its role in spurring both artistic creativity and private patronage.[34] Thus, in a display of classic subgovernment politics, the arts policy triad exercised governance autonomy in the face of presidential opposition. Through the 1980's, the arts subgovernment seemed capable of protecting its primary interest, maintaining the NEA's appropriation at around $160 million and even edging the budget up somewhat late in the decade.

The initial success of the arts subgovernment in meeting and turning back the budgetary and reorganizational challenges of the early Reagan Administration demonstrated the effectiveness of the triad alliance on distributive policy matters. Throughout the decade of the 1980's, subgovernment efforts focussed on preserving, restoring, and incrementally increasing the NEA's budget. After decreases in FY 1982 and FY 1983 to $143 million, financial ground was recovered in FY 1984 to $162 million, followed by subsequent incremental increases to $169 million for FY 1989.

Meanwhile, developments in each triad partner seemed to strengthen the arts subgovernment. In Congress, CAC membership grew, diversified and stabilized.[35] The arts community also developed a stronger emphasis and became better organized for advocacy activities. In 1981, the American Council for the Arts (ACA) began organizing an annual Arts Advocacy Day in Washington designed to bring together national arts policy-makers and arts advocates and to send delegations of local arts constituents into as many individual member offices as possible. In 1988, the arts community took a pro-active campaign stance, not only seeking policy positions and commitments from presidential candidates George Bush and Michael Dukakis, but also developing and presenting their own policy agenda.[36]

Even the new Reaganite leadership of the NEA seemed to settle into a supportive pattern. The appointment of career political executive and former Foreign Service officer Frank S. M. Hodsoll as the fourth chairman of the NEA was initially greeted with guarded enthusiasm. An experienced public administrator whose experience in the arts was limited to his staff assignment with the 1981 Task Force on the Arts and Humanities, Hodsoll was politically dependable but not a Reaganaut ideologue. Hodsoll soon came to be regarded as a cautious conservator of NEA resources, willing to work with his agency's constituency and its congressional supporters.

Indeed the proof of the vitality of the arts subgovernment was seen in its defeat of President Reagan's early budget-cutting proposals.[37] In this, the arts subgovernment exhibited the policy veto capacity associated with special interest politics. As manifest in the 1980's, such subgovernment veto behavior reflected the mutual and complimentary interests of the system's component members. The constituency, seeking to preserve its benefits, called upon the assistance of its Congressional and bureaucratic allies who, in turn, shared these concerns. As long as the primary issue remained a distributive one -- that is, preserving or incrementally improving the annual arts funding level -- the policy system operated fairly effectively. However, amidst such success, each component of the policy triangle experienced erosion while the entire policy system was buffeted by externally imposed pressures.

Leading legislative supporters such as John Brademas (D-IN), Jacob Javits (R-NY), Fred Richmond (D-NY) and Frank Thompson (D-NJ) left Congress, thus depleting the ranks of arts supporters. As the decade progressed, resolute leadership of the Congressional Arts Caucus gave way to cautious caretaking. Fred Richmond's (D-NY) high-profile, founding leadership focussed on bipartisan information but legislative neutrality. This shifted to the more institutional advocate role assumed by the second chairman, Tom Downey (D-NY).[38] Between September 1982 and December 1986, Downey led the Caucus to take supportive positions on specific legislation (especially arts appropriations). Informally, he lobbied his colleagues by testifying at various Congressional committee proceedings concerning the arts. Formally, through his membership on the Ways and Means and the Budget Committees, he guarded arts interests within the broader and more indirect contexts of tax reform and budget construction.

Although the arts subgovernment became complacent with its ability to preserve the NEA's budget, it proved less effective in securing funding increases. Indeed, the Agency's optimistic projections that budget growth would continue at the exponential rate of the 1970's to reach $300 million in FY 1984 were utterly frustrated.[39] Yet the financial needs of an increasingly diversified, specialized, and widely distributed arts community faced with rising production and operating costs continued to grow. Thus, while NEA funding remained symbolically important to the arts community at large and valuable to specific grantees, the relative proportion of federal funding in the entire arts support system actually decreased. At the individual level, relatively few artists receive direct federal grants, for relatively modest sums of money. Indeed, more individual artists are turned down for grants than win awards. For example, in FY 1992, the ratio of successful to unsuccessful individual applicants was 1:40 for visual arts fellowships, 1:23 for literature fellowships, 1:9 for dance choreographers and 1:8 for music fellowships.[40] Even for the arts service organizations, oversight of with federal arts policy and the political fortunes of the NEA is but one of the services they provide to their members.

As initial opposition turned to benign presidential disinterest, the agency itself was less politically proactive in the 1980's. The Federal Council for the Arts and Humanities fell into disuse as the NEA pulled backed from inter-agency arts advocacy and coordination efforts. Concomitantly, the arts endowment did less in terms of its public information and congressional relations. In sum, the subgovernment policy system became less efficient in securing resources for distribution among its participants while also neglecting to replenish its long-term political capital.

During the second half of the 1980's two general trends of importance also emerged. On the one hand, issues not distributive in nature arose as arts policy topics. Concurrently, the mutuality of interests among subgovernment allies became less reliable.

Other issues that were of concern to the arts which arose during the mid to late 1980's included recurrent tax revisions, copyright concerns and record labelling and colorization controversies. While many of these issues directly concerned the commercial arts and entertainment sector, they nonetheless were of peripheral interest to the nonprofit arts community. As they occasioned public debate, each of these issues engaged interests beyond those of the arts subgovernment, thus introducing new and different political actors into the arts policy arena. Coincidentally, a multi-year controversy raged over Richard Serra's public sculpture in New York City entitled "Tilted Arc." Although "Tilted Arc" was a General Service Administration commission, not an NEA project, this affair presaged concerns about artists rights and community standards that would arise later over publicly supported art more generally.[41]

Controversies over the nominations of individuals to head other federal cultural agencies indicated some divergence of interests among agencies, subcommittees and constituencies in the cultural realm. Although NEA Chairman Hodsoll had avoided serious questions about his credentials for the post in 1981, as the decade wore on, issues of job qualifications arose more intensely with regard to other cultural agencies. For example, in 1985, scholarly opposition to the nomination of Edward Curran to head the National Endowment for the Humanities led to critical congressional scrutiny and eventually to his rejection for the post. Similarly, in 1986, the nomination of Lois Shepard as Director of the Institute of Museum Services was challenged on the related question of inadequate qualifications for the post, while the nomination of former Deputy Chairman of the NEH, John Agresto, as Archivist of the United States was opposed over the issues of both inappropriate credentials and ideological posture. The upshot of such contention may have been a budding awareness of a broader set of related "cultural" issues, rather than just a narrowly perceived set of arts issues. In any event, the appearance of new and more numerous issues as well as controversy concerning similar programs and agencies certainly stirred up the environment around the largely quiescent NEA.

Beginning in 1985, relations among the components of the arts subgovernment began to show signs of stress and variance. Three Republican Texas Congressmen -- Tom DeLay, Richard Armey and Steve

Bartlett -- launched an attack on the NEA during consideration of its FY 1986 appropriations, criticizing the agency for supporting what they called "pornographic poetry."[42] During the NEA's reauthorization that same year, Bartlett also sharply criticized the NEA for "cronyism" among its panelists, staff and grantees which, he said, led to an "imbalance" in the makeup of panels and to conflicts-of-interest among the panelists.[43] Although the outcome of these criticisms did not appreciably affect either appropriations or reauthorization in 1985, the issues would resurface at the end of the decade. One concrete consequence was that Congress asked for studies of panel operations at both the NEA and the NEH in the agencies' 1985 reauthorization; the studies were sent to Congress in 1987.

In 1987 and 1988, Congress and the NEA were repeatedly at odds over two issues, both of which touched on panel operations. In 1987, the Martha Graham Dance Company sought a $7 million line item directly from Congress to support creation of an archive and to videotape the Graham repertoire for preservation. Both the NEA Chairman and the National Council strenuously objected to the tactic of a line item as setting a "dangerous precedent against...competitive peer review." The issue was dropped, but returned the following year, in the form of funds added to the Endowment's budget but earmarked for the project. Again the Agency successfully opposed this legislative proposal.[44]

During much of 1988, disagreement flared between NEA Chairman Hodsoll and Interior Appropriations Subcommittee Chairman Sidney Yates over a proposal to bring into panel deliberations computerized data on the relative size of grant award recommendations. The Chairman's proposal provoked an outcry from panels and the arts community, as well as from the National Council. The issue came to a head during the FY 1989 appropriations process, with Representative Yates taking a strong stand against the data use plan, and Chairman Hodsoll stating that he felt it would be "...irresponsible for a Federal official such as himself to fail to put into effect budgetary accountability now that he had the tools to do the job."[45] At its May 1988 meeting, the National Council on the Arts passed a formal resolution rejecting the data use plan saying "...judgments that require artistic merit cannot be reduced to formulas."[46]

Meanwhile, conservative opinion in the nation became better organized and more vocal about an expanding domestic issue agenda. The partisan tensions of divided government were intensified by resurgent ideological differences. The federal deficit grew and budget priorities shifted; consequently, new federal funds for the arts became more difficult to obtain. Thus, when controversy expanded the types of arts policy issues, the traditional arts subgovernment system had already experienced considerable stress even though its expectations and practice of politics-as-usual prevailed.

These subtle developments not only affected the prospects for positive subgovernment policy action, but also its capacity to weather controversy and external criticism. In order to advance arts policy, all three subgovernment allies must engage in active collaboration as well as secure presidential support, as happened during the early 1970's. Furthermore, both the legislative and agency partners must be capable of exercising leadership in their respective domains, while the constituency must have the capacity to align behind a common articulation of its interests. Presidential indifference, neutrality or merely lack of opposition, as seen during the late 1970's and into the 1980's, seemed to allow only for incremental and intra-system adjustment. Conflict -- whether among members of the subgovernment, with the president, or with opposing interests -- was likely to impose political costs on all arts policy players.

A Changed Policy Politics

Since 1989 federal arts policy has changed from a subgovernment with politics typical of distributive policy to an issue network concerned with policies that encompass not only distributive, but redistributive and regulatory aspects as well.

In 1989, 1990, and 1991, the distributive politics that had typified NEA's annual appropriations process were eclipsed by ideological "culture wars" that encompassed issues of obscenity and censorship, public accountability and artistic freedom as well as the legitimacy and propriety not only of the NEA's decision-making procedures, but of the agency itself. Exaggeration, misrepresentation and passion substituted for reason, accuracy and balance as the debate became increasingly polarized. Indeed, the debate took on ever larger connotations, from feminism to religious bigotry, from the effects of the end of the Cold War and the failure of communism to the spiritual decline of the Western world, from campaign fund-raising devices to negative campaign tactics. The NEA controversy was considered a symbol of many causes. A few examples will make the point:

> "...more than an argument over arts: it was a debate over competing social agendas and concepts of morality, a clash over both the present and future condition of American society...."[47]

"...[an] attempt to appease the homophobic, misogynist and racist agenda...must be understood in the context of the Government's continued indifference to the AIDS crisis and inaction toward it..."[48]

"...a classic example of the power highly organized citizen pressure groups have to electrify Congress, and the difficulty Congress has in resolving touchy controversies that pit abstract rights such as freedom of expression against the tangible and occasionally shocking products of that freedom."[49]

Clearly, criticism of a few artistic projects supported by NEA grants had provoked new interests and issues -- in other words, the stable arts policy system had exploded into a highly volatile issue network. Furthermore, this transformation occurred during an executive transition. Newly elected President Bush had not yet made his selection to head the NEA, so the Agency had only an Interim Chairman at the helm throughout the crucial months between April and September of 1989. Preoccupied with installing his presidency and pursuing his own policy priorities, President Bush avoided direct involvement in the controversy as it unfolded.

Importantly, some of these new issues had regulatory aspects -- whether concerning content or procedure. The freedom of expression-censorship-obscenity-homoeroticism cluster focussed on possible content restrictions. This generated intense, largely unmanageable, regulatory conflict as First Amendment absolutists faced off against conservative fundamentalists. In October of 1989 as part of the NEA's FY 1990 appropriations bill, Congress voted to impose content restrictions on publicly funded art, barring the use of federal funds for art judged obscene under the judicial standards the Supreme Court had defined in the Miller case in 1973. The newly-installed NEA Chairman John Frohnmayer chose to implement this restriction by requiring that, as a condition of receiving their award, grantees sign a pledge not to use agency funds to create obscene works of art. Thus content regulations assumed both a statutory and an administrative character; both were denounced by the arts community and a few artists even sued the agency for infringement of their constitutional rights.[50]

As the volume of the controversy continued unabated, the Congressional arena of debate widened, moving out of supportive subcommittees to contentious floor debate and cross-pressured conference negotiations. Meanwhile questions about the propriety and fairness of grant-making procedures arose from artists who felt unjustly denied grants and scapegoated in the name of political expediency, from opponents who considered certain grants either wasted on the trivial and trendy or an offensive and outrageous misuse of public money, or from administrative reformers who found some of the NEA's procedures inconsistent or questionable. Such challenges undermined the procedural legitimacy of NEA grant decisions at the very time that specific grant decisions as well as the fundamental principle of public support for the arts were being questioned. Thus, defenders of the agency found themselves in a lethal crossfire, unable to establish a consensus on principle, purpose or procedure.

Both proponents and opponents in these regulatory debates concerning arts policy exacerbated the inherent conflict potential by characterizing the issue in ideological terms that seemed to pit liberals against conservatives over the right of artistic freedom versus the responsibility for public accountability. Consequently, prospects for compromise, conflict management, or bargaining for other tangible benefits (such as budget increases) were rejected both by vocal elements of the arts constituency as well as by extremist elements of a fundamentalist opposition. Thus, the conflict raged through the 1989 appropriations process and into the 1990 reauthorization hearings.

As the regulatory conflict continued unresolved, moderate congressional elements sought possible conflict management tools. One attempt to mediate the conflict involved the creation of a blue ribbon, bipartisan Independent Commission to study the NEA's grant-making standards and processes. The Co-Chairmen, former Democratic Representative John Brademas and former Republican presidential assistant Leonard Garment, led the philosophically diverse group in forging a unanimous set of recommendations that helped reestablish a middle ground in the debate, thus facilitating the reauthorization of the NEA.[51] However, the legislation renewed the agency for only three years (not five), required a number of procedural changes, mandated some new spending priorities, and directed the Chairman to consider "general standards of decency and respect for the diverse beliefs and values of the American public" when making grant decisions. And again, controversy was sparked as its new Chairman, John Frohnmayer, floundered in an attempt to devise a consistent, fair, and politically acceptable position as additional grants aroused complaint and criticism.

Another conflict management tactic that the congressional authorizing committees employed in 1990 -- one that backfired and provoked different conflicts -- involved setting new distributive priorities for the Endowment in an effort to craft a policy solution that avoided the regulatory conflict over content restrictions. These mandates included an increased emphasis on decentralized public access to the arts through the states, a new focus on reaching under-served communities, and an emphasis on arts education. In each case, funds for these purposes were increased while the overall agency budget remained static. The result was to redistribute funding allocations within the NEA so that less money was available for discretionary allocations to discipline-based projects that were of vital interest to much of the arts community. The magnitude of this redistribution was substantial; in FY 1993 it would have required an appropriation of $256 million merely to restore the Endowment's discipline programs to their FY 1990 pre-reauthorization dollar levels. Furthermore, this redistribution occurred within a general environment that was increasingly redistributive because of the federal budget deficit. Therefore, there was little prospect of securing budget increases for the Agency sufficient to mitigate the impact of these funding shifts.

Of course, the effects of this de facto redistribution prompted a political response characterized by highly ideological debate, wide-ranging and visible conflict, and the involvement of a diffuse issue network of contentious groups and individuals. Intramural conflicts broke out among components of the arts community over both scarce and shifting resources as well as over advocacy tactics and determination of priorities. In effect, new layers of political conflict stoked the all ready combustible regulatory fires while also interfering with the effectiveness of the distributive policy subgovernment.

Although active presidential participation might have helped develop a resolution, it was politically improbable given the potentially high intra-party costs and risks of presidential involvement. Indeed, in arts policy, the historical pattern has shown presidents willing to exert supportive leadership when it presented them with an opportunity to secure political benefits at little or no political cost. Instead, strong presidential action in the early 1990's risked just the reverse -- possibly incurring high political costs while securing few benefits.

Despite surviving bruising appropriations considerations later in 1990 and again in 1991, the NEA continued to reel from a succession of new grant controversies. For example, four performance artists denied grants initiated a suit against the Agency charging improper procedure. A grant to independent film-maker Todd Haynes for "Poison" was denounced by the American Family Association president, Donald E. Wildmon.[52] Two literary anthologies entitled "Live Sex Acts" and "Queer City" prompted a flurry of protesting letters and congressional inquiries. Both NEA and the Corporation for Public Broadcasting shared the controversy over a "Point of View" program, "Tongues Untied," that focussed on black gay men. Indeed, during the 1992 presidential primaries, clips from this program were prominently featured in a 1992 negative campaign advertisement against President Bush by conservative challenger for the Republican presidential nomination, Pat Buchanan.

Throughout 1990 and 1991 and into 1992, Congress continued to be barraged by letters and news stories critical of the Endowment, while it was also criticized by various arts advocates for not doing more to defend the agency, artists, and artistic freedom. Indeed, various members of Congress grew weary of the persistent crisis and the costs it was imposing in terms of time, attention and political capital. Organized arts interest groups were stretched nearly to the point of exhaustion by the necessity for constant vigilance and defensive action. Meanwhile, the leadership ranks of the NEA suffered first from key vacancies, then from extraordinary turnover, which culminated in the resignation of Chairman Frohnmayer as Pat Buchanan's threat to make the NEA a campaign issue loomed ominously, following his strong showing against President Bush in the New Hampshire primary.

Clearly, a danger of such prolonged controversy lay in the possibility that key policy subgovernment components would lose the stamina or capacity to continue. Alternatively, one of the subgovernment parties, particularly elective officials in Congress, might decide that the political calculus of continued support for federal arts policy indicated that the costs were outrunning the potential benefits -- particularly since total NEA grant awards were such a minuscule part of the federal budget each year.

Thus, the decade of the 1990's finds the formerly stable, cooperative arts policy subgovernment transformed into a loose, volatile and conflictual issue network. This issue network is characterized by debate over both indirect administration (through third party organizations, such as nonprofit arts organizations and non-federal arts agencies) and indirect decision-making (via advisory peer panels and an advisory National Council). The issue network also involved varied interest group participants none of which could dominate the policy process and for which emotional commitment could override direct, tangible interests. Indeed, debate saw exertions of power more commensurate with issue knowledge than with policy responsibility.

Such a network does not replace the once stable distributive subgovernment, but rather overlays its political reference points with new dynamics that complicate calculations, decrease predictability, confound bargaining capacity, and severely strain executive leadership.[53] In short, as arts policy in the United States has had to grapple with new and different types of policy issues, the political challenge to all of the original subgovernment participants has expanded.

Indeed, the arts policy issue network faces multiple tests in the near future amidst an environment of considerable change. In 1993, the National Endowment for the Arts was subject to annual appropriations and the confirmation of a new Chairman. Although reauthorization hearings were informally deferred for another two years, a major concern of the NEA's next reauthorization is likely to be an assessment of the changes mandated in 1990. These included a set of formula driven substantive priorities, a number of procedural changes, and provisions concerning content. By increasing the state formula percentage, by instituting an under-served set-aside formula, and by creating an arts education override formula, Congress effectively set the agency's major policy priorities for the next few years. Reauthorization hearings are likely to examine the implementation and effect of these mandates as well as assess their impact on the Agency's ability to address its other policy priorities, especially providing grant support for individual artists and for arts organizations in the various artistic disciplines.

Adjusting to such a complex and changed policy environment may require the equivalent of a paradigm shift -- that is, a redefinition of the purpose, expectations and conceptual grounding of federal arts policy. Ultimately, such a exercise in redefinition might be both a way to defuse the present maze of policy conflict as well as a creative response to significant economic, demographic, technological and cultural changes in American society. For nearly 30 years, arts policy has retained the original language and policy logic of the Great Society era that gave rise to the NEA and to the public art movement. That logic focussed on public support and subsidy, on addressing need and deficits, on winning parity with other intellectual activities (e.g., science and humanities), and on thinking in terms of specific arts disciplines. During the intervening years, it has now become apparent, society and the polity have moved on -- away from deficit spending to fiscal responsibility, away from entitlement needs to societal capabilities and mutual responsibility, and away from spending on special interest subsidies to making productive public investments. Government is beginning to "reinvent" itself, with federal agencies shifting from "rowing" to "steering" organizations. Programmatic linkage and policy integration are becoming the preferred approach rather than specialized and segmented policy formulation and implementation.

Possible elements of a new arts policy paradigm may include:

- a realization that support for the arts represents a public investment, rather than a subsidy;
- recognition that the continuum of art and entertainment may constitute an interrelated and multifaceted industry of significant economic scope and impact with some shared interests and potential new allies;
- awareness that the arts and humanities together are related pillars of a more broadly conceived cultural policy; and
- and using the arts as a dynamic resource to other domestic policy issues and program activities.

A new policy paradigm is also likely to require a reconsideration of what might be the most appropriate federal role in the arts and cultural affairs for the twenty-first century and what means and methods will be most efficacious in fulfilling that role. Other questions may need to be asked, such as: Do current grant practices represent the most effective use of federal funds, particularly as the economic value and appropriated amounts of such monies continue to decline? What leadership responsibilities and opportunities can the NEA provide and how can these best be realized? What is likely to be the most productive relationship among public arts agencies at different levels of government and among cultural agencies at the federal level?

The prospects for formulating any new policy paradigm will, however, depend on the political and conceptual creativity of the core members of the arts policy system -- the subgovernment members. Any potential policy successful of a new paradigm will, in turn, depend on articulate leadership, committed constituency support, and political and economic circumstances conducive to opening a "window" of opportunity for positive policy action.

Notes

1. For some of the basic scholarly work that distinguishes among types of public policy see Randall B. Ripley and Grace A. Franklin, *Congress, the Bureaucracy and Public Policy*, 5th ed. (Pacific Grove, CA: Brooks/Cole Publishing, 1991). R.H. Salisbury, "The Analysis of Public Policy: A Search for Theories and Roles" in Austin Ranney, ed.,*Political Science and Public Policy* (Chicago: Markham, 1968); Theodore J. Lowi: "Four Systems of Policy, Politics and Choice," *Public Administration Review*, Vol 32 (July/August 1972), pp. 298-310 and "American Business, Public Policy, Case Studies and Political Theory," *World*

Politics, Vol. 16 (July, 1964), pp. 677-715; Carl E. Van Horn, Donald C. Baumer and William T. Gormley, Jr., *Politics and Public Policy* (Washington, DC: Congressional Quarterly Press, 1989).

2. Hugo Heclo, "Issue Networks and the Executive Establishment" in Anthony King, ed., *The New American Political System* (Washington, DC: American Enterprise Institute, 1978), pp. 87-124. See especially pp. 102-105 for a comparison of subgovernments and issue networks.

3. August Heckscher, "The Quality of American Culture," *Goals for Americans* (Report of the President's Commission on National Goals and Chapters Submitted for the Consideration of the Commission), (Englewood Cliffs, NJ: Prentice-Hall/Spectrum Book, 1960), pp.127-146.

4. Terri Lynn Cornwell, "Party Platforms and the Arts," in Judith H. Balfe and Margaret Jane Wyszomirski, eds., *Art, Ideology and Politics* (New York: Praeger, l985), p. 249.

5. There was little organized support for the bill from the arts community. Indeed, significant portions of the arts community were either unenthusiastic or opposed to the proposal. See Milton C. Cummings, Jr. (Ch. 4).

6. It is not uncommon for high-level political conflict resolution to be accomplished through a presidential strategy of redefining a redistributive issue as a distributive one. See Ripley and Franklin, p. 122.

7. Fannie Taylor and Anthony Baressi, *The Arts At a New Frontier, The National Endowment for the Arts* (New York: Plenum Press, 1984),pp. 115-117; Kevin V. Mulcahy, "The Politics of Congressional Oversight of the Arts," in Margaret J. Wyszomirski, ed., *Congress and the Arts: A Precarious Alliance?* (New York: American Council for the Arts, l988).

8. For a fuller account of Nancy Hanks' executive leadership strategy and achievements at the NEA, see Margaret J. Wyszomirski, "The Politics of Art: Nancy Hanks and The National Endowment for the Arts" in Jameson W. Doig and Erwin C. Hargrove, eds., *Leadership and Innovation: Entrepreneurs in Government* (Baltimore: The Johns Hopkins University Press, 1987)

9. For example, Hanks helped Tricia Nixon host a White House pumpkin-carving contest and succeeded in getting a monumental modern sculpture which the president removed from the lawn of the Corcoran Gallery. On the latter incident, see Michael Straight, *Twigs for an Eagle's Nest* (New York: Devon Press, 1979), pp. 31-33.

10. This style of interest group formation is discussed by Jack L. Walker, "The Origins and Maintenance of Interest Groups in America," *American Political Science Review*, Vol. 77, No. 2 (June 1983), pp. 390-405.

11. Dick Netzer found that between 1966 and 1974, government arts subsidies helped to effect a substantial increase in the earnings of those engaged in artistic production. *The Subsidized Muse, Public Support for the Arts in the United States* (New York: Cambridge University Press, 1978), pp. 97-110. In a more recent study, he extends this analysis and points out that by the 1980's, earnings increases were neither a policy goal nor an implicit effect of public subsidies except in emerging art fields such as folk arts or expansion arts; Netzer, "The Distributional Consequences of the Non-Profit Sector -- Arts and Culture," in *Who Benefits from the Nonprofit Sector?* edited by Charles Clotfelter (Chicago: University of Chicago Press, 1992).

12. National Endowment for the Arts, "National Council on the Arts: Policy and Planning Committee Report on Service Organization Support" (Washington, D.C.: Mimeographed, 1980), pp. 50,68.

13. Wyszomirski, "The Politics of Arts," p. 230-1.

14. Straight, *Twigs for an Eagle's Nest*, Taylor and Baressi, *The Arts at a New Frontier*, pp. 115-117.

15. Netzer, *The Subsidized Muse*, p.73.

16. *The New York Times*, September 4, 1977, p.18.

17. On the activities and personalities engaged in congressional oversight of the arts, see Mulcahy, "The Politics of Congressional Oversight of the Arts."

18. Barbara Hinckley defines a subgovernment as "an agent for a policy area...that exists separately from presidential government." *Problems of the Presidency* (Glenview, Illinois: Scott, Foresman, & Co., 1985), p. 154.

19. Lawrence D. Mankin, "The National Endowment for the Arts: The Biddle Years and After," *Journal of Arts Management and Law*, Vol. 14, No. 2 (Summer 1984), pp. 59-80.

20. As quoted on p. 24 of an insightful discussion of the evolution of arts advocacy through the early 1980's: Joseph Wesley Zeigler, "Passionate Citizenship," *American Arts*, May 1983, pp. 22-26. Also see his "Friendly Persuasion: The Arts Arrive on Capital Hill," *American Arts*, July 1983, pp. 22-24.

21. National Endowment for the Arts, *Annual Report 1978*. (Washington, DC: 1979), p. 15.

22. U.S. Congress, House of Representatives, Committee on Appropriations, Surveys and Investigations Staff, *Report on the National Endowment for the Arts* (March 22, 1979), pps. 71. For the Endowment's written response to the investigative staff report, *Department of Interior and Related Agencies appropriations for 1980, Hearings*, Part II before the House Appropriations Subcommittee on the Department of Interior and Related Agencies, 96th Congress, 1st Session, 1979, p. 952.

23. Taylor and Baressi, *The Arts at a New Frontier*, pp. 179-88; Laurence Leamer, *Playing for Keeps in Washington* (New York: Dial Press, 1977), pp. 46-7; Wyszomirski, "The Politics of Art," pp. 234-5.

24. Anthony J. Radich, ed., *Economic Impact of the Arts, A Sourcebook* (Denver Colorado: National Conference of State Legislatures, May 1987), contains some excellent articles on the development and limitations of economic impact studies.

25. For coverage of the formation of AAA, see *The New York Times*, November 15, 1977. For a discussion of the development of arts interests groups, see Margaret J. Wyszomirski, "Art Policy-making and Interest Group Politics," *Journal of Aesthetic Education*, Vol. 14, No. 4 (October 1980), pp. 28-34.

26. On the cohesiveness and effectiveness of this arts support network, see Mary L. Weaver, "The Politics of Congressional Arts Policy," in *Congress and the Arts*, pp. 53-56.

27. Most nonprofit arts organizations are legally 501(c)(3) organizations registered with the Internal Revenue Service.

28. John K. Urice, "Using Research to Determine, Challenge, or Validate Public Arts Policy," *Journal of Arts Management and Law*, Vol 13, No. 1 (Spring

1983), pp. 198-206, especially, p. 205; "Planning at the National Endowment for the Arts: A Review of the Plans and Planning Documents, 1978-1984," *Journal of Arts Management and Law*, Vol. 15, No. 2 (Summer 1985), pp. 79-91.

29. A limited, but erratic, exception to this disinterest in university-based research concerned arts education. For an overview see James Hutchens, "Policy Research in Arts Education," in David B. Pankratz and Valerie B. Morris, eds., *The Future of the Arts, Public Policy and Arts Research* (New York: Praeger), pp. 47-61.

30. Margaret Jane Wyszomirski, "Philanthropy, the Arts and Public Policy," *Journal of Arts Management and Law*, Vol.16, No.4 (Winter 1987), pp.5-29

31. *The New York Times*, January 13, 1981.

32. On the establishment, membership and leadership of the CAC during the 1908's, see Margaret Jane Wyszomirski, "Budgetary Politics and Legislative Support" in *Congress and the Arts*, edited by Margaret J. Wyszomirski (New York: American Council in the Arts, 1988). "The Arts in Congress" and on the cohesiveness and effectiveness of their arts support network see Weaver, "The Politics of Congressional Arts Policy."

33. Margaret Jane Wyszomirski, "The Reagan Administration and the Arts: 1981-1983," Paper presented at the Annual Meeting of the American Political Science Association; Chicago, Illinois, September 1-4, 1983, pp. 5-6.

34. Presidential Task Force on the Arts and Humanities, *Report to The President* (Washington, DC: GPO, October 1981), p. 3. For a brief overview of arts politics in the 1980's see Milton C. Cummings, Jr., "Government and the Arts: An Overview," in Stephen Benedict, ed., *Public Money and The Muse* (New York: W.W. Norton & Co., 1991) pp. 56-79.

35. By 1986, the Caucus maintained a membership that averaged 38 percent of the House, including most Democratic House leaders and representatives from 43 states. Wyszomirski, "Budgetary Politics and Legislative Support," pp. 20-23.

36. Independent Committee on Arts Policy, "The Nation and the Arts: A Presidential Briefing Paper," (New York: ICAP, October 1988).

37. For greater detail on the early Reagan Administration arts policy, see Margaret Jane Wyszomirski, "The Reagan Administration and the Arts: Early Indications," Paper presented at the annual meeting of the American Political Science Association, New York, NY, September 1981 and "The Reagan Administration and the Arts: 1981-1983."

38. Wyszomirski, "Budgetary Politics and Legislative Support," pp. 23-27.

39. The growth projection was set out as part of the agency's first plan. National Endowment for the Arts, *General Plan, 1980-1984*, (Washington, D.C.: Office of Policy and Planning, April 1979), p. 150.

40. The proportions were calculated from grant and application figures contained in the NEA's FY 1992 budget justifications submitted to Congress. The actual number were Choreographer Fellowships: 403 applications and 47 grants; national Literature fellowships: 2350 applications and 100 grants; Music fellowships: 687 applications and 82 grants; and Theater fellowships: 400 applicants and 35 grants.

41. Sherril Jordon, ed., *Public Art, Public Controversy: Tilted Arc on Trial* (New York: American Council for the Arts Books, 1987).

42. *The Washington Post*, September 12, 1985; Allison Gamble, "NEA Under Fire for 'Pornographic' Poetry" and "Congressman DeLay Leads the Attack" in *New Art Examiner*, November 1985, pp. 31-2.

43. Mulcahy, "The Politics of Cultural Oversight," p. 69.

44. *The New York Times*, October 21, 25, 26, 1987 and December 18, 1987; *The Washington Post* June 10, 1988.

45. *The New York Times*, 21 April 1988; *The Washington Post*, March 17, and May 9, 1988.

46. *The Washington Post*, May 9, 1988.

47. Richard Bolton, "Introduction," in Richard Bolton, ed., *Culture Wars* (New York: New Press,1992), p.3.

48. Holly Hughes and Richard Elovich, "Homophobia at the N.E.A." *The New York Times*, July 28, 1990, reprinted in Bolton, *Culture Wars*, pp. 254-55.

49. George Hager, "Every Voter's a Critic on Arts Funding," *Congressional Quarterly Weekly*, August 19, 1989, p. 2174.

50. One of these was choreographer Bella Lewitzky, who subsequently won her case.

51. Independent Commission, *Report to the Congress on the National Endowment for the Arts*, (Washington, D.C.: September 1990).

52. George Archibald, "NEA to Defend Male-rape Film," *Washington Times*, March 29, 1991, pp. 1-10.

53. Heclo, "Issue Networks and the Executive Establishment," p. 105.

3

Federal Arts Patronage in the New Deal

Lawrence D. Mankin

The national government's attitude toward the arts changed in the 1930's to reflect a broader conception of the government's proper role in society.[1] Thousands of artists were among the ranks of the unemployed. Twenty-thousand theatrical people alone were out of work.[2] Employment was the number one priority of the Roosevelt Administration. Out of this goal, the government became involved with the arts as it never had been before. Relief Administrator Olin Dows stated that:

> Human economic relief was the motive behind all the New Deal's art programs. That is why they were so easily accepted by the public and the politicians. If it had not been for the great depression, it is unlikely that our government would have sponsored more art than it had in the past.[3]

Dows exaggerates the ease with which these programs were accepted. Administration critics waited for the proper opportunity to launch an attack against these programs, but more will be said about this below.

New Deal Programs: The Support

The Public Works Art Project (PWAP) was the first cultural program to be initiated in the New Deal. Operated under the auspices of the Treasury Department, it was better run than the other New Deal art projects which would follow it. Historically, it marked "the first time the government had subsidized an art project of national dimension."[4] Roosevelt had established a tone for the PWAP by telling its supporters "I can't have a lot of young enthusiasts painting Lenin's head on the Justice Building."[5] Funds for the project were supplied by the Civil Work Administration to employ painters and sculptors to create works for public buildings. The PWAP employed about 3,750 artists at low daily wages. They provided over 15,600 works of art...The total cost was approximately $1,312,000, which makes the cost per artist $350.[6]

This program expired in June, 1934 after seven months of operation and was succeeded at the Treasury Department by what was eventually known as the Section on Fine Arts. Through this program, sculpture works and murals were created for buildings throughout the nation. Local panels recommended artists for projects in their areas. This program was quite successful and only ended in 1943 because of the economic constraints imposed by World War II.

During its nine years of activity, the Section awarded 1,124 mural contracts for which it paid $1,472,199 and 289 contracts for sculpture costing $563,529.... 1,205 individual artists placed their work in federal buildings. The average price for the mural commission was $1,356 and for sculpture $1,935. Administrative costs were $393,516.[7]

A number of factors accounted for the program's success. Edward Bruce, who designed the program, combined the skills of artistic ability and appreciation with those of a pragmatic administrator. Olin Dows observed that:

> Being a lawyer, businessman and economist and knowing most of the important politicians and administrators informally, Bruce would talk to them in their own language, and so inspired their confidence in what he was trying to do.[8]

His relations with members of both political parties were good and he was the chief architect of strategies to cope with political questions such as congressional relations.[9]

Cordiality characterized the relationship between the Section and the local judging panels. No selection of an artist by a local panel was changed by the Section.[10] This avoided internecine warfare, which can consume the resources and energy of an agency, and sabotage its goals. Adding to the political success of the Section, as Edward Lucie-Smith observes, was the tempering of elitist attitudes of program administrators by their desire to have the Section's works popularly accepted.[11]

The Section's fortunes were further advanced by the enthusiastic support of President and Mrs. Roosevelt and Secretary of Treasury Henry Morgenthau and his wife.

> The Section of Fine Arts was stronger than was warranted by its subordinate position in the Treasury Department table of organization. Many officials knew that President and Mrs. Roosevelt and Secretary and Mrs. Morgenthau were interested. The latter especially kept in close touch with our activities. Her wise, sympathetic and intelligent advice was a great asset. Although she helped to solve a few difficult administrative matters, there was never any question of professional interference or pressure.[12]

For the most part, the Section on Fine Arts shunned projects which might result in controversy, but it was not entirely successful in escaping criticism. The Section, rather than refuting criticism, worked with it by placating powerful elements within communities. On only a few occasions was the Section unable to have a mural accepted.[13] Most criticism was directed at the authenticity of images or events regarding the communities in which the murals were to be placed.[14] The themes reflected in the works commissioned by the Section were chosen to provide a sense of security to a nation in the midst of the "Great Depression." During the war, the Section encouraged murals and sculptures related to defense efforts.[15] Both the PWAP and the Section on Fine Arts commissioned projects by artists who were not usually unemployed or destitute since employment was no longer a central program goal.[16]

The Treasury Arts Relief Project, created in July 1935 as the third cultural program which the Treasury Department administered, was not subject to the above criticism. Funding for this program was provided by the Works Progress Administration and Treasury Arts Relief Project under their administrative guidelines. For most of the Project's existence, 75 percent of the people employed by it came from the relief rolls[17] and, like the other Treasury programs, it commissioned artists to provide murals and paintings for federal buildings. The program, employed approximately 330 persons and existed for four years at a total cost of $735,700.[18] In these Treasury Department art programs federal expenditures were pumped into the economy to acquire the services of artists whose finished projects demonstrated artistic competence. Controversial projects were avoided. On the other hand, the Works Progress Administration (**WPA**) Art Projects were constantly surrounded by controversy and its operations were dramatically affected by it.

Experimental, idealistic, political and frustrating are all terms which aptly describe the WPA art projects. Never had the government engaged in such a program, nor has it since. Under favorable conditions it would have been difficult to determine whether the program would have flourished, but given the conditions under which it was conceived and operated, only a constant struggle for survival was guaranteed. Faced with the need to alleviate the economic plight of thousands of artists and lobbied by cultural organizations, the government proposed the WPA Arts Projects as a solution. The Emergency Relief Act of 1935 was the authorizing legislation for the creation of the WPA. Jerre Mangione noted that:

> An inconspicuous but significant clause in the act authorized assistance to educational, professional and clerical persons; a nationwide program for useful employment of artists, musicians, actors, entertainers, writers...and others in these cultural fields.[19]

The WPA, an agency mainly concerned with construction work, was created by an executive order on May 6, 1935 and the arts projects were begun on September 12, 1935. The following five projects constituted the arts programs of the WPA: (1) Theater Project, (2) Writers' Project, (3) Art Project, (4) Music Project, (5) Historical Survey. (The Historical Survey, as a special case, is not reviewed in this study.) Although their priorities at times became blurred, the goals set for the art projects were clear. The President and Harry Hopkins (the Administrator of the WPA) envisioned the program to be primarily one of economic relief with secondary emphasis on artistic competence and achievement.[20] At times the administrators of the various projects, who were artists themselves, tended to forget this ordering of priorities but all were in agreement that the projects should instill an appreciation of the arts in people. It was hoped that support from the people would obviate further national government underwriting of the arts.

The day the WPA came into existence was the first day it confronted its enemies. Congress at best was passive in its support of the new agency. William F. McDonald states that:

> At no time can it be said that Congress, as a whole, truly and generally supported the principle of work relief. Congress merely permitted its use, because in 1935 it was afraid to do otherwise and, having started the WPA, was after 1935, afraid to stop it.[21]

McDonald summarizes the sentiments upon which arguments and opposition to the arts were based.

> Music, drama, literary activities, painting and sculpture were in the layman's mind avocations that existed either for the delectation of those who could pay for them or for the self-satisfaction of those engaged in them.[22]

The press was unsympathetic and even hostile in its attitude toward the WPA and its Arts Projects.[23] Jane DeHart Mathews says of the Director of the Federal Theater Project that:

> In nearly every batch of press clippings that poured in from across the country, Hallie Flanagan found references to the government's ill-advised venture into show business.[24]

When the Dies Committee investigated the Arts Projects in 1938, it found a sympathetic press willing to publicize its activities.[25] It is estimated that three quarters of those who read the newspapers supported the committee.[26]

The Arts Projects also faced the problem of incorporating creative people within the confines of a governmental bureaucracy. Creativity requires freedom and to the artist rules and regulations can be like ropes tied around a pair of creative hands. Paperwork, wage and hour regulations frustrated working relationships and delayed the completion of projects. McDonald notes that:

> Within a given project unit, workers in different categories worked a different number of hours a month; even workers in the same category (e.g., professional and technical) did not work the same number of hours a week if the prevailing hourly rate for each group was not the same. This made it difficult, and at times impossible, to synchronize hours of work of workers on a given project. Thus, both quality and continuity of supervision suffered, and the proper proportion of skilled to unskilled workers, necessary for efficient operation, was not as readily maintained.[27]

If all of the above didn't present enough of an obstacle to the success of the Arts Projects, the organizational design in which the Arts Projects operated was an additional burden. In the early months of their existence, the Arts Projects were officially given a great amount of autonomy. This, unfortunately, led to a high degree of intra-organizational conflict. Each WPA state administrator had a director for each of the Arts Projects, but this was only a formality. In fact, the state directors were controlled by the Arts Projects; national office and state directors, in turn, controlled district supervisors. The state directors and district supervisors of the WPA provided services for the state and district directors of the Arts Projects rather than the reverse. Mathews states that for "reasons of economy" the Arts Projects were placed in the administrative framework of district and state WPA offices.[28] This reflected a lack of awareness of the possible political consequences of such an organizational design. Control over the finances and personnel of the Arts Projects were in the hands of its own officials. As McDonald notes, "the only privilege left with the state and district WPA officials was that of protest."[29]

Tension between the Arts Projects and its host agency was also heightened by differences in loyalties and perspectives of state WPA administrators and state arts directors. The appointment of state administrators required senatorial confirmation, so they were subject to the practice of senatorial courtesy. Most state administrators owed their appointment to a senator from their state. Although Harry Hopkins had formal control over WPA state administrators, he confronted political limitations which constrained his authority. McDonald discussed these limitations:

> In the first place, the WPA did not exist by virtue of a substantive law, but merely by virtue of appropriations acts previously noted. Congress, and especially the House, could at any time either refuse money or, as indeed it did, progressively reduce appropriations. The state administrators, who for the most part held their appointments because of senatorial connections, were in a position to make their point of view powerful in Congress. Harry Hopkins could resent, at times fight, this power but never defy it. In the second place, the philosophy of the state governments expressed itself naturally through pressures upon their senators and representatives who, in turn, brought this philosophy to bear upon national issues.[30]

In addition to these strains, many states were opposed to the concept of work relief and resented the federal controls which came with the welfare funds.[31] The state directors exercised effective control over their staffs, but tension between arts personnel and the non-arts personnel in the WPA was apparent throughout the existence of the Arts Projects.

President Roosevelt was personally involved in trying to shape the policies of Federal One as the Arts Projects were known.[32] He was alert to the political sensibilities that would be affected by the creation of an arts project and, therefore, understood the need to have a broad base of support. Roosevelt believed that to insure public support the art project had to be (1) part of a larger relief project, and (2) appreciated by the common man across the nation.[33]

The Arts Projects were designed as a relief project and levels of competence varied within and between projects. Nevertheless, the Federal Art Project maintained a fairly high level of staff competence.[34] This was not the case with the Federal Writers' Project where "White collar workers who could not be fitted into any other WPA agency were likely to wind up in the Writers' Project."[35]

Resulting intra-organizational tensions prevented effective cooperation between the arts personnel and the non-arts personnel in the WPA bureaucracy. State WPA officials attempted to sabotage some arts programs. Mangione reports that in Idaho there was an attempt "to pack the Project's staff with former inmates of mental institutions."[36]

Plans to spread theater across the nation also encountered difficulties. Theater personnel could be loaned or transferred from one state to another, but in the Midwest this practice was hindered by WPA state administrators.

> Anyone who thinks a state boundary line is an imaginary affair, or states rights an expression out of history books, should have tried to move companies or even individuals across the former or to make plans which, seemed in the minds of state administrators, to conflict with the latter. Midwest state administrators for the most part, refused to allow people from our talent sources, Chicago and New York, to be brought into their state, even when expenses, plus return fare, were guaranteed out-of-state funds. Illinois state officials on the other hand did not like the idea of personnel or equipment, paid for with "Illinois money," being sent to other states. Such aspects hindered effective operation of the program.[37]

During this period of struggle for power within the WPA bureaucracy, state administrators gradually received concessions from the Washington WPA office that increased state control over the Arts Projects, including the authority to close state arts projects, which they secured in 1937.

WPA Art Programs: The Attack

The **WPA Arts** projects began at a time of high popularity for the Roosevelt Administration, and although critics denounced the program, they lacked the power to damage it. The Federal Theater Project, in particular, incited opponents of the arts program because they judged it to be a propaganda vehicle of the Roosevelt Administration. Statements by Harry Hopkins to the effect that some of the Living Newspaper reproductions were propaganda only served to fire critical tempers.[38] In 1938, critical voices became serious threats to the Federal Theater Project. Roosevelt, who then appeared to be a lame-duck president, had suffered serious setbacks in the congressional elections and his own attention was shifting from domestic policy to the ominous signs from Europe. For Roosevelt's detractors, there was no better program to challenge him on than one that symbolized his domestic welfare programs. More extreme critics saw the opportunity to strike out at a program that they believed had been captured by radicals and leftists.

> The plain fact was that Communists were exceedingly active in the WPA Theater and Writer's Projects; they did all they could to get their own people into it and to turn the whole enterprise into an agitprop machine.[39]

But such activity could not sustain a charge of Communist domination of the projects. Motives for such charges ran deeper than the mere exposure of Communist infiltration of the arts program. Robert Vaughn concludes that the Dies Committee, which became the focal point for charges of Communist infiltration of the Theater and Writers' Projects, was used as an instrument to discredit the policies of the Roosevelt Administration.[40]

Those who directed and staffed the Federal Theater Project were professional theater people unfamiliar with the political machinations needed to survive in Washington. Dedicated to the principle that the theater was both a vehicle for entertainment and a means of social enlightenment, they concentrated their energies on program content. Their dream was that the nation would adopt the theater to its breast but their conception of theater was considered dangerous by other political actors. Like crusaders before them, Federal Theater bureaucrats viewed the world through blinders and Anthony Down's description of the administrative "zealot" best characterizes the Federal Theater official.

> The peculiarities of zealot's behavior spring from two characteristics; the narrowness of their sacred policies, and the implacable energy they focus solely upon promoting those policies. The narrowness of their interests causes zealots to be poor general administrators. They tend to concentrate their energies and resources on their

sacred policies regardless of the breadth of their formal responsibilities, thereby ignoring important bureau functions. Moreover, they antagonize other officials by their refusal to be impartial and their willingness to trample all obstacles.[41]

Administrative survival, and the consequent need to develop political sophistication, was an ignored but important bureaucratic function. Hallie Flanagan, director of the Federal Theater Project, came from the world of stage and academe. She rather naively accepted Hopkins's promise that the Federal Theater Project would be uncensored and, thereby, illustrated the politically fictitious world in which the Project operated.[42]

After several controversies concerning Theater Project productions, a centralized board was established with responsibility for approving plays before they were performed. This did little to still the voices of criticism. Productions appeared to be as controversial as ever and political wisdom dictated the need to place some limits on the politically unanointed leaders. An administration in the midst of an emergency program to overcome a depression could not afford inviting antagonism from a hostile Congress; this is exactly what some productions brought. On several occasions, the WPA did intervene to modify the content of a play or to prevent its performance.[43]

Theater operates in the world of ideas and therefore will never be the sole property of those who are theater professionals. Political sensitivities of audience members can be offended by ideas expressed in the theater and demands for censorship can result. As one of the major cultural conveyors of the thirties, the Federal Theater Project was more vulnerable to attack than it might have been in the era of television. As Vaughn remarks:

> With the exception of the cinema, the cultural atmosphere of the thirties may indeed have been influenced by the Federal Theater Project in the sense that more people saw plays than any other form of entertainment.[44]

Given the important communications dimensions which the Federal Theater Project had, plays which were critical of congressmen could have only resulted in attacks upon the Project. As Vaughn states:

> Mrs. Flanagan's decision to use federal subsidies to produce plays condemning her subsidizers is another example of an impolitic decision that might have been avoided by less idealism or more political pragmatism.[45]

But such pragmatism was lacking. Instead of courting the approval of Congress, the Project alienated it. Wider support from Congress might have been forthcoming if, as said earlier, the presentations were less controversial or if the Theater Project was a truly national one. The Theater Project was not given the opportunity to function in most congressional districts or to develop grass roots support which might have been converted into congressional support. Jane DeHart Mathews notes that there was a critical difference between the controversial Federal Theater Project and the nearly as controversial Federal Writers' Project. The Theater Project was

> ...restricted initially to those areas where twenty-five qualified professionals could be formed into a local company, forced subsequently to disband these small and often artistically inferior units. As such it could only count on active support from congressmen from New York, California, Illinois and a few other states which local projects had served loyally and well. But the backing of these members was simply not enough. The more geographically dispersed Writers' Project, on the other hand, could present every congressman in Washington with a guidebook to his particular state.[46]

While the Dies Committee listened to charges by witnesses of large-scale Communist infiltration of the Theater Project, WPA officials and Theater Project personnel remained strangely quiet.[47] Some did not even consider the Committee's investigations to be a serious threat. When the Dies Committee was willing to hear a defense of the art projects, such a defense was lacking. Ellen Woodward, Director of the related Women's and Professional Project, attempted to defend the Theater Project but she was too distant from its everyday operations to make a convincing case.[48] Hallie Flanagan next tried valiantly to parry the onslaught of charges the Dies Committee unleashed at her. Determined to find the Project subversive, the Committee spewed out a variety of questions ranging from her alleged Communist sympathies to whether she approved of profanity in plays.[49] Her answers were direct but lacked political tact. Chairman Dies was successful in having Mrs. Flanagan admit that in some cases the Federal Theater Project did serve propagandistic purposes. She too could not adequately defend the Theater Project.[50]

Further investigation by the Dies Committee, as well as a special committee to investigate the WPA, and a House Appropriations subcommittee inquiry, continued to haunt the Federal Theater Project, and signaled its imminent demise. Changes in the domestic and international political climate in the brief period since the establishment of the Federal

Theater Project meant trouble for the Roosevelt Administration's social programs in general. When the House Appropriations Committee failed to provide funds for the continuation of the Federal Theater Project in 1939, there was little the Administration could do, or would do, to save it. Administration officials would not put the entire relief program in jeopardy to save the Federal Theater Project. Hallie Flanagan noted that:

> WPA officials were in a difficult situation. They had to push through a tremendous appropriation or else millions of people on July 1 would be thrown out of work. How could they placate the opponents of WPA enough to get the largest possible appropriation through. These opponents were out to hang the New Deal. Perhaps a hanging in effigy would do. Federal Theater was ideal for the purpose; although small, it was potent enough to allow the opponents of WPA to trumpet a victory through the press. I do not mean to say that the abandonment of Federal Theater by the WPA was discussed in just those terms, it didn't need to be.[51]

From its inception, the Federal Theater Project was a political program -- something which its zealous administrators failed to realize. It ended not because of its failure as a professional project, but rather because of its failure as a political project.

> For many opponents of the New Deal in that raucous, rancorous congressional session, the ban on the Theater, like the embargo in the Neutrality Act and provisions in the tax and farm bills provided another opportunity to take a slap at the administration.[52]

And as Flanagan came to realize:

> It was ended because Congress, in spite of protests from its own members, treated the Federal Theater not as a human issue or cultural issue, but as a political issue.[53]

The Emergency Relief Act of 1939 radically changed the character of all of the Arts Projects. An abrupt end was brought to the Federal Theater Project and state sponsors were required to provide support for the other projects. Mangione states that:

> More and more the sponsors tended to use the writing staffs for their own purpose -- programs that had little or no relationship to what the Writers' Project had set out to do. In Washington, as well as in the states, supervisors found it expedient to pay close attention to the demands of the sponsors. Survival rather than quality of work became the chief consideration, and they were unhappy about that.[54]

The extinction of the programs was grimly awaited by personnel who remained with projects until they finally ended in 1943.

Accomplishments of WPA Arts Projects

Internal and external organizational pressures interfered with the complete attainment of the goals of the Arts Projects. But given the context in which they operated, it is amazing how much was accomplished. Artistically gifted individuals were saved from pursuits in which their talents would have been wasted. The Projects were more than busy work. An investment of $5 million in the Arts Projects produced a body of "unofficial art" conservatively valued around $450 million.[55] *The Living Newspaper*, a dramatization of controversial current events, was a new form of theater. They had a definite slant, which was often less than subtle. The following speech by Harry Hopkins before the cast of *Power*, a play about the electrical industry, gives one an idea of the nature of these productions.

> People will say it's propaganda. Well, I say what of it? It's propaganda to educate the consumer who's paying for power. It's about time someone had some propaganda for him. The companies have spent millions on propaganda for utilities. It's about time the consumers had a mouthpiece. I say more plays like Power and more power to you.[56]

The Federal Art Project was fairly well received by the nation although not uniformly acclaimed by arts professionals. Art historian E. P. Richardson says of them:

> In general the mural paintings done at this time amount to rather unsuccessful illustrations pasted on the wall with little understanding of the architectural effect..... Regionalism in mural painting became identified with sentimental hometown subject matter presented in a horrid melange of ill-digested modernism.[57]

While the artistic merits of some of the murals may be subject to some debate, the Project did make a technological breakthrough with the development of the silk screen process.

Art education centers were established by the Art Project throughout the nation. Local citizens could pursue art interests by attending classes taught by members of the Arts Project. Approximately eight million people took advantage of the opportunities presented by the program.[58] Richardson concludes:

> There is no question in my mind that these played a part in getting people all over the United States working in some medium -- paint, wood, textile, clay -- not as a livelihood, but as a pleasant part of their daily lives.[59]

A research division, the Index of American Design, collected information on various art forms practiced throughout the history of America. Although only about ten percent of the Art Projects personnel were employed on the Index, it became the most popular part of the project.[60] The Art Project, like the other WPA art programs, never received the popular acclaim it deserved for its original contributions to the art world.

The Federal Music Project was the least controversial of the Art Projects although pressure to ease its hiring standards was exerted by the American Federation of Musicians.[61] The Project conducted a number of different programs. Musicians were employed in newly formed symphonic orchestras. "By March 1938, thirty-four symphony orchestras under the Federal Music Project were employing 2,533 musicians."[62] Some of these orchestras stayed in existence even after the Federal Music Project ceased to exist. Although a number of operas were sponsored by the Project, actual productions were limited because of their cost. With the approval of a panel of judges, a composer could hear his work performed by an orchestra. A nationwide program of music education, both appreciation and practice, was a large part of the Project. "A summary compiled at the end of the fiscal year June 30, 1939, listed 1,197,936 classes held by project leaders with aggregate pupil attendance of 13,849,919."[63] The Music Project, like the Art Project and the Writers' Project became involved in historical research and the preservation of art forms. The Index of American Composers, an unfinished project, attempted to list all major American composers, their works and critical reactions to them.[64] A collection of folk music from throughout the United States was gathered by the Music Project as a part of a WPA folks arts project. Members of the project were sent on the road to obtain recordings of Southern folk music. The state music projects cooperated by researching and collecting folk music in their respective states and making this material available to the national project.[65]

The Federal Writers' Project shared the spotlight of controversy with the Federal Theater Project. Although it was fortunate to employ in its ranks writers such as Nelson Algren, Richard Wright and Saul Bellow, many others who claimed to be writers were frankly incompetent. There were also ideological tensions dividing staff members of Trotskyist and Stalinist beliefs.[66]

The composition of its staff and sensitivities to the political climate of the time dictated that programs of the Writers' Project focus on nonfictional works. Most of the Project's writers lacked creative writing ability and it was felt "that if writers were allowed to work on their own subjective efforts Congress and public opinion would soon put the Project out of business."[67] The American Guide series was the Project's major work. Each state program was directed to compile a geographical, descriptive and historical account of their respective states, and important localities. Yet, even what seemed to be a useful and politically safe project was not free from controversy. Emphases on certain events as well as their interpretations were questioned. It was claimed that the Massachusetts guidebook, for example, was written with a pro-labor bias and placed too much emphasis on certain controversial events.

> Several mayors throughout the state decided to ban the book. Governor Hurley ordered the state legislature to examine the book for all objectionable passages and asked the writer responsible for them to be identified and dismissed.[68]

However, the Massachusetts case was not the typical reaction to the guidebooks. For the most part, they were well-received.

A folklore study, conducted by the Writers' Project, sought to catalog popular customs, beliefs and legends. The study not only explored the past but also delved into contemporary American views and attitudes. Reflections and life-perspectives were recorded by interviewers. A related program, Social-Ethnic Studies Program, recorded the ways in which various groups helped to mold their local communities and the nation itself.[69]

There were several other programs that the project conducted. Mangione sums up the contributions of the Writers' Project with the following:

> In less than four years the Project had produced some three hundred twenty publications, of which almost one hundred were full-sized books. Besides state, city, small town and highway guides, the list included works on subjects as diverse as ethnic studies, place names, folklore and zoology. More than six hundred other books were in various stages of completion. It made quite an impressive record, especially when one considers the difficulties of conducting a project made up largely of workers with little or no writing experience, most of whom had to qualify as paupers before they could be employed.[70]

The above account of the four Arts Projects is not meant to be an exhaustive list of the programs they conducted, but rather to indicate that under very trying circumstances they made an original contribution to the American culture. Ideologies, partisan political loyalties, intra-organizational conflicts and lack of traditional popular support for the arts all threatened the operation of the Projects. What could have been, if there had been more cooperation and less tension, can only be imagined. The Project not only made an original contribution to American culture and provided emergency relief for the artist but, more importantly, offered a model for future governmental support for the arts. Though this support would take a different form, the precedent for wide-scale public support for the arts had been set with the WPA.

Conclusion

There is little to note in the way of programmatic support for the arts from the end of the New Deal until the establishment of the National Endowment for the Arts. President Eisenhower appointed an advisor on the arts, but there were not any notable changes in government support for the practicing artist. Those governmental efforts that led up to the Endowment's enabling legislation in 1965 are discussed in the next chapter.

Prior to the 1930s, government encouraged the development of the arts symbolically, rather than financially. The WPA years represented the highest point of government support for the arts, but the support emanated from a need for economic recovery, rather than from any deeply held societal value in support of the arts. The WPA programs demonstrated that the American government could nourish the arts as is the case with a number of European countries. The New Deal Arts Projects also demonstrated that the government can harass and retard the arts. Public support for the arts must continue to be examined to determine the effects of government's relationship to culture. Certainly, the question can be raised whether government can be a neutral patron of the arts. Our early experience with government as patron has revealed its uneven temperament.

Notes

1. Parts of this chapter appear previously in the *Journal of Aesthetic Education* and appear with the permission of the University of Illinois Press.
2. Jane Dehart Mathews, *The Federal Theater 1935-1939* (Princeton, NJ: Princeton University Press, 1967), p. 27.
3. Olin Dows, "The New Deal's Treasury Art Programs," *Arts in Society 2* (Spring-Summer 1963): 52.
4. Jerre Mangione, *The Dream and the Deal* (Boston: Little, Brown and Company, 1972), p. 34.
5. Steven Dubin, *Bureaucratizing the Muse* (Chicago: University of Chicago Press, 1987), pp. 10-11. Dubin cites the quote from Gerald Monroe, *The Artists Union of New York* (Ed.D. diss. New York University, 1971).
6. Dows, "The New Deal's Treasury Art Program," p. 56.
7. Ibid., p. 58.
8. Ibid., p. 55.
9. Ibid., pp. 72-73.
10. Ibid., p. 83.
11. Edward Lucie-Smith, *Art of the 1930's: The Age of Anxiety* (London: Weidenfeld and Nicolson Limited, 1985), p. 14.
12. Dows, "The New Deal's Treasury Art Program," p. 72.
13. Marlene Park and Gerald E. Markowitz, *The Democratic Vistas: Post Office and Public Art in the New Deal* (Philadelphia: Temple University Press, 1984), p. 22.
14. Ibid., p. 23.
15. Ibid., pp. 22-23, 29, 42, 47.
16. Mangione, *The Dream and the Deal*, p. 33. The employment of artists who were not in economic need served as a source of criticism of the PWAP.
17. Dows, "The New Deal's Treasury Art Program," p. 52.
18. Ibid.
19. Mangione, *The Dream and the Deal*, p. 39.
20. William F. McDonald, *Federal Relief Administration and the Arts* (Columbus, OH: Ohio State University Press, 1968), pp. 187, 238; and Mangione, *The Dream and the Deal*, p. 39.
21. McDonald, *Federal Relief Administration and the Arts*, p. 112.
22. Ibid., p. 113.
23. Ibid.
24. Mathews, *The Federal Theater*, p. 54.
25. Mangione, *The Dream and the Deal*, p. 294.
26. ibid., p. 39.
27. McDonald, *Federal Relief Administration and the Arts*, p. 177.
28. Mathews, *The Federal Theater*, p. 41.
29. McDonald, *Federal Relief Administration and the Arts*, p. 145.
30. Ibid., p. 111.
31. Ibid.
32. Ibid., pp. 208, 237, 238, 240.

33. Ibid., pp. 185, 238.

34. Ibid., p. 402. Although Orr-Cahall urged the exercise of care in the selection of artists for the Federal Art Project, Robert McKinzie notes that "most states took a high percentage of mediocre if not incompetent artists." Richard McKinzie, *The New Deal for Artists* (Princeton, NJ: Princeton University Press, 1973) p. 87.

35. Mangione, *The Dream and the Deal*, p. 107.

36. Ibid., p. 79.

37. Hallie Flanagan, *Arena* (New York: Benjamin Blom, 1940), pp. 132-133.

38. Mathews, *The Federal Theater*, p. 115.

39. Walter Goodman, *The Committee* (New York: Farrar, Strauss and Giroux, 1968), p. 44.

40. Robert Vaughn, *Only Victims* (New York: Putnam, 1972), p. 50.

41. Anthony Downs, *Inside Bureaucracy* (Boston: Little, Brown, 1966), pp. 109-110.

42. Flanagan, *Arena*, p. 28.

43. Mathews, *The Federal Theater*, p. 177.

44. Vaughn, *Only Victims*, p. 40.

45. Ibid., p. 72.

46. Mathews, *The Federal Theater*, p. 311.

47. U.S. House of Representatives, Special Committee on Un-American Activities, *Investigation of Un-American Activities in the United States Hearings*, on H. Res. 282, Vols. 1, 4, 75th Cong., 3rd Session, 1938.

48. Ibid., pp. 2729-2830.

49. Ibid., pp. 2838-2885.

50. Mathews, *The Federal Theater*, p. 224.

51. Flanagan, *Arena*, p. 353.

52. Mathews, *The Federal Theater*, pp. 308-309.

53. Flanagan, *Arena*, pp. 334-335.

54. Mangione, *The Dream and the Deal*, pp. 344-345.

55. Roger L. Stevens, "The State of the Arts: A 1966 Balance Sheet," *Saturday Review*, March 12, 1966, p. 25.

56. Mathews, *The Federal Theater*, p. 115.

57. E. P. Richardson, *A Short History of Painting in America* (New York: Thomas Crowell Company, 1963), p. 300. For additional criticism of the work produced by the Art Project see Harold Rosenberg, *Art on the Edge* (New York: MacMillan Publishing Company, Inc. 1975), p. 199.

58. Dows, "The New Deal's Treasury Art Program," p. 85.

59. Richardson, *A Short History of Painting in America*, pp. 298-299.

60. McDonald, *Federal Relief Administration and the Arts*, pp. 422, 453.

61. Ibid., pp. 609-610.

62. Ibid., p. 619.

63. Ibid., p. 630.

64. Ibid., p. 643.

65. Ibid., pp. 637-642.

66. Mangione, *The Dream and the Deal*, pp. 136-137.

67. Ibid., p. 244.

68. Ibid., pp. 217-218.
69. McDonald, *Federal Relief Administration and the Arts*, p. 727.
70. Mangione, *The Dream and the Deal*, p. 8.

4

To Change a Nation's Cultural Policy: The Kennedy Administration and the Arts in the United States, 1961-1963

Milton C. Cummings, Jr.

Prologue

Policies of the United States government have had an impact on the nation's literature and other forms of art since the founding of the Republic. Yet until the 1960's, at least, the indirect effects of policies designed primarily for other purposes often had a greater influence on the arts world than did government actions which were consciously designed for their impact on the arts.

In the nineteenth century, several types of policies inadvertently had an influence on the development for American culture. American copyright law had a major influence on the development of American literature in the nineteenth century. Before 1891, only an American author could copyright his work in the United States. This rankled Charles Dickens; but it also had the curious effect of hurting American writers, who had to compete with royalty-free editions of the works of established British authors such as Scott, Dickens, and Thackeray. Similarly the establishment of the second class postal rate in 1879 was profoundly important for American literature. The second class postal rate facilitated the subsequent rapid growth of American magazines, which provided, among other things, a commercial outlet for the short story. Had Edgar Allan Poe lived 40 years later, he might not have starved.

Alternatively, in the 1930's, as part of his New Deal effort to combat high unemployment, President Franklin D. Roosevelt conducted one of the largest arts patronage programs in the history of the world. Moreover, for most of the 20th century, American tax laws -- by making contributions to many arts groups tax-deductible -- have represented the single most important policy decision by government that affects the arts. (In 1991, the cash value of the tax deductibility of contributions by private donors for "arts, culture and humanities" almost certainly exceeded two billion dollars; and it may have been closer to three billion dollars.[1])

Most of the massive New Deal arts programs were cut back sharply in 1939, in a political backlash stimulated in part by Congressional anger over what many Congressmen regarded as radical plays presented by the Federal Theater Projects. In addition, after World War II many American artists began to be leery of the federal government playing a substantial role in the arts. In the late 1940's and early 1950's, the widely publicized congressional investigations of entertainment and arts figures for alleged subversive activities widened the gulf between government and the arts.

By the 1950's, artistic activities in the United States were supported primarily at the box office, and by a truly remarkable (and tax deductible) system of private patronage. This private patronage was provided mainly by individual donors, but also, and increasingly, by private foundations.

Even so, by the 1950's there were four broad types of arts activities in which the federal government had a continuing interest: international cultural exchanges; the design and decoration of public buildings; government collections such as the National Gallery of Art; and the design of coins and stamps. During the 1950's the role of the national government in several of these spheres increased. Part of this growth came from an increasing use of art as an instrument of United States foreign policy in the "Cold War." Under International Cultural Exchange legislation passed in 1954 and 1956, 111 attractions -- ranging from Dizzy Gillespie to the New York Philharmonic -- were sent to 89 countries in the program's first four years. In addition, the Office of Foreign Buildings of the Department of State launched a ten-year 200 million dollar program in 1954 to build new embassies and consulates on four continents.

Initiatives were also taken which would have a direct impact on the arts at home. In March, 1958, a bill was passed to save the Patent Office Building, which had been designed by Robert Mills (who also designed the Washington Monument) during the administration of Andrew Jackson. The bill was backed by Representative Frank Thompson (D-NJ) and

Senators Hubert Humphrey (D-MN) and Clinton P. Anderson (D-NM). In September 1958, Congress authorized the building of a National Cultural Center on the banks of the Potomac River in Washington. Under the act, co-sponsored by Senator J. William Fulbright (D-AR) and Representative Frank Thompson (D-NJ), the federal government would donate the land if private funds could be raised to build the Center within five years.[2]

These actions moved the government into the periphery of arts support, but all of them were cautious and tentative. However, by the end of the 1950's, a network of relationships between government and the arts had clearly developed, and some political leaders, such as New York's Jacob Javits and New Jersey's Frank Thompson, were advocating a greater federal role.

This, then, was the general status of federal government policy concerning the arts as the 1960 presidential campaign between Richard M. Nixon and John F. Kennedy began. During the campaign, both candidates took cautious positions on a national cultural policy without committing themselves to specific programs. Nixon placed special emphasis on the encouragement of private initiative, but recognized the need for the federal government to play an indirect role through "scholarships and exchange programs, encouragement, rather than subsidy."[3] Kennedy pointed to the already existing role of the federal government as art patron, which had developed gradually over the years. Moreover, like Nixon, Kennedy advocated the creation a new presidential advisory agency for the arts.[4]

There was, therefore, not very much distance between the positions the two candidates took on arts policy, with one exception. In an article that appeared shortly before the election in *Equity Magazine*, the official publication of Actor's Equity, Kennedy was quoted as follows:

> I am in full sympathy with the proposal for a Federally-supported foundation to provide encouragement and opportunity to non-profit, private and civic groups in the performing arts. When so many other nations officially recognize and support the performing arts as a part of their national cultural heritage, it seems to me unfortunate that the United States has been so slow in coming to a similar recognition.[5]

The *Equity Magazine* article was based on a series of questions that were sent to both Kennedy and Nixon by Dick Moore, the magazine's editor. The Kennedy statement on the arts foundation was probably hastily drafted by a Kennedy staff member during the heat of the campaign. There is no indication that Kennedy himself either focussed on that campaign commitment or emphasized it during his three years as president. But it did give supporters of new federal arts legislation in the Kennedy Administration something to point to. As one of the staffers said later, "I don't think...he came to power committed in any way to establish a National Arts Foundation. Later on, however, I did feel that having it on the record, we could emphasize that more strongly."[6]

The Beginning

In November, 1960, John F. Kennedy was elected president by a very narrow margin over Richard Nixon. Attention among Kennedy's advisors soon focussed on the problems of staffing the new administration -- and on plans for the inauguration. One of the president-elect's friends and Georgetown neighbors, Miss Kay Halle, suggested that a group of leaders in the nation's cultural life should be invited to the inaugural ceremonies as special guests of the President and Mrs. Kennedy. The proposal was approved, and telegrams of the invitation were sent to 168 "creative Americans in the Arts, Sciences, and Humanities." Fifty-eight attended -- among them Arthur Miller, Robert Lowell, Mark Rothko, Franz Kline, and John Steinbeck.

The weather the afternoon before Inauguration Day was terrible. (A foot of snow had fallen on Washington on January 19th.) Nevertheless, according to Miss Halle's own report, John Steinbeck was "so astonished and thrilled to have been invited that he was quite willing to mush to every event."[7] And the comments of many of those who had been invited, "revealed delight that President and Mrs. Kennedy were moved to consider them the equals of the politicians."[8]

Inauguration Day was sunny and crisp. In the ceremonies, Robert Frost forecast "the glory of a next Augustan age...a golden age of poetry and power, of which this noonday's the beginning hour." Several months later, two albums filled with letters from the artists, writers, and scientists invited to the Inauguration were given to President and Mrs. Kennedy. A gracious note of thanks was sent to each contributor by the President, to which he added: "Mrs. Kennedy and I would be particularly interested in any suggestions you may have in the future about the possible contribution the national government might make to the arts and scholarship in America."[9] But, most important for future presidential interest in the arts, the special invitations to the nation's artists to attend the Kennedy Inauguration received much favorable publicity. Several days after the inauguration, the *New York Times* ran a special story reporting that the inaugural invitations had been widely "hailed" in the arts world.[10] In her report on the undertaking, Miss Halle stressed the many news stories the event had prompted "here and abroad."[11] And she could not resist noting, with a touch of national pride, "General de Gaulle's recent invitation to a reception at the Elysee Palace for the creative French leaders in the Arts, Sciences, and Humanities." De Gaulle, she added, "is reported to have said that he had 'taken a leaf out of Mr. Kennedy's book.'"[12]

The Inaugural ceremonies set a tone for the relations between government and the arts in the Kennedy Administration. The gesture was direct and personal, involving all the majesty of the presidency in a bow of recognition to the arts. And it was quite economical. President Kennedy was always worried about things that might be costly in the arts policy area.

The events of Inauguration Day created an air of expectation among members of the arts world. As one of them who later came to Washington to develop a Kennedy arts program said of the President:

> I don't think he had any idea of the reverberations or the expectations that it would create in the mind of the artistic community itself. They all said, now the president has done this, what is he going to do next? And I felt later on that really I had been called down to Washington in large part to see that the expectations evoked on that first day were not let run out in the shallows of frustrations, that it would not look, in the end, like an empty gesture but would look like the real beginning of something important.[13]

Groping for a Policy

In the days and weeks following the Inauguration, the energies of the individuals who had joined the new Kennedy Administration -- like those of the President himself -- were absorbed in a wide variety of activities, challenges, and crises. Plans for the Alliance for Progress, a new program of economic aid for Latin America, were launched. There was a major fight in the House of Representatives over the power of the Committee on Rules -- rightly regarded as hostile to much of the Kennedy legislative program. In April came the failure of the Cuban invasion. In June the Berlin crisis began.

Yet there were, in the White House and elsewhere in the Administration, a number of individuals with a strong interest in seeing the federal government play a more active role in assisting the arts. Their cause was aided by the favorable public reaction to indications of Mrs. Kennedy's interest in the arts, and to the announcement in February that Mrs. Kennedy was starting a project to furnish the White House with furniture of the period when the White House was constructed.[14] First among these arts advocates in the Administration was Arthur Schlesinger, Jr., who as Special Assistant to the President had responsibilities for maintaining a liaison between the Administration and the intellectual community. Pierre S. Salinger, the President's Press Secretary, also had interests in the arts, as did Frederic G. Dutton, another White House staff member. Outside the White House, Philip Coombs, the Assistant Secretary of State in charge of the International Cultural Affairs program had an obvious concern for arts policy, and Secretary of Labor Arthur Goldberg, along with his able Assistant Secretary, Daniel Patrick Moynihan, took a strong interest in the arts.

During the first Spring and Summer of the Kennedy Administration, members of the Administration with a concern for the arts held a number of informal and formal meetings to discuss possible steps the Administration might take in this area. Several of these meetings were organized by either Schlesinger or Salinger. Before a meeting set for July 20, 1961, Philip Coombs circulated a memorandum prepared by his associate, Max Isenberg, titled "A Strategy for Cultural Advancement." The memorandum proposed a plan of action for the Kennedy administration:

> In his Inaugural address, following upon Robert Frost's prophecy of 'a next Augustan age,' the president called for encouragement for the arts and for a global alliance to 'assure a more fruitful life for all mankind.' By this, and other declarations, this administration has committed itself, before the country and the world, to cultural advancement as a major national aim. It must now address itself to fulfilling this commitment.[15]

Such a commitment, Isenberg argued, would have benefits in both domestic and international affairs.

> At least a serious effort to improve the quality of American Cultural life would be a boost to national morale. It would inevitably be more. It would confirm that in the endless striving for peace and material well-being, we have not lost sight of why we want them....

> In our international relations, establishment of cultural advancement as a major aim of the United States could not fail to make us more effective. Among nations of like heritage and development, it would make the less developed nations think better of us as a model; and to the nations of the Soviet bloc, it would show devotion on our part to humanism transcending political differences, a demonstration which holds more promise than any other approach tried thus far for bringing forth affirmative, even conciliatory, response from their side. Arts, letters, and learning are the only goods for which a world common market exists.[16]

In developing a "program of cultural advancement," Isenberg declared, "the President and Mrs. Kennedy, whose personal identification with the arts, letters, and learning is universally known and respected, are ideally suited for leadership in this field."[17] Isenberg suggested the establishment of a steering committee, composed of representatives of the White House, the State Department, the Library of Congress, the Smithsonian Institution, and other agencies with a special interest in cultural affairs, to undertake a twofold task: "(1) to develop a theory...of the place of cultural advancement in national and international policy; and (2) to work out and set in motion a plan of action to achieve agreed goals."[18]

The July 20th meeting did not lead immediately to the establishment of a formal steering committee. But, in September, about a dozen individuals from various parts of the government met at the Occidental Restaurant near the White House for dinner to make plans for the next step. Arthur Schlesinger was unable to attend the meeting, but most of those who were there recommended that the President should appoint a full-time Special Assistant for Cultural Affairs, charged with the task of developing a national cultural policy.

When Schlesinger heard this recommendation, he objected strenuously in a memo to Salinger. "I do not think," he argued, "that the appointment of a Special Assistant for Culture would be a good idea at this stage; nor do I think that any existing Special Assistant could get free enough from more urgent jobs to do the cultural assignment justice." Instead, Schlesinger recommended that a person be "brought in from the outside as a White House consultant on a part-time basis...charged with conducting discussions around the government on all issues connected with culture...and instructed to come up...with a general program."[19] In addition, Schlesinger told Salinger that he had a man in mind for the job -- August Hecksher, Director of the Twentieth Century Fund.

Defeat in the House of Representatives

Meanwhile, on September 21st, supporters of federal assistance for the arts were reminded of just how weak support for their cause was in Congress. In July, a bill had been reported out of the House Committee on Education and Labor to establish a Federal Advisory Council on the Arts. The Council would be authorized to recommend ways to increase the nation's "cultural resources," to propose methods for encouraging private initiative in the arts, and to act as a coordinating group between private and government activities in the arts.[20] The bill was sponsored by Representative Frank Thompson (D-NJ); Representative John Lindsay (R-NY); and Representative Carroll Kearns (R-PA). However, the House Committee on Rules, sometimes called the "traffic cop" of the House, refused to grant a rule for the measure to be debated and voted on by the full House.

The bill's sponsors then tried to bring the bill to a vote by a suspension-of the-rules procedure -- a move which required a two-thirds affirmative vote in the House to be successful. It did not even come close -- 166 supported the motion, 173 opposed it.[21]

Opponents focussed on the question of whether it was really possible to define what the arts were. Representative W. Smith (D-VA), Chairman of the Rules Committee, was a leader in opposition to the bill. In a sally which evoked chuckles from some of his colleagues on the floor of the House, he declared:

> Well, I hate to ask this question. I always hesitate to display my ignorance, of which I have a plenty. But, this bill has been pending up in the Committee on Rules for about 3 or 4 weeks, and there is no interest up there in it. We sort of put it away in the cooler, waiting until it got more enthusiastic endorsement. But, the thing that troubles me is -- and since it was brought to the floor this afternoon I have asked everybody that seemed to know anything about this bill -- what are the arts? And, here is where I display my ignorance. I do not know. What does it include? What is it about? I suppose fiddle players would be in the arts and the painting of pictures would be in the arts. It was suggested that poker playing was an artful occupation. Is this going to subsidize poker players that get in trouble?[22]

The defeat of the Advisory Council bill showed how much weaker support for the arts was in Congress than in the executive branch. The experience made Kennedy more cautious in his support for the arts at a time when he was already having difficulty getting support in the House for major items in his New Frontier legislative program. The vote also showed how much work still remained for the arts supporters to do. As Arthur Schlesinger wrote to Representative Kearns:

> I fear that the Federal Advisory Council on the Arts bill ran into traffic difficulty this year; but we anticipate passage in the next session. A motion to suspend the rules requires, of course, a two-thirds vote. I gather that this motion was supported by 135 Democrats and 31 Republicans and opposed by 70 Democrats and 103 Republicans. I hope both sides will do better next time![23]

A Special Consultant to the President for the Arts

Despite this weakness in Congress, several developments in 1961 increased the public's identification of the presidency with the arts. Early in the administration the President and Mrs. Kennedy began attending cultural events. This presidential interest generated extensive coverage in the news media. Moreover, behind these public presidential actions there often lay persistent suggestions and prodding by White House staff members. Just one week after the inauguration, Fred Dutton sent a memo to the keeper of the President's schedule, Kenneth O' Donnell:

> If the President is looking for any relaxation this evening ... you might consider his going to the African Ballets at the National Theater here...Just the mere going would indicate the energy which the public so likes in their Presidents and which shows so much in this one. The African aspect would be widely reported in that critical and sensitive area, and it would also point up here at home the personal interest that the President has in Africa. This particular ballet would also constitute a very fresh way of implicitly re-emphasizing the cultural interest which the President wants to bring more fully to American life.
>
> A couple of notes of warning: the show tonight does not begin until 9:30 p.m. At least one number has bare bosomed women -- highly respectable, the reviews said![24]

Another public move by the president in support of the arts was triggered by an announcement on August 7th that the 1961-1962 season of the Metropolitan Opera was to be cancelled. The cancellation took place because the Metropolitan Opera Association and the American Federation of Musicians union had been unable to agree on the musicians' wages.

The distinguished American mezzo soprano, Rise Stevens, appealed to President Kennedy to intervene to save the Met's season.[25] A few days later, Kennedy designated Secretary of Labor Arthur Goldberg to arbitrate the dispute.[26]

After ten days of intense negotiations, Goldberg's efforts were successful. The Association and the musicians agreed to submit the issue to "final and binding" arbitration; and the Met opened its season on October 23rd.[27] When the terms of the arbitration award were announced in December, Goldberg issued a set of accompanying remarks, in which he argued that the performing arts, in order to survive economically, would require a mixed partnership of patronage -- involving business, private philanthropy, and the government.[28] The Goldberg statement was prophetic of the course that future arts policy was to take in the United States.

A third development that emphasized presidential interest in the arts was a series of glittering state dinners that were held at the White House. These were planned with Mrs. Kennedy's personal involvement and supervision; and, in several of them artists and members of the intellectual community were the guests of honor. One of the most memorable of these evenings featured a concert at the White House by Pablo Casals on November 13, 1961. Casals had not played in the White House since 1904, during the administration of President Theodore Roosevelt.[29]

The enormously favorable public reaction to the Casals evening persuaded Arthur Schlesinger that the time was ripe to try to persuade the President to take another step forward in developing a federal government cultural policy. On November 22nd, he wrote Kennedy a two page memorandum entitled "Moving Ahead on the Cultural Front:"

> The Casals evening has had an extraordinary effect in the artistic world. On the next day, when the advisory council for the National Cultural Center met, a number people said to me in the most heartfelt way how much the administration's evident desire to recognize artistic and intellectual distinction meant to the whole intellectual community. You probably saw John Crosby's column this morning ("President Kennedy is the best...friend culture has had in the White House since Jefferson").
>
> All this is of obvious importance, not only in attaching a potent opinion-making group to the Administration, but in transforming the world's impression of the United States as a nation of money-grubbing materialists. And it is notable that all this has taken place without any criticism, so far as I am aware. Contrary to the

expectations reported by Crosby, no editorial writer has used the Casals dinner to accuse you of fiddling while Berlin burns.

I wonder whether this might not be an appropriate time to carry the matter one step further. You will recall that Pierre Salinger and I gathered together a group of people around government concerned with areas where public policy has an impact on cultural matters. The group recommended that the White House should have a Special Assistant for Culture. Pierre and I thought that anything like this would be premature. We would recommend instead bringing in someone from the outside as a part-time White House consultant to survey areas of actual or possible government impact on culture (from airport construction to tax policies to honors lists to direct government sponsorship or subsidy) and to come up at the end of six months with a report and, hopefully, a program.

The mere existence of this White House inquiry would do a good deal to generate concern through the bureaucracy for the government's cultural responsibilities. At the end, we would have a much better idea of the resources, possibilities and problems in the area.

My first thought was of the man to do the job is August Heckscher of the 20th Century Fund. Heckscher wrote the essay on "The Quality of American Culture" for the Eisenhower commission on National Goals. He is a man of intelligence, and cultivation; he understands that government at best can only play a marginal role; and he is deeply committed to the subject. He use to be editor of the New York Herald Tribune editorial page but resigned because he could not face the thought of writing editorials in favor of Nixon. He supported you in the campaign...Can we go ahead and get a man down to carry out this assignment?[30]

This time Schlesinger's proposal fell on receptive ears, and, on December 5th, the President sent a letter, the first draft of which had been written by Schlesinger, to August Heckscher. The day after the Kennedy letter went out, Schlesinger sent a copy to Pierre Salinger with a covering memorandum. This memo contained only one word -- "Enfin!"[31] This new initiative in the arts was tentative; it was cautious; it was only a "modest scheme."[32] But the plan for which a small group of White House staff members had been pressing for several months was under way.

The Job of the Special Consultant

After obtaining approval from the trustees of the Twentieth Century Fund, August Heckscher made plans to take on the assignment of Special Consultant to the President for the Arts. But before the White House formally announced the appointment, the *New York Times* broke the news with a front page story in February, 1962. The reaction in the press and among arts groups was generally highly favorable. Although initially Kennedy had said he wanted "a quiet inquiry, without fanfare," the President was obviously pleased by the favorable reaction which news of the assignment had received.[33]

Heckscher then went to work. The looseness with which his job responsibilities were defined gave him considerable latitude to decide what he would emphasize in his assignment. Considering himself a temporary consultant, Heckscher hoped to achieve three main goals during his stay in Washington: (1) contribute to the establishment of a Federal Advisory Council on the Arts; (2) prepare a report, to include policy recommendations for the future, on the arts and the national government; and (3) obtain a permanent successor, thereby institutionalizing the role of a Special Assistant to the President for the Arts.[34] In addition, Kennedy, who was always concerned with achieving practical, tangible results, was strongly interested in seeing a National Cultural Center built in Washington during his Administration.[35] Primary responsibility for that, however, fell on Roger Stevens. Stevens, a successful theater producer and real estate investor -- and a former Democratic campaign manager for Adlai Stevenson, was appointed by Kennedy in September, 1961, to serve as head of the Board of Trustees for the Cultural Center.

Heckscher's job inevitably expanded. Increasingly he became the Administration's spokesman for the arts, which included making speeches, getting the President to issue statements on arts matters, being alert to what other government agencies were doing, and raising concern for the arts in other parts of the government. (Heckscher called this "day-to-day surveillance.")[36] He also inherited the task of defining what the arts were for the government:

> I think that one of the useful things that I did ... was to enlarge the definition of 'The Arts'. I was always careful to maintain that they weren't simply painting, the ballet, the opera, and the theater, but they included the whole environmental condition of the nation's life and that architecture and city planning and so on were very important. ... At that time government was doing nothing in the field

of performing arts, but spending billions of dollars on architecture. So here was a good place to begin....[37]

Heckscher spearheaded continuing efforts to use the White House as a stage for official recognition of the arts, often with the active cooperation of Mrs. Kennedy. One of the most publicized of these efforts was a state dinner on April 29, 1962 at which 49 Nobel Prize winners from the Western Hemisphere were honored.[38] In his after-dinner remarks, the President said the event had brought together "the most extraordinary collection of talent, of human knowledge, that has ever been gathered together at the White House, with the possible exception of when Thomas Jefferson dined alone."[39]

Not every effort to stimulate symbolic leadership for the arts was successful. As Heckscher later recalled, "We were always trying to get Mrs. Kennedy to do things which she wouldn't do."[40] And although Mrs. Kennedy was both generally interested in the arts and enormously helpful to Heckscher, she was also "a somewhat ambivalent figure in all this."[41] "Mr. Heckscher, I will do anything for the arts you want," she once said. "But, of course, I can't be away too much from the children and I can't be present at too many cultural events. After all, I'm *not* Mrs. Roosevelt."[42]

During his tenure, Heckscher also undertook an extensive survey of the things various agencies of the government were already doing that affected the arts. The President, quite correctly, felt the government was doing more to assist the arts than was generally realized. For instance, he initially wanted Heckscher to get a dollar figure for the tax deductibility of contributions to arts organizations. This, Kennedy reasoned, amounted to a very substantial sum, and constituted an indirect subsidy of the arts by the government. However, when it was pointed out to the president that, by that line of reasoning, the federal government was also subsidizing the Catholic Church, he quickly dropped the point. The "religious issue" had been a major problem for Kennedy, the first Roman Catholic to win the presidency, in the 1960 presidential campaign.

By early 1963, Heckscher had completed a draft of his report on *The Arts and the National Government.*[43] Taken as a whole, it was a remarkable document -- one which presaged arts policy-making during the next decade. The report surveyed existing federal programs with a direct or indirect impact on the arts. It urged the many existing government agencies to keep the interests of the arts in mind while formulating and administering their policies. It recommended the establishment of a Federal Advisory Council on the Arts and the appointment of a permanent arts advisor to the President. It also proposed the creation of a Federal Arts Foundation to make grants for the arts. The report was approved by the President and formally released on May 28, 1963.

The Advisory Council on the Arts

Progress towards a Federal Advisory Council on the Arts was slow. After the September 1961 defeat of the bill to create the Council, House sponsors, led by Representative Frank Thompson, tried once more to move the measure to the floor for a vote in the 1962 session of Congress. Kennedy himself asked for this legislation in a special message to Congress on aid to education in February of 1962.[44] But on May 17th, the bill was blocked once again by the House Committee on Rules.[45]

At this point, some of Kennedy's advisors urged that, instead, the President establish an Advisory Council by Executive Order. The negotiations which followed were long and tortuous. In the Senate, there were powerful potential sponsors of legislation to establish an Advisory Council, including Senators Jacob Javits, Claiborne Pell, and Hubert Humphrey. These men felt, almost certainly correctly, that the necessary votes could be obtained in the Senate.

In the House, which on arts legislation as on many other parts of the Kennedy program was much more resistant, supporters of legislation were not as sure that they had the votes they needed. However, they were prepared to try again to get a favorable vote in the Rules Committee after the May, 1962 setback. For a while Representative Lindsay, in particular, was quite optimistic that the necessary switch of votes in the committee could be obtained from some of his Republican colleagues.

The President, again characteristically cautious, for many months preferred to rely on the legislative route to create the Council. As late as February, 1963, Heckscher reported that "the President still feels that this would have greater permanency and prestige if accomplished through legislation."[46] Moreover, Kennedy and his legislative advisors were concerned that members of Congress might feel that "executive action had been taken to by-pass Congress," if the president went ahead alone.[47]

By early 1963, however, the pressures on Kennedy from his own staff to establish an Advisory Council began to grow. On January 13, Heckscher summarized his position on the issue in a memo to Arthur Schlesinger:

A direct move in regard to the establishment of an Advisory Council on the Arts now seems urgent.

1. The Congress is being restrained only with difficulty from putting in bills for this purpose. Such bills almost surely would remain, as heretofore, bottled up in the House.

2. Senator Humphrey is, in particular, urging us very strongly to go ahead.

3. Major elements in the arts constituency have been assured that the President is going forward on this, and our failure to do so would be judged adversely.[48]

Shortly thereafter, Schlesinger urged the President to make a statement "as soon as possible announcing your intention to set up the Council and saying that the order and the names will follow. Heckscher has prepared a draft statement."[49]

> If we don't do this, various Congressmen will put in bills for this purpose. Then we will have to decide whether or not to make a fight for them; and failure to do so will be judged adversely. The executive order approach could bypass this; and, since the legislators involved are interested in the result rather than the method, they say that they would not regard the executive order as an invasion of legislative prerogative.[50]

The President listened to this advice, but evidently wanted to be sure that understandings had been reached with the Congressmen most concerned. After Thompson and Lindsay both agreed that the President should go ahead, plans got under way to issue the executive order, which was released in June, 1963. It now remained, or so Heckscher thought, only to prepare a list of names of persons to be appointed to the Council.

The Role of the Arts Constituency

Throughout the struggle to establish an Advisory Council on the Arts, legislative supporters were hampered by the inadequate political support which came from arts groups. Few individual artists and arts institutions were accustomed to or organized for political action. Most had had little experience in exerting political pressure for such legislation. Even on the basic issue of whether there should be federal government subsidies for the arts, there were sharp differences among the arts groups.

A few arts organizations were active politically in 1962 and 1963. Actors' Equity, the union of professional actors, had a lobbyist, Jack Golodner, working for the Administration's arts proposals.[51] The American Federation of Musicians urged its members to write to their Congressman in support of arts-related issues.[52] But many other elements of what might be a political constituency for the arts were still politically naive and unorganized. In some arts fields, such as dance or opera, national organizations were not even formed yet. In addition, one of the potentially most politically potent groups -- symphony orchestras -- evidenced only lukewarm support for and some outright opposition to an explicit federal role in the arts. The symphony orchestras were relatively well organized in the early 1960's: the American Symphony Orchestra League had been established in 1942; the Boards of Trustees of symphony orchestras often included many of the economic and social elite of their community; and the orchestras were one of the largest, most long established, and geographically dispersed sets of arts institutions in the country.

A systematic survey of the attitudes of symphony orchestra board members toward the role of the federal government in the arts was taken by the League in 1953. As the League's Executive Secretary reported:

> The responses came in quickly from the boards and the opinions were decisive...91 percent of the governing boards responding to the surveys were unalterably opposed to any governmental program in the arts which would relate to local performing organizations, and under no circumstances did they want any form of federal subsidy of the arts.[53]

During the years following 1953, major changes began to take place in the music world which increased both the cost of maintaining a symphony orchestra and the amount of contributions needed to supplement income from the box office. The weekly earnings of orchestra musicians remained low, but they were increasing under union demands. Pressures were also brought by the musicians' unions to lengthen the season -- and the number of weeks during which musicians would be paid. Following a new survey in 1962, the League's Executive Director, Helen Thompson, reported that there had been a "tremendous change in the last nine years in the attitudes of community and civic leaders (from whose ranks symphony orchestra boards are now drawn) towards the role of the federal government in the arts."[54] There was also "an increasing awareness that symphony orchestras and the arts generally have become a matter of national concern."[55] Mrs. Thompson added: "Apparently, the increased receptivity to the concept that the federal government might assume a more active role...stems largely from increased awareness that greater economic stability must be developed for the performing musicians."[56] However, there is still no clearcut mandate from the orchestras either in support of or in opposition to any particular arts legislation.

There were also differences of opinion related to the size of different symphony orchestras. The smaller, community orchestras were more strongly in favor of an expanded federal role in the arts than were the large, more prestigious orchestras.[57] The overall ambivalence of the symphony orchestras was also reflected in a survey which the *New York Times* conducted in September, 1962. This focussed on attitudes among 24 major and 13 lesser United States orchestras. Most of them, the *Times* reported, opposed subsidies by the federal government for symphony orchestras, and instead favored cash gifts or subsidies on the local level.[58]

The Final Months

Once his report had been released and the Executive Order establishing a Federal Advisory Council on the Arts had been issued, August Heckscher cut back on his time in Washington, thinking his job was nearly over. His third objective, securing a permanent successor, appeared to be achieved when it was agreed that Richard Goodwin should take the post of Special Assistant for the Arts. In the Summer of 1963, Goodwin was working at the Peace Corps, and he had played an active role as a speechwriter in Kennedy's presidential campaign in 1960. Kennedy, however, asked Heckscher to stay on until Goodwin's appointment could be formally made.

As he prepared to leave his job in Washington, Heckscher felt a sense of satisfaction.

> I felt that the time I spent there had been tremendously worthwhile. When I'd finished, I had done a report for the President which had been well-received by him and well-treated by the press. It looked as if this report was not going to be one of those that just lay on the shelf because the President had agreed to the thirty names which would make up the Advisory Council. The Advisory Council was to be appointed in the very near future, and would take up this report as their first order of business, to say how it could be implemented and what portion should be given priority. The President had, at the same time, which was crucial to me, agreed to name a full-time

successor in my place, which was the one thing which I had asked. So I could feel that...the things I had asked for had all been accomplished. Maybe I'd put my sights too low but I had gotten the Advisory Council on the Arts, I'd gotten the report, and I'd gotten a permanent successor. From the first day, I said to the people in my office -- Barbara Donald, Nancy Newhouse, "When you make up the files you must realize that we are not just putting up files; we are really starting something -- an office which I hope will continue here in the White House forever."[59]

During the Summer, however, Heckscher was away from Washington for several weeks, and "things...began to slip very badly."[60] The names of the persons to be appointed to the Advisory Council had not been formally approved. Kenneth O'Donnell, one of Kennedy's closest aides whom Heckscher regarded as "rather hostile" to the arts world, had held up the routine security investigation of the names.[61] In addition, Goodwin's appointment was being delayed until he completed the work in which he was involved with the Peace Corps.

Once Heckscher was back in Washington, he and Schlesinger were able to get action started again on clearing the names of the Advisory Council. In mid-November Kennedy told Frank Thompson, in what was to be the President's last telephone conversation with the Congressman, that he planned to announce the appointments to the Advisory Council "as soon as I get back" from a planned trip with Mrs. Kennedy to Texas.[62] On November 21, the President and Mrs. Kennedy began a two-day tour of Texas. On the morning of November 22nd, the *New York Times* announced that Richard Goodwin would be appointed as a full-time Special Assistant to the President for the Arts and ran a profile of Goodwin. Early that afternoon, John F. Kennedy was assassinated in Dallas.

Epilogue

The list of names John F. Kennedy approved for what would have been the first Federal Advisory Council on the Arts was not acted upon. Yet, in the 22 months that followed, under Kennedy's successor, President Lyndon B. Johnson, federal action and legislation to assist the arts moved forward at a rate that would have seemed unthinkable in the early Kennedy years.

In the immediate aftermath of Kennedy's death, there was apprehension in the arts world that Johnson might not give the arts the same emphasis that Kennedy had. On November 29th, 1963, Arthur Schlesinger wrote Johnson a two-page memorandum on the "Future of the Arts Programs." After detailing what had happened since Heckscher was appointed in March, 1962, Schlesinger said: "The question is whether you will want to go ahead with this effort. I hope very much that you will...."[63] After indicating what the program could do to benefit the arts, Schlesinger also added a practical political argument: "It can strengthen the connections between the Administration and the intellectual and artistic community -- something not to be dismissed when victory or defeat next fall will probably depend on who carried New York, Pennsylvania, California, Illinois and Michigan."[64]

Very soon after the assassination, Johnson supported legislation renaming the National Cultural Center the John F. Kennedy Center for the Performing Arts and providing up to $15,500,000 in federal matching grant funds for its construction. Then, as the Johnson Administration faced the staggering task of taking over the reins of power and managing an election campaign, it did little on the arts front. In May 1964, activity resumed with Roger Stevens being appointed as Special Assistant to the President for the Arts. Later that Summer, prompted by skillful lobbying by Stevens, legislation creating a Federal Advisory Council on the Arts was finally passed by Congress.

In June 1964, another event which was eventually to be of importance for the arts took place. A special nongovernmental Commission of scholars in the humanities released a report on the status of the humanities in American life. The Commission had been created by the American Council of Learned Societies, Phi Beta Kappa, and the American Council of Graduate Schools. Dr. Barnaby Keeney, the President of Brown University, was its chairman. In its report, the Commission called for the establishment of a National Foundation for the Humanities, with broad similarities to the National Science Foundation. In September, while on a tumultuous campaign tour of Providence, Rhode Island, President Johnson visited Brown University. In a major speech there, he declared that he looked "with the greatest of favor" on the Keeney Commission's proposal for a National Foundation for the Humanities.[65]

In November, Johnson was elected to a four-year presidential term by a landside. At the same time, heavy Democratic gains in Congress altered the balance of power in the House of Representatives, bringing it more into line with the liberal activist White House. In the process, many Congressmen who had opposed federal arts legislation were defeated.

In early 1965, a political compromise brought the supporters of arts legislation and supporters of humanities legislation together to work for the passage of legislation creating a National Foundation on the Arts and Humanities. The Foundation was to have a separate National Endowment for each field. This alliance added to the forces working for the arts higher education's political constituency -- which then had nearly five million students, several hundred thousand faculty members, and colleges, universities or junior colleges in every congressional district in the country.

On March 10, 1965, the Administration submitted its legislative proposal to create the National Foundation. And in September, after a spirited floor fight in the House of Representatives, the bill was passed. Thus began a National Endowment for the Arts, for which the Congress has since appropriated more than three billion dollars.

John F. Kennedy and the Arts -- An Assessment

Once, when August Heckscher and John F. Kennedy were having a meeting to talk about the arts, the discussion turned to a more general evaluation of the record of previous presidents. Heckscher had written a book on Woodrow Wilson and much admired him. He was, therefore, disappointed to find that Kennedy rated Wilson fairly low. Wilson, Kennedy said in effect, had not won his greatest battle -- the League of Nations. He had articulated goals for the nation, but he had been unable to achieve them.[66]

It is one of the ironies of John Kennedy's brief presidency that in the development of public policy for the arts -- as in many other policy areas -- he was better able to articulate the goals than he was to persuade Congress to pass legislation to help implement those goals. When Kennedy died, legislation to establish an Advisory Council on the Arts had not been passed. The creation of a National Foundation on the Arts had not become a formal presidential proposal. And even the membership of an Advisory Council created by Executive Order had not been appointed -- though if Kennedy had had a little more time, it would have been.

The record of the president's interest in the arts is one of gradual evolution and growth. At the beginning he had no over-all plan. As Heckscher later recalled:

> Everything that was done in this field of the arts -- everything President Kennedy did in regard to it -- was a trial step. President

> Kennedy would do something; he would be surprised by the reverberation it caused, then he would go on and do something else. I don't think he ever had any grandiose -- he would have hated the word "grandiose" -- any larger plan from the beginning.[67]
>
> He said, "Of course, you're going to need legislation," I mean he was very clear that we would have an arts bill of some magnitude sometime. But he was never anxious -- and I think he was right in this -- to get out and fight a lonely battle for culture in advance of an interest which had already been shown by the public at large.[68]

In retrospect, it seems clear that the President was both leading and riding a tide that made it almost inevitable that a larger federal role for the arts would evolve. A number of social and political trends seemed to be coming together in the early 1960's.

1. While the notion of a "cultural explosion" in the United States in this period could be -- and was -- greatly exaggerated, participation and interest in some forms of cultural activities were expanding at the time when Kennedy came to power. Museum attendance was up. New artistic organizations were being formed, sometimes in communities which previously had not had them. And audiences for some of the performing arts, notably dance, were increasing. Perhaps more important than any actual increases in cultural activities during this period, it was widely believed that interest in the arts was expanding and as a result, the news media were giving greater attention to the role of the arts in American society.

2. Economic and social trends were raising the costs of artistic activities. They were also increasing the pressures on artists and arts organizations to seek new sources of funding.

3. The American national government itself began to seem a less forbidding institution for the arts world to embrace. The congressional investigations of artists for alleged subversive activities in the early days of the "Cold War" were receding from memory. A government headed by John F. Kennedy seemed much more attractive to many members of the artistic community.

4. During the 1950's there had developed in the Congress a cadre of key legislators who were genuinely committed to arts legislation. Representatives Frank Thompson and John Lindsay, and Senators Jacob Javits, J. William Fulbright, and Hubert Humphery were willing to do the hard work which was necessary to promote

115

legislation in this area. And in 1960 a man who was to be one of the strongest advocates of new government programs for the arts, Claiborne Pell (D-RI), was first elected to the Senate.

5. Kennedy appointed to positions of great power in his Administration a number of men who had a strong interest in the arts. The White House staff members, Arthur Schlesinger, Jr. and Pierre Salinger, were of crucial importance in launching the Administration's cultural program. Other Kennedy appointees such as Arthur Goldberg and Daniel Patrick Moynihan elsewhere in the Administration, also played a major role.

6. The generally favorable public reaction to the initiatives that the President and Mrs. Kennedy took for the arts did much to keep the program going and to expand it. At a time when many of the president's major programs such as aid-to-education and medicare were going nowhere in Congress, Kennedy, shrewd politician that he was, recognized that his expression of interest in the arts was a political asset. As Heckscher said of some of the other members of the White House staff, "I think they were always rather...pleased by the amount of good will that came to the Administration and amused by the fact that it costs so little money."[69]

7. Other political considerations also made it desirable for the President to be associated with the arts. One of his closest advisors, Theodore Sorensen, felt that Kennedy's arts concern won him good will among board members of artistic organizations -- often well-to-do members of the business community and, frequently, Republicans. As Sorensen later wrote, "They warmed to an intellectual president who patronized the arts when his position on fiscal and other matters might well have cooled them."[70] In New York State, a Republican governor, Nelson Rockefeller, was also making a record in the arts world by establishing the Arts Council of New York. Rockefeller had been seriously considered as a possible presidential candidate in 1960 and it was thought that he might be Kennedy's opponent in 1964. It was better to lead than to lag behind.

8. Finally, individuals and institutions involved in the arts were re-evaluating their own attitudes toward the role of the federal government in the arts. They were also beginning to acquire some practical experience in testifying before Congress and exerting pressure in the executive and legislative branches of government

on behalf of government actions that they favored. This growth in the political sophistication of the arts world still had a long way to develop. But it had begun.

The Kennedy Administration was only the beginning in the efforts to encourage the national government to give greater assistance to the arts. Little that was firm or institutionalized was completed by 1963. Yet many of the seeds of future federal government policy towards the arts were planted during the three brief years of the Kennedy Administration: the idea of one or more White House staff members with an explicit interest in the arts; the idea of a National Foundation on the Arts, now given concrete expression through the National Endowment; the idea of a broad definition of the arts, including architecture, now reflected in many of the government's arts policies; and the idea that a mixed arts support system of patronage would be most appropriate to help support the arts in the United States -- relying heavily on business corporations, individual donors, private foundations, and the states and localities, as well as on the federal government. These have been key elements of the system that have developed substantially since 1963.

These concepts -- and their successful launching -- were solid accomplishments. But Kennedy had an impact on the nation's arts policy in another way -- even though it was a way that he himself professed to consider of secondary importance. The American presidency is both a highly visible theater from which to dramatize new ideas, and a bully pulpit. During his three years in office, Kennedy articulated a vision of an expanded relationship between government and the arts in a way that few American presidents before him had ever done. And the voicing of that vision set in motion forces which would change a nation's cultural policy. As Kennedy once said in words that now stand on the wall of the Center for the Performing Arts that bears his name:

> There is a connection, hard to explain logically but easy to feel, between achievement in public life and progress in the arts. The age of Pericles was also the age of Phidias. The age of Lorenzo de Medici was also the age of Leonardo da Vinci. The age of Elizabeth was also the age of Shakespeare. And the New Frontier for which I campaign in public life, can also be a new frontier for American art.

Notes

1. The American Association of Fund-Raising Counsel reported total private giving of 8.81 billion dollars for the "Arts, Culture and Humanities" in 1991. Most of these donations came from individual givers, business corporations, or private foundations; and most of these individuals or organizations were able to claim tax deductions for their gifts to cultural organizations. *Giving USA*, 1992 Edition (New York: American Association of Fund-Raising Counsel Trust, 1992).

2. Most of the principal federal arts activities in the 1950's are summarized in Milton Bracker, "U.S. Role in the Arts Is Found to Have Increased in Decade Since World War II," *New York Times*, December 8, 1958.

3. Quoted in William Howard Adams, "National Policy on the Arts: The Candidates' Views," *Cultural Affairs* 4 (1968), p. 4.

4. *Ibid.*

5. "The Presidential Candidates: Vice President Nixon and Senator Kennedy Discuss the Theater's Problems," *Equity Magazine* 45, no. 10 (November 1960), p. 10.

6. August Heckscher, recorded interview by Wolf von Eckhardt, December 10, 1965, p. 4. Oral History Program, John F. Kennedy Library.

7. "Report on Inaugural Committee Project Concerning Invitation of President and Mrs. Kennedy to 168 Creative Americans in the Arts, Sciences and Humanities to Attend their January 20, 1961 Inaugural Ceremonies," June, 1961, p. 1. Files of August Heckscher, John F. Kennedy Library.

8. *Ibid.*

9. Letter from President John F. Kennedy to Professor Jacques Barzun, September 13, 1961. White House Central Files, John F. Kennedy Library.

10. *New York Times*, January 31, 1961, p. 30.

11. "Report on Inaugural Committee Project Concerning Invitation of President and Mrs. Kennedy to 168 Creative Americans in the Arts, Sciences and Humanities to Attend their January 20, 1961 Inaugural Ceremonies," June, 1961, p. 1. Files of August Heckscher, John F. Kennedy Library.

12. *Ibid.*, p. 2.

13. August Heckscher, recorded interview by Wolf von Eckhardt, December 10, 1965, pp. 3-4. Oral History Program, John F. Kennedy Library.

14. *New York Times*, February 24, 1961, p. 1.

15. Memorandum, "A Strategy for Cultural Advancement," July 10, 1961, p. 1. Files of August Heckscher, John F. Kennedy Library.

16. *Ibid.*

17. *Ibid.*, p. 2.

18. *Ibid.*, p. 3.

19. Memorandum for Pierre Salinger from Arthur Schlesinger, Jr., Subject: "The Cultural Offensive," September 27, 1961, p. 1. Files of August Hecksher, John F. Kennedy Library.

20. *1961 CQ Almanac* (Washington: Congressional Quarterly, Inc., 1962), p. 387.

21. *Congressional Record*, September 21, 1961, p. 20535.

22. *Congressional Record*, September 21, 1961, pp. 20499-20500.

23. Letter from Arthur Schlesinger, Jr. to Congressman Carroll D. Kearns, October 19, 1961. White House Central Files, John F. Kennedy Library.

24. Memorandum to Kenneth O'Donnell, from Fred Dutton, January 27, 1961. White House Central Files, John F. Kennedy Library.

25. *New York Times*, August 8, 1961, p. 31.

26. *New York Times*, August 19, 1961, p. 19.

27. *New York Times*, October 24, 1961, p. 1.

28. *New York Times*, December 15, 1961, p. 1.

29. *New York Times*, November 14, 1961, p. 1.

30. "Memorandum for the President, Subject: Moving Ahead on the Cultural Front," Arthur Schlesinger, Jr. to John F. Kennedy, November 22, 1961, White House Central Files, John F. Kennedy Library.

31. Memorandum for: Pierre Salinger, from Arthur Schlesinger, Jr., December 6, 1961. White House Central Files, John F. Kennedy Library.

32. August Heckscher, recorded interview by Wolf von Eckhardt, December 10, 1965, p. 9. Oral History Program, John F. Kennedy Library.

33. *Ibid.*, p. 13.

34. *Ibid.*, p. 52.

35. Roger Stevens, recorded interview by August Heckscher, January 22, 1964, p. 17. Oral History Program, John F. Kennedy Library.

36. August Heckscher, recorded interview by Wolf von Eckhardt, December 10, 1965, p. 61. Oral History Program, John F. Kennedy Library.

37. *Ibid.*, p. 16.

38. U.S. President, *Public Papers of the Presidents of the United States, John F. Kennedy, 1962* (Washington: United States Government Printing Office, 1963), p. 347. The Nobel guests included 46 United States citizens; one Canadian, Lester Pearson, a winner of the Nobel Peace Prize; and two Europeans who were then living in the United States.

39. *Ibid.*, p. 347.

40. August Heckscher, recorded interview by Wolf von Eckhardt, December 10, 1965, p. 49. Oral History Program, John F. Kennedy Library.

41. *Ibid.*, p. 48.

42. *Ibid.*, p. 51.

43. 88th Congress, 1st Session, Document No. 28: *The Arts and the National Government*, Report to the President, submitted by August Heckscher, Special Consultant on the Arts, May 28, 1963 (Washington: United States Government Printing Office, 1963).

44. *New York Times*, February 7, 1962, p. 20.

45. *New York Times*, May 18, 1962, p. 33.

46. Letter, August Heckscher to Senator Hubert H. Humphrey, February 13, 1963. Files of August Heckscher, John F. Kennedy Library.

47. "Notes on Meeting to Discuss White House Policy on Advisory Committee on the Arts, May 12, 1962." Files of August Heckscher, John F. Kennedy Library.

48. Memorandum for Mr. Arthur Schlesinger, Jr., from August Heckscher, January 17, 1963. Files of August Heckscher, John F. Kennedy Library.

49. "Memorandum for the President, Subject: Federal Advisory Council for the

Arts," not dated, Arthur Schlesinger, Jr., to John F. Kennedy. White House Central Files, John F. Kennedy Library.

50. *Ibid.*

51. Memorandum, Barbara Donald to August Heckscher, May 24, 1962. Files of August Heckscher, John F. Kennedy Library.

52. Letter from Hal Leyshon, Director, American Federation of Musicians, to August Heckscher, July 20, 1962. Files of August Heckscher, John F. Kennedy Library.

53. American Symphony Orchestra League, "Report on Survey of Opinion of Governing Boards of Symphony Orchestras on the Role of the Federal Government in the Arts," June 21, 1962, Prepared by Helen M. Thompson, Director, for the League Board of Directors (Charleston, West Virginia: American Symphony Orchestra League, 1962), p. 3. Files of August Heckscher, John F. Kennedy Library.

54. *Ibid.*

55. *Ibid.*

56. *Ibid.*, p. 7.

57. *Ibid.*, p. 8.

58. *New York Times*

59. August Heckscher, recorded interview by Wolf von Eckhadt, December 10, 1965, pp. 52-53. Oral History Program, John F. Kennedy Library.

60. *Ibid.*, p. 53.

61. *Ibid.*

62. Frank Thompson, recorded interview. Oral History Program, John F. Kennedy Library.

63. "Memorandum for the President, Subject: Future of the Arts Program," Arthur Schlesinger, Jr., to Lyndon B. Johnson, November 29, 1963, p. 1. Files of August Heckscher, John F. Kennedy Library.

64. *Ibid.*, p. 2.

65. Lyndon B. Johnson, "Remarks in Providence at the 200th Anniversary Convocation of Brown University," September 28, 1964. U.S. President, *Public Papers of the Presidents of the United States, Lyndon B. Johnson, 1963-64*, Book 2 (Washington: United States Public Printing Office, 1965), p. 1141.

66. Address by August Heckscher, "Kennedy; The Man Who Lives On," Larchmont Temple, November 29, 1964. Files of August Heckscher, John F. Kennedy.

67. August Heckscher, recorded interview by Wolf von Eckhardt, December 10, 1965, p. 3. Oral History Program, John. F. Kennedy Library.

68. *Ibid.*, p. 62.

69. *Ibid.*, p. 54.

70. Theodore C. Sorensen, *Kennedy* (New York: Harper & Row, 1965), p. 388.

5

The Organization of Public Support for the Arts

Margaret Jane Wyszomirski and Kevin V. Mulcahy

The Constitution gave only one specific direction with regard to arts and culture. Article I of the Constitution gave Congress the power to "promote the progress of science and useful arts by securing for limited times to authors and inventors the exclusive right to their respective writings and discoveries." Through the "necessary and proper" clause, it also left open the possibility that the artistic and cultural well-being of the nation might be addressed. Indeed, federal policies concerning the arts have typically been indirect, through such activities as extending copyright protection, sponsoring international cultural exchanges, or providing subsidized postal rates. The most significant indirect subsidy has come through tax expenditures that allow both individuals and corporations to make tax deductible donations to cultural organizations.[1]

Furthermore, American attitudes toward the arts have been ambiguous and contradictory. On the one hand, since colonial times, Americans have often felt themselves to be in "the backwash of European artists and cultural achievements,"[2] and, therefore, sought to imitate or import European artists and artworks. On the other hand, modern America has become a dynamic center of artistic creativity and excellence in fields ranging from dance and opera to musical theater, popular music and movies as well as architecture and painting, of which its citizens are justifiably proud. However, neither the public nor its elected representatives have developed a clear public philosophy about the value and place of art either in their personal lives or in society at large. Therefore, no consensus has evolved regarding the legitimate relationship between government and the arts in the United States.[3]

A Range of Federal Arts Activity

Direct federal patronage has, however, never been completely absent. Early on, Congress, understanding the symbolic significance that the City of Washington would represent to the new nation, funded the design, building, and decoration of the Capitol as its first act of direct support of the arts. Over the years, federal support for some of the nation's major cultural institutions has also been forthcoming. Congress established the Library of Congress in 1800 and reestablished it, with the help of Thomas Jefferson's personal library, after the British burned Washington during the War of 1812. The Smithsonian Institution, chartered by Congress in 1846, has grown from the "nation's attic" to a complex of museums and galleries on and around the Mall in Washington, D.C. that is visited by approximately 25 million people each year. Historically, state and local governments have also granted cultural institutions exemptions from property taxes and have supported a variety of arts, historical and natural science museums as well as commemorative sites and "cultural parks."

Nonetheless, until the 1960's, such government support for the arts was largely indirect, episodic and marginal. No public arts agency existed on the national level comparable to the British Arts Council (founded in 1945), let alone at the magnitude of state support found in West Germany or central government subsidy in France. Indeed, in the United States, even the principle of public subsidy for the arts has been the subject of enduring political debate.

Federal government support for the arts developed in the 1960's against the backdrop of the political legacy of the New Deal arts programs.[4] The political controversies that resulted from the cultural projects of the Works Progress Administration (WPA) served to dramatize the dangers as well as the benefits for the arts that might come with an official, albeit awkward, embrace.[5] Subsequent public art agencies have been very sensitive to charges of ideological or partisan bias and have sought to avoid them in both their procedural operations and programmatic policies. A few major assumptions frame the contemporary character of federal support for the arts.

First, government patronage plays only a circumscribed role in the nation's culture. Private support for the arts is considered paramount as recognized in the preamble of the National Foundation on the Arts and Humanities Act of 1965, which states that "...the encouragement and support of national progress...in the humanities and the arts...[is] primarily a matter for private and local initiative." Consequently, the NEA has not functioned as a national "ministry of culture" responsible for comprehensive cultural planning or managing the nation's artistic activities. Rather it has promoted the arts in limited and collaborative ways.

Second, the federal role, led by the NEA, has developed in close relationship to state arts agencies, and more recently, with regional and local arts agencies. These "little NEA's" have complemented the federal agency in advancing a broad range of national cultural objectives, including increasing public accessibility and funding. Together, the federal, state, regional, and local arts agencies have evolved into an intergovernmental system for the administration of arts policies.

Third, the limited nature of the federal commitment to the arts has been underscored by the limited amount of public funding that has been made available. Even though the total involved has grown significantly since 1965, appropriations for the Arts Endowment (as well as for state arts agencies) remain small compared to other policy areas. At approximately $175 million per annum, the NEA budget represents approximately one-hundredth of one percent of the federal budget (approximately $1.5 trillion). This, in turn, restrains the federal government from providing general operating support for arts organizations, from assuming direct responsibility for artistic production, or from becoming the guarantor of our national cultural heritage.

Fourth, the guiding decision-making principles for the Arts Endowment have been commitments to excellence and to "cultural pluralism" -- that is, a definition of the arts capacious enough to allow broadly distributed support for a diversity of cultural expressions meeting professional standards of excellence.

Overall, the Arts Endowment has sought to build a base of public support both from within the arts world and outside, while also increasing the nation's cultural resources, both as to variety and availability. In keeping with the American pluralist tradition, public support has come to be associated with greater access to and awareness of the arts, even as the NEA has sought to foster excellence without becoming identified with any particular artistic perspective.

Both the National Endowment for the Arts and the National Endowment for the Humanities provide discretionary funding on a competitive basis to underwrite partially the costs of specific projects undertaken by private or locally supported cultural institutions. While the NEA is involved primarily in artistic creation, exhibition and performance, the NEH places more emphasis on aesthetic criticism, history and philosophy as well as on a different range of disciplines. The constituency of the NEH is aligned with the major universities and humanistic research centers of the United States, while the NEA's constituency is focussed in the professional nonprofit arts organizations of the nation.

In addition, the enabling legislation of the two Endowments also provided for a Federal Council on the Arts and Humanities (FCAH) as a coordinating entity among twelve member agencies.[6] Except during the Carter Administration and except for its ongoing implementation of the Arts and Artifacts Indemnity Act of 1975 (which underwrites insurance for foreign art works traveling for exhibition in American museums), this Council has been largely inactive. During the 1980's, a President's Committee on Arts and Humanities (PCAH) undertook efforts to stimulate additional private support for cultural endeavors such as the Fund for New American Plays or the conservation and care of cultural collections in museums, archives and libraries. However, the Clinton Administration has been slow to make appointments to PCAH or to determine a role for it. As both the fates of FCAH and PCAH demonstrate, inter-agency coordination has been episodic at best. Rather, the two Endowments have functioned as separate bureaucratic entities, evolving different internal structures and procedures even though their political and budgetary fates have been intertwined.

In 1976, the Institute of Museum Services (IMS) was established to administer a grant program to aid museums, particularly through provision of general operating support grants, through support for conservation projects, and via the Museum Assessment Program. In 1984, the IMS was placed within the NFAH and in FY 1993 had a budget of approximately $27 million.

While the NEA is the flagship of federal arts support, the cultural programs of the federal government are fragmented, located in a variety of agencies, overseen by different congressional committees, supported by and responsive to a variety of interests and reflective of the policy perspectives of a range of segments of the cultural constituency. The 1980 *Cultural Directory II* listed over 300 federal programs that provided funds or services for arts activities which were administered by thirty-eight agencies.[7] A more recent estimate counted over 200 federal government programs that provided resources or sponsored activities for the arts.[8]

For example, the Interior Department funds economic development programs for indigenous culture that help support Native American arts and crafts. It also supports historic preservation efforts in cooperation with the (private) National Trust for Historic Preservation and maintains the National Register of Historic Places. In addition, the Park Service also maintains a number of commemorative sites and historic monuments. The Corporation for Public Broadcasting receives federal funds which help non-profit radio and television stations around the country to provide non-commercial cultural, educational and public affairs programming. These stations form a loose network with locally supported member stations providing the bulk of the programs. Although CPB is a government-owned corporation for which funds are appropriated biennially, it is not a government agency.

Other government programs that are concerned with cultural matters as ancillary activities, include the Library of Congress, the National Archives, the U.S. Department of Education, and the United States Information Agency (USIA). The General Services Administration has commissioned art work to decorate federal buildings through its Art-in-Architecture Program.

This institutional segmentation reflects the diffuse nature of artistic activity in the United States, as well as the ad hoc evolution of public concern with the arts and cultural matters. It also derives from a fear that a single cultural bureaucracy might inhibit artistic freedom. Thus, as a minority stakeholder in the nation's culture, the federal government has eschewed the idea of establishing an official culture. Concomitantly, federal policies that affect the arts and culture are often implicit and certainly fragmented. Thus, coordination among programs and agencies has been erratic; information collection and policy research has been limited; the development of a cultural policy agenda and options has been haphazard; and the articulation of the public value and benefit of the arts and humanities has been impeded.

The National Endowment for the Arts

Public Law 89-209 created the National Foundation for the Arts and the Humanities in 1965. This enabling legislation defined the arts broadly as including, but not limited to:

> ...music (instrumental and vocal), dance, drama, folk arts, creative writing, architecture and allied fields, painting, sculpture, photography, graphic and craft arts, industrial design, costume and fashion design, motion pictures, television, radio, tape and song recording, the arts related to the presentation, performance, execution, and exhibition of such major art forms, and the study and application of the arts to the human environment.[9]

Although the NEA does not provide direct support for the operation of artistic institutions, for employing artists, or for the creation of specific cultural products, it can provide project grants to nonprofit organizations, to other public agencies (state, local or regional), and to individuals of exceptional talent. By law, the Endowment cannot provide more than 50 percent of the costs of any project; thus, all grants to organizations must be matched by other monies. (Grants to individuals are generally awarded in the form of non-matching fellowships.) On average, grants to organizations cover less than 10 percent of project costs. In general, the larger the project budget and the organizational applicant, the more likely the proportion of federal support is to be far less. Consequently, the NEA is only a minority partner in most of the activities that it supports. Nevertheless, no other single public or private arts funder enjoys a comparable stature or exerts a similar influence on such a range of artistic institutions and activities in the nation.

Historically, the agency has hosted discipline-oriented programs, such as Literature, Dance, Music, Visual Arts, Museums, Theater, Opera/Musical Theater, or Design. It has also developed programs that are inter-disciplinary or multi-disciplinary, such as Folk Arts, Expansion Arts, or Inter-arts. Yet other programs are essentially functional (and multi-disciplinary) such as Arts-in-Education, Presenting and Commissioning (formerly Inter-arts), Challenge, Advancement, and the new International program. Similarly, the States and Local Arts Agencies programs foster inter-governmental partnerships that assist artists and arts organizations in a variety of disciplines and activities.

Today of the NEA's eighteen program divisions, only eight are distinctly discipline-oriented, another nine cannot be characterized this way.[*] One program -- media -- has a mix of categories, some of which are oriented toward media as an arts discipline, while others serve a multi-disciplinary

---

[*]The disciplinary programs include Dance, Design, Literature, Museums, Music, Opera-Musical Theater, Theater, and Visual Arts. The Non- or multi-disciplinary programs include: Arts in Education, Expansion Arts, Folk Arts, InterArts/Presenting and Commissioning, State and Regions, Challenge, Advancement, Locals, International, and Fellows. In 1992, the grant obligations figure for the non-disciplinary programs includes underserved set-aside funds that were allocated to Folk Arts, Expansion Arts, States, Locals and Presenting. That portion of Media program funds that supported programming in the arts on television and radio were consistently counted as non-disciplinary, while remaining media program funds were counted as disciplinary obligations.

clientele using media as an access mechanism. Thus, the assertion that the NEA is organized along discipline lines is less true than it once was.

Indeed, the relative funding balance between discipline and non-discipline programs has recently experienced an historic shift. Using figures for obligated funds in the NEA Annual Reports, it is evident that in 1975, discipline programs accounted for 62 percent of agency grant obligations, while non-discipline programs accounted for only the remaining 38 percent. In 1980, 1985 and 1990, the proportions of the two types of programs had become virtually equal. However, in 1992, following reallocations mandated in the 1990 reauthorization, non-discipline programs, for the first time, accounted for a greater proportion (55 percent) of grant obligations than did discipline programs (45 percent). Thus, NEA program activity, both in terms of number of programs and in terms of grant obligations, is more functional and inter-disciplinary than it is disciplinary.

During the nearly thirty years of the agency's existence the total number of separate programs has increased and the internal organization of each of these programs has undergone some evolution. Most programs address concerns for supporting individual artists, arts organizations, audience/public access, and general field services. The relative priority and mix among these concerns varies from one program to another. Although some programs, such as States, Locals, Advancement, Education, and Challenge, do not provide support directly to individuals, they do fund activities and organizations that provide indirect support, re-grant programs, or services for artists. Each of the programs accepts applications in a variety of grant categories -- ranging from three in Folk Arts to 18 in Music. Each year, the Agency reviews approximately 18,000 applications resulting in the award of over 4,200 grants.

The NEA is an independent government agency: thus it is not within the jurisdiction of any cabinet department and its chairman reports directly to the President. For a small agency, the Arts Endowment has a complex administrative structure and layered decision-making apparatus. For example, with approximately 270 employees, it sustains 18 grant processing program divisions as well as a dozen administrative and staff offices. In assessing applications in over 100 grant categories, the agency convenes approximately 150 advisory panel, task force, and council meetings each year. In other words, the administrative style of the agency is highly specialized, consultative with its artistic constituency and funding partners, and incessantly process-oriented.

The formal hierarchy of authority is short and flexible as well as augmented by an extensive advisory network. Its executive officer is the Chairperson, appointed by the President for a four-year term and subject to Senate confirmation. By statutory provision, the Chair is responsible for making grant decisions. The Chairperson may appoint subordinate line and staff officials as necessary. Such administrative arrangements have varied with different incumbents. Generally, there is some complement of Deputy Chairmen. Initially, there was only one Deputy Chairman -- a role that may presently have evolved into the Senior Deputy position. For more than a decade, it has been customary to have two other Deputy Chairpersons -- one for programs and one for partnership.[10] Briefly, in the late 1970's, there was a Deputy Chairperson for Policy and Budget. In the 1980's, a position of Deputy Chairperson for Administration was created. The Chairperson also makes senior staff appointments for positions such as the Congressional Liaison, the Public Affairs Director, the policy planning director, the General Counsel, and occasional special assistants.

In addition, the Chairperson can appoint the directors of the grant programs for renewable contract terms. While a few program directors have accrued extended terms, others turnover every two to five years on average. During his tenure as Chairman, Livingston Biddle announced a preference for a 5-year rotation policy concerning program director appointments.[11] These programs have, historically, been the basic administrative building blocks of the agency. Thus, it is at the program level, involving agency staff and advisory panelists, that application review and panel discussion largely determine grant decisions and shape federal cultural policy and programming.

The formal authority structure is augmented by an extensive advisory system composed of grant advisory panels and the National Council for the Arts (NCA). The NCA is a 26-member body of distinguished artists, arts administrators, arts patrons, trustees and supporters, who are presidentially appointed for staggered six-year terms and are subject to Senate confirmation. The Council meets quarterly to review grant applications and forward recommendations to the Chairperson. The NCA also offers advice on the programs and policies of the agency. The 1990 reauthorization of the NEA stipulated that the National Council should make recommendations concerning the amount of financial assistance to be provided to each applicant it endorsed and that the Chairman could not approve an application which the Council had judged negatively.[12]

Grant advisory panels have come to bear the principal burden of evaluating applications at the NEA. In 1992, the agency asked 1132 individuals to participate in 133 panel meetings. The NEA's panel system has come to constitute the broadest, most comprehensive, national arts evaluation system in the country. Furthermore, the NEA panel system plays a role unique among government agencies using some variant of peer review. While the review panels that NSF and NEH use in their grant-making activities are prestigious and influential, such panels are not the only national peer review systems in either set of disciplines, nor are they the primary form of professional validation. Yet, an NEA grant has come to be considered an invaluable imprimatur, a sort of "good housekeeping seal of approval" in the arts world. In contrast, both scientists and humanists have national discipline-based peer review systems focussed around the university tenure system as well as around accepting research manuscripts for publication in scholarly journals. There are also many prestigious professional prizes, awards, endowed chairs, and research appointments that recognize professional accomplishment and attest to excellence and leadership in the scientific and humanistic realms.

In contrast, the arts have few other national professional validation and recognition systems. None of these others address as wide a range of artistic disciplines and activities or possess the national perspective of the NEA panel system. While a few major foundations have a national viewpoint, they tend to be concerned with only select arts fields. State arts agencies service a diverse set of arts interests, but from a local perspective. Specific prize, award, and competition committees select from a national pool, but are highly specialized in their impact. Therefore, the NEA's panel system assumes a significance within the professional arts world that is greater than peer panels in other federal agencies.

The use of review panels at the NEA was allowed in the original authorizing legislation of 1965, but not mandated. The Chairperson was authorized "...to utilize from time to time, as appropriate, experts and consultants, including panels of experts..."[13] Very quickly, Chairmen and National Council members recognized the utility of review panels. By 1967, advisory panels were common throughout the agency and their significance increased as the size and workload of the agency grew rapidly during the 1970's.[14]

Panels may include between five and 20 members. Panel members are appointed by the NEA Chairman for one-year terms (renewable up to three years) on the recommendation of NEA staff, arts lobbyists, Council members, elected officials, and other concerned members of the cultural community. Panelists are selected for their expert knowledge, with an eye toward geographic, gender, ethnic, racial, and aesthetic diversity. Panel members serve as individuals, not as representatives of their institutions. To assure diverse representation and fairness, panel membership rotates annually, with at least one-third of each panel changing each year (and with total turnover on fellowship review panels).

Review panels play a key role in the allocation of scarce and sought after resources. Indeed, the award of federal grant money is not only financially important to grantees, but is symbolically crucial as an indicator of the capabilities of the awardee and of the quality and significance of the project. Because of the influence that panel recommendations have on grant decisions and because of their political legitimizing function, the panel system has been the subject of considerable comment, both favorable and critical.

The Congress, exercising its oversight authority, has frequently commented upon or specified requirements of panels. In general, these specifications have sought to broaden the representativeness of panels or to ensure fairness by minimizing conflicts of interest. For example, in 1973, the House Committee on Education and Labor was concerned that broad geographic representation would help avoid the domination of any one part of the country.[15] In 1979, a report of the House Committee on Appropriations was concerned that "cronyism" among panelists resulted in "closed circle" decisionmaking that was not representative of general public interests. In 1990, Congress enacted a strong conflict of interest prohibition as well as mandated that panel membership be expanded through the inclusion of informed laypersons. As a result, the number of panelists used by the Arts Endowment increased from 985 in 1989 to 1,132 in 1992, while the number of panel meetings rose from 118 in 1990 to 133 in 1992.

Over time, panels have evolved as a mechanism for assessing the artistic quality of projects awarded federal grants as well as a means of engaging the arts world in the work of the NEA. They also serve as a mechanism for assuring representative and fair procedures in grant review. Thus, panels have historically served to rationalize application review, to minimize the influence of political patronage, and to justify the artistic wisdom of each NEA grant. They have also been employed as a procedural channel for addressing many of the thorniest public demands, expectations, and constraints upon federal arts policy.

For example, during the NEA's 1973 reauthorization, the Senate oversight committee noted, with favor "...the involvement of panels of experts who aid the two Endowments and Councils in reaching their decisions and which broaden the base of private citizen participation...."[16] In 1980, a Senate report underscored "...the importance of advisory panels to the work of the Endowments ...[noting] favorably that there is a broader representation of viewpoint on each panel and that all styles and forms of expression which involve quality in the arts are being more equitably treated...."[17] The 1981 Presidential Task Force on the Arts and Humanities reaffirmed that the panel system was a tested principle and called for its continuation. In 1990, the report of the Independent Commission on the National Endowment for the Arts both endorsed and criticized the NEA's review panels. On the one hand, the Independent Commission found that "...The grant advisory panels provide a valuable source of expert knowledge and judgment to the Endowment and are essential to the evaluation of applications for grants...." But it went on to emphasize that panels were only one of several sources of advice and were merely the first step in the review process. The Commission noted that "...these grant advisory panels have come to dominate the process of grant making. This development does not satisfy expectations about public accountability nor does it reflect the purposes of Congress when it created the agency. The Chairperson, who is accountable to the President, Congress and the American people, is the only person with legal authority to make grants...."[18]

Despite the repeated occurrence of comment about the operation of the NEA's panel review system, the panel principle itself is firmly established. Periodic concerns have led to both public validation as well as to necessary administrative adaptation. While, the expertise, flexibility and utility of the system is generally recognized, government's use of peer panels in a variety of public purposes -- not only the arts -- has attracted increasing attention.[19] At one level, peer panel systems in government reflect enduring tensions between informed and participatory decisionmaking, between expert and public authority, and between technical and political considerations. In the arts, advisory panels strive for decisions that are both well-informed and broadly participatory. They must also attempt to reconcile the protection of creative freedom of individual applicants with the agency's need for accountability to a general public and its representatives.[20]

Indeed, part of the recent debate over the role of grant advisory panels at the NEA may stem from asking panels to do too much. Panels are expected to represent the diversity of America's peoples and cultures; to insulate the arts from centralized government control, yet help government make decisions concerning the arts; to act upon assumptions regarding the value and definition of art, artistic excellence and cultural priorities when such a consensus has not been politically forged; to make essentially subjective, qualitative decisions in ways that are seen to be fair and equitable; and even to embody standards of decency.

Panels have the expertise for the job of assessing artistic excellence; elected and appointed officials are responsible for the task of setting policy priorities and addressing these goals by supporting activities that meet standards of professional excellence and artistic significance. As articulated by Congress, policy priorities have included developing the appreciation and enjoyment of the arts by all citizens through increased availability and through education; of reaching and reflecting our diverse cultural traditions, including those of minority, inner-city, rural or tribal communities; and of recognizing the primacy of private, state and local initiatives, while developing productive partnerships in support of the arts. Each component of the NEA's complex and layered decision-making process is called upon to exercise discretion and judgment. Each element sees itself as meeting the demands and expectations of a particular role, representing a particular constellation of interests, and articulating certain values. A considerable congruence of these roles, interests and values is necessary for the agency to function effectively, however, it is not uncommon for differences to arise stemming from varying knowledge and interpretation, in an effort to act fairly, equitably, and legitimately. What is noteworthy is how little tolerance for incongruence there has been even as the Agency and its constituency have faced the most concerted and intense opposition of its existence.

The Intergovernmental System of Support for the Arts

Before the establishment of the National Endowment for the Arts, seven states and less than one hundred communities had local arts agencies.[21] Today, each of the 50 states plus six special jurisdictions have state arts agencies; there are six regional arts organizations, and approximately 3,800 local/community arts agencies. In short, since 1965, an extensive intergovernmental system for administering support for the arts and for distributing artistic benefits to the public has evolved. Federal money has served as a catalyst for establishing state arts agencies, for increasing state and local arts funding, and for stimulating local and regional private support. In turn, the state, local and regional system has served as partners in reaching more artists, arts organizations and audiences, provided a delivery mechanism for national programs, and acted as an advocacy support network for the NEA.

Congress provided an impetus for the stimulation of state arts agencies in the Endowment's enabling legislation when it stipulated that the NEA make available one-time, non-matching grants of $25,000 to each state to "conduct a survey leading to the establishment of a state agency."[22] In its *1967 Annual Report*, the NEA noted that it had provided "the stimulus for fifty states, the District of Columbia, Puerto Rico, the Virgin Islands, and Guam to survey their cultural resources and develop programs, facilities and services at the community level."[23] That same year, the NEA began making block grants of $50,000 to states to implement their arts programs. Initially, almost one-third of the Agency's program funds were devoted to this purpose. Then as the Agency's budget grew rapidly during the early 1970's, the proportion fell to around 20 percent, where it was set legislatively in 1974.

By 1974, the Agency was awarding $12 million in block grants (of no less than $200,000 each) to state arts agencies (SAAs) in 55 states and special jurisdictions which were appropriating a combined total of over $31 million for support of the arts.[24] A decade later, in 1983, SAAs were receiving $18 million in basic state grants as well as another $5.3 million from other NEA programs. Changes in the 1990 reauthorization of the NEA stipulated that the proportion of programs funds allocated to the states increase from 20 percent to 25 percent in FY 1991 and further to 27.5 percent in FY 1993. As a consequence, SAAs received $27.2 million in basic grants from the NEA in FY 1993.[25] In addition, another 5 percent of program funds in FY 1991 was set-aside for grants to states for projects in rural, inner city and other artistically underserved communities. This proportion rose to 7.5 percent in FY 1993, amounting to an additional $9 million beyond the basic state grants.[26] Annually, the states receive another $5 million from the NEA's Arts-in-Education program.

During the 1970's, the development of local arts agencies (LAAs) in communities all over the country was spurred by access to state funds as SAAs supported local arts activity, sometimes through decentralization plans that provided block grants to counties. Indeed by 1976, 43 states were directly involved in the creation of local arts councils and these LAAs were eligible to apply in over 30 of the Endowment's funding categories.[27] In the mid-1970's, states, with federal encouragement, created Regional Arts Organizations (RAOs) to address their shared concerns to expand public access through the presentation and touring of arts performances, exhibitions, and residencies as well as to administer certain national programs (such as dance touring, the Regional Visual Arts Fellowships, and the National Jazz Presenting Network). In 1982, RAOs were receiving a total of $2.5 million from NEA state funds; by 1992, the amount had risen to $3.85 million. In addition, the Regional Organizations won another $3.16 million in grants from other NEA programs, raised nearly $3 million more in private funds, and earned $900,000.[28]

Following the rapid growth of the late 1960's and early 1970's, the states and the NEA undertook a year-long reassessment in 1977 that revised the partnership concept. Recognizing that the State Arts Agency movement had matured, the new NEA Chairman, Livingston Biddle announced that state arts agencies would no longer compete for a quarter of the 20 percent funds designated for the states, but rather that states would receive funding on the basis of their total state plan and a funding formula based on the state population and its state arts agency legislative appropriation. Thus, the Endowment no longer decided whether or not to grant federal funds to state agencies, but rather worked with the states to make the best use of the available funds within the general policy purposes set out for the NEA statutorily. As a consequence, state arts agencies have developed a regular statewide planning process that includes board and staff members, service organizations, individual artists, planning committees and panels, other arts organizations and the general public. In addition, the NEA created a new position of Deputy Chairman for Public Partnership, reflecting that the states were not merely another programmatic grantee of the federal agency, but rather a full-fledged partner.

During the 1980's, the capabilities, range, and resources of state, regional, and local arts organizations expanded considerably. For example, the range of their partnerships with the federal agency grew. The NEA initiated a test program of support for local arts agencies (LAAs) in January of 1983, which developed into the Locals Program. The first 11 grant projects were able to generate $12 million in new local and state funds in support of 46 LAAs that served 681 communities, 3,239 arts organizations and hundreds of artists.[29] Today, over 3,000 LAAs are acting as cultural chambers of commerce, helping to oversee the long-term cultural development of their communities and incorporating the arts into the fabric of everyday life. Meanwhile, the SAAs and RAOs had come to constitute a national distribution and implementation network for a number of programs and initiatives, including arts in education, the presentation of dance on tour (as well as other performing arts), regional visual arts fellowships, fostering the folk arts, and helping develop local arts agencies. The states and their service organization, the National

Assembly of State Arts Agencies, developed a National Standard for Arts Information Exchange to report on publicly supported arts activities. This data base, which is maintained through a cooperative agreement between NASAA and the NEA, could constitute a valuable resource for policy debate, formulation and advocacy at both the state and national levels, particularly if the NEA could adapt its grants information to be comparable to the state data.

Significantly, the level of financial and public support for the arts at the state level also increased during the 1980's. In 1979, NEA grant funds were about 80 percent greater than combined state arts appropriations. By 1990, state arts appropriations reached a peak of $292 million, which was 93 percent greater than NEA grant money (program, treasury and challenge funds) of only $151 million. In other words, a dramatic reversal in federal and state budgetary resources for the arts had occurred within the decade.[30] The implications of this reversal for policy leadership, political support and program implementation have yet to be fully understood. Indeed, it has led various members of the arts policy community to call for a comprehensive assessment of the intergovernmental arts support system to reconsider roles, responsibilities, and resources.

An important contributing factor to the growth of state support was the emergence of state arts advocacy groups. The growth of such organizations is, in part, a logical outgrowth of the development of the public arts movement and, in part, a reflection that development of local constituencies for the arts followed (rather than preceded) the creation of state arts agencies.[31] Today virtually every state has an arts advocacy group and since 1983, the State Arts Advocacy League of America (SAALA) has helped strengthen the movement through the creation of a network facilitating communication and the exchange of information, and offering peer support among the separate state efforts.[32] Unlike most national arts advocacy groups which represent specific arts interests (such as museums, dance, theater, etc), state arts advocacy groups speak for the general arts constituency and audience of a particular geographic area. Although state groups realize that federal issues can affect each of their states, these usually small, sometimes informal organizations, generally focus on what is happening in their own states and with their own state legislatures, rather than on national issues or trends. Collectively, however, state arts advocacy efforts have helped increase both financial and public support for the arts in the states, and therefore, have stimulated more resources for the arts nationally.

The steady growth in state arts agency appropriations peaked in FY 1990 at $292 million. During the next two years, SAAs collectively experienced substantial decreases as many states faced general fiscal crises, resulting from constitutional requirements to balance their budgets, recession induced shortfalls in revenues, and rising demands for social services in the wake of increasing federal mandates and decreasing federal revenue sharing. In FY 1991, aggregate state arts appropriations declined to $273 million, down 7 percent; 22 states experienced cuts ranging from less than one percent in Montana and New Hampshire to 41 percent in New Jersey. New York and New Jersey lost eight million dollars each that year, while Massachusetts lost over five million dollars.[33] The following year aggregate state funding dropped an additional 22 percent, the largest single decline in twenty-three years. New York dropped nearly another $20 million, while Massachusetts, Michigan and Virginia saw cuts of over 50 percent each. In FY 1993, only minor decreases were experienced, down $4 million, or 2 percent, to a combined total of $209 million. In all, 47 SAAs saw a reduction sometime during this three-year period, prompting agencies to reduce staff, to reorganize grant categories, and to place an increasing emphasis on service provision (rather than grant-making).[34] In at least seven states, elected officials even proposed to abolish the arts agency or to cut it back so drastically as to make it ineffective. In those cases, the possibility that such action would precipitate the loss of federal funds from the Endowment proved to be an argument against draconian state action.[35] Thus, at the very time that the effect of the NEA's 1990 reauthorization changes were sending a larger proportion of national funds to the states, many states, coping with decreasing general revenues, were reducing funding. As a consequence, many states experienced a net decrease of public funds for the arts.

What the future will hold for state arts funding is open to debate. As the recession abates, state revenues may allow state funding for the arts to revive, providing that public interest and support of the arts is strong in each state. On the other hand, if federal-state relations experience a general reconsideration, then subsequent changes might affect the arts partnership. For example, David Osborne, an influential policy analyst known for his book, *Reinventing Government*, argues that, over the years, the federal government has become overloaded with too many programs that might better be left to the discretion of state and local governments. Asserting that this situation leads to a diffusion of accountability and a resulting loss of public faith, Osborne proposes rigorous standards for justifying federal action and avoiding the inefficiencies of program fragmentation. According to these criteria, Osborne recommends eliminating categorical grants to the states for programs in the arts and humanities. Abolishing these and other categorical programs would, Osborne argues, "...free state and local governments from many restrictive rules and allow them to eliminate functions they now fund only to get federal money or meet federal mandates...."[36] Thus, even as the state arts policy situation restabilizes after the recession shocks of the early 1990's, a widened policy debate over federal and state roles and responsibilities may have an impact upon the intergovernmental arts partnership.

Public Support for the Arts: The Record and Future Challenges

Since the establishment of the Arts Endowment, public cultural investments have helped build a national institutional infrastructure for the production and distribution of the arts in America. Composed of artists and arts organizations, this system has grown dramatically in the past thirty years. Where there were only 56 professional non-profit theaters in 1965, there are over 400 today. The number of professional orchestras with budgets of over $280,000 has more than doubled in that time to 230 while professional dance companies have increased from 37 to 250. Meanwhile the number of artists in the country has risen to 1.7 million. Today, these artists and arts organizations are reaching many more citizens throughout the country, than they did 30 years ago.[37]

In addition, public support has added to our nation's artistic assets in numerous ways. It has helped stimulate new kinds of arts organizations, from culturally specific organizations to regional media arts center, from folk arts organizations to visual arts organizations and small literary presses. Similarly, it has invested in the creation of new art works, from works of art in public places, to new repertoire in dance, theater, music and opera, to new works in literature, film or the visual arts. Public funding, in partnership with private support, has invested in the careers and professional development of creative artists in a range of disciplines and art forms, providing opportunities for them to create, collaborate, and to imagine.

As for the NEA itself, by the end of President Nixon's tenure in office, the basic contours of the cultural budget and the intergovernmental arts support system had been established as the Arts Endowment passed through its "initial survival threshold." A sign of having navigated this passage is the allocation of enough resources so that an agency can rapidly expand to meet the needs its members have long been advocating.[38] The rapid and steady growth in the NEA's budget and the rise in state arts appropriations through the 1970's provided the necessary resources for this to occur. The challenge and cutbacks of the early Reagan Administration, marked the end of this initial developmental stage, as well as another milestone for public support for the arts. The idea of public support for the arts seemed to be validated and a certain level of budgetary resources maintained (albeit at eroded purchasing power) throughout the decade of the 1980's. In all the debate about the Endowment's budget during these years, it was easy to lose sight of the magnitude of the issue in financial terms. The NEA's budget was less than one-hundredth of one percent of total federal spending and represented only a small proportion of the operating expenses of arts organizations in the United States. Nonetheless, federal arts funding (and the other public and private support that it helps to attract) can provide a financial margin of survival for arts activities and can be a factor in determining the hours that even the largest museums can afford to be open or whether and how extensively a symphony or dance company can afford to tour.

Beyond this financial importance, it is possible to identify three qualitative contributions provided by government support for the arts. First, an NEA grant constitutes an imprimatur for artistic projects and productions as well as for smaller and newer arts organizations. This professional recognition has, in turn, proven helpful in generating additional support from other sources. Second, an Endowment grant often assists cultural institutions to undertake activities that they might otherwise not be able to consider, such as bringing exhibitions and performances to smaller and less accessible communities, supporting new and traditionally specific creative work, or providing educational opportunities for children and adults. Third, as a public arts agency, the Endowment (and its intergovernmental partners) has taken a leadership role in addressing issues of cultural equity, through efforts to further the accessibility of the arts to people of different socio-economic and ethnic backgrounds than have historically characterized the culture-consuming public. This is a role that is likely to be even more challenging in the years ahead as the demographic character of the nation changes in ways that will effect many aspects of our lives.[39]

In sum, a primary goal of Endowment policy has been to democratize access to artistic opportunities. As such, government support for the arts cannot be characterized simply as a "transfer payment for the upper-middle class"[40] nor as a form of "cultural imperialism" that threatens the artistic autonomy and cultural vitality of "non-high cultural taste publics."[41] Although some have argued that public art outreach efforts diminish artistic excellence, others have argued that too little has been done, particularly to reach the sizeable group of Americans who are "cultural dropouts" -- those who have no creative or expressive pastimes, enjoy no performances of any kind and are equally immune to the claims of galleries, zoos, or public parks.[42]

Over the past three decades, with the NEA's leadership, an intergovernmental arts support system has developed that helps service and sustain a truly national artistic infrastructure of artists and arts organizations throughout the country. Now, this system confronts the challenges of adequate maintenance and full utilization. Significant progress has been made in bringing more of a wider range of artistic opportunities to more people in more communities. The NEA helped spur much of this growth and, in the process, has broadened the notion of "culture" and helped reconcile it with a mass public in an effort to gain the support that is necessary for such a specialized public policy. However, these successes mean that the public is more likely to encounter some types of art which they find unfamiliar, even unintelligible and perhaps offensive. At the very least, this raises new challenges for arts education efforts. It also points to a need for genuine public debate about the standards and purposes of public support for the arts in order to re-establish a workable consensus within which public arts agencies can effectively operate.

Public support is particularly important to many small, emerging, culturally-distinct, rural or experimental arts groups. Similarly, new and more diverse audiences might not be reached without targeted governmental programs and the incentives that provide public subsidy to established arts organizations. Nonetheless, a challenge for the future is not merely to expand the arts audience, but to fully engage the citizenry in the arts and to integrate the arts into everyday lives. State, local and regional arts agencies help to identify and address the artistic needs of their communities and can further promote aesthetic pluralism and cultural democratization. In this sense, the administrative construction of America's commitment to the arts resonates with the political culture in which it is rooted: limited, segmented, intergovernmental, pluralistic, and evolving.

Notes

1. See Alan L. Feld and others,*Patrons Despite Themselves: Taxpayers and Arts Policy* (New York: New York University Press, 1983). The authors estimate that two-thirds of public support for the arts comes in an indirect form, principally through federal income tax deductions and local property tax exemptions.

2. Carl Degler, *Out of Our Past* (New York: Harper and Row, 1962), pp. 40-42.

3. For example, reporting in February 1993 on a poll it commissioned on "The Importance of the Arts and Humanities to American Society", the National Cultural Alliance found that 80 percent or better of the respondents felt that the arts and humanities contribute to the economy, make their local community a better place to live, enrich the education of their children and provide a form of expression essential in a democratic society. However, 68 percent reported that the arts and humanities played only a minor or no role at all in their own lives.

4. On the New Deal arts programs and their political legacy, see, for example, William F. McDonald, *Federal Relief Administration* (Columbus: Ohio State University Press, 1968); Jerre Mangione, *The Dream and the Deal* (Boston: Little Brown, 1972); Richard McKinzie, *The New Deal for Artists* (Princeton: Princeton University Press, 1973); Jane DeHart Mathews, *The Federal Theatre, 1935-1939* (Princeton: Princeton University Press, 1967); Karal Ann Marling, *Wall to Wall America: A Cultural History of Post Office Murals in the Great Depression* (Minneapolis: University of Minnesota Press, 1982), and Judith H. Balfe and Margaret Jane Wyszomirski, "Public Art and Public Policy: The Case of Tilted Arc," *Journal of Arts Management and Law*, Vol. 15, No. 4 , (Winter 1986), pp.5-29.

5. See Gary O. Larson, *The Reluctant Patron: The United States Government and the Arts, 1943-1965* (Philadelphia: University of Pennsylvania Press, 1983); and Joan Simpson Burns, *The Awkward Embrace, The Creative Artist and the Institution in America* (New York: Alfred A. Knopf, 1975).

6. Pursuant to the National Foundation on the Arts and Humanities Act of 1965, Section 9(b) and Reorganization Plan No. 2 of 1977, the membership of the Federal Council for the Arts and the Humanities included the Chairmen of the National Endowments for the Arts and for the Humanities, the U.S. Commissioner of Education (now Secretary), the Secretary of the Smithsonian Institution, the Director of the National Science Foundation, the Librarian of Congress, the Director of the National Gallery of Art, the Chairman of the Commission of Fine Arts, the Archivist of the United States, the Commissioner of the Public Buildings Service of the General Services Administration, the Director of the International Communication Agency (now US Information Agency), and a member designated by the Secretary of the Interior. In addition, a member may be designated by the Chairman of the Senate Commission on Arts and Antiquities as well as another designated by the Speaker of the House of Representatives. The President may also change the membership of the FCAH as federal cultural programs and agency structure changes.

7. Federal Council for the Arts and Humanities, *The Cultural Directory II: Federal Funds and Services for the Arts and Humanities*, compiled by Linda C. Coe, Rebecca Denney, and Anne Rogers (Washington, D.C.: Smithsonian Institution Press, 1980).

8. For a broad discussion of the variety of federal programs of concern to the arts and of the possibility of bringing these into coordination through a Department of Cultural Resources, see Joni Maya Cherbo, "A Department of Cultural

Resources: A Perspective on the Arts," *Journal of Arts Management and Law*, Vol. 22, No. 1 (Spring 1992), pp. 44-63. On the 200 federal programs, Cherbo cites Susan Boren, "Arts and Humanities: Funding Issues in the 101st Congress," *Congressional Research Service Issue Brief*, January 7, 1991.

9. PL 89-209, Section 952 (sec. 3)(b).

10. The Deputy Chairperson for Programs generally has jurisdiction for the discipline-based programs, while the Deputy Chairperson for Partnership has jurisdiction over the public partnership programs of States, Locals, and Arts in Education. The location of a few programs has been subject to some shifting, for example the Challenge program has variously reported to one or the other of the deputy chairpersons.

11. A *New York Times* article, "Arts Endowment Keeps Aides Past 5-Year Limit" by Karen DeWitt on 1 May 1979 discusses the implementation of Biddle's 5-year program director rotation policy.

12. Sec 955, Sec 6 (f) of P.L. 89-209 as amended 1990.

13. Sec. 10 (a)(4).

14. For an extensive study of the evolution and operations of NEA panels as well as a comparison with NEH panels, see Ann Mary Galligan, "The National Endowment for the Arts and Humanities: An Experiment in Cultural Democracy" (Dissertation: Teachers College of Columbia University, 1989).

15. Cited in Independent Commission, *Report to Congress on the National Endowment for the Arts* (Washington, D.C., September 1990),p. 27, as coming from a Report of the House Committee on Education and Labor, June 5, 1973.

16. Quoted on page 9 of the National Endowment for the Arts, *Panel Study Report*, (Washington,D.C.: NEA, October 1987).

17. *Ibid*, p. 10.

18. Independent Commission, *Report to Congress*, p. 71. For an example of congressional concern over the dominance of panels in the decisionmaking process, see comments by Representative Steve Gunderson, "Rescuing NEA with New Goals," *The Washington Times*, July 18, 1990. He states that "...panel recommendations have become ipso facto the final word...panel members are neither civil servants nor appointees. In effect, they are accountable to no one, though their loyalties are firmly grounded in the art communities they serve..."

19. This can certainly be seen in science, where a number of government agencies employ peer review or expert advisory mechanisms. See for example, Daryl E. Chubin and Edward J. Hackett, *Peerless Science: Peer Review and U.S. Science Policy* (Albany, N.Y.: SUNY Press, 1990); also see, Bruce L.R. Smith, *Advisers: Scientists in the Policy Process* (Washington, D.C.: Brookings Institution, 1992). Robert H. Dahl in *Democracy and Its Critics*, (New Haven: Yale University Press, 1989), argues that over-reliance upon expertise in policy-making can challenge democratic principles by encouraging what Plato called a "guardianship" government directed by a knowledgeable, but elite, minority which implies that ordinary people are not qualified to govern themselves. See especially Chapters 4 and 5.

20. For further discussion of the NEA's panel system, see, for example, Kevin Mulcahy and Charlotte Murphy, "The Controversial Role of Peer Panels," *ArtsInk*, Vol. 3, No. 1 (Fall 1992) (The newsletter of the MidAtlantic Arts Foundation); and Margaret Jane Wyszomirski, "The Art and Politics of Peer Review," *Vantage Point* Spring 1990, pp. 12-13.

21. Utah was the first state to create an arts agency (in 1899). Next came New York in 1960, which also instituted a matching fund requirement. Other states that acted to establish arts agencies in the early 1960's included California, Georgia, Minnesota, Missouri, and North Carolina. See Arthur Svenson, 'State and Local Arts Agencies" in Mulcahy and Swaim, *Public Policy and the Arts* (Boulder, CO: Westview Press, 1982), pp. 195-211. According to a "Compendium of State Arts Agency Enabling Legislation," Washington, D.C.: National Assembly of State Arts Agencies, 1979), pp. 4-6, New York, Utah, California, Illinois and Missouri had arts agencies by 1964; eleven other states had either an executive order or legislative authority to form an arts agency by 1965. According to the NEA's *Annual Report, 1966*, seventeen states and Puerto Rico had created official arts agencies before 1965, while the District of Columbia and nineteen more states created arts agencies in 1966; the Virgin Islands, Guam and fourteen states followed suit in 1966. The authors are especially thankful for the informed thoughts and suggestions of Ronya McMillen, former information specialist at NASAA, on the development of this section on sub-national public arts support and issues.

22. Reported by the then-Deputy Chairman for Partnership Anthony Turney in his Advocacy Day speech, American Council for the Arts, Washington, D.C., April 8, 1987.

23. National Endowment for the Arts *Annual Report, 1967* (Washington, D.C.: National Endowment for the Arts, 1967).

24. John Urice,"The Future of the State Arts Agency Movement in the 1990's: Decline and Effect" *Journal of Arts Management, Law and Society*, Vol 22, No. 1 (Spring 1992), p. 21.

25. For a review of the evolution of the state and regional program at the NEA, see, National Endowment for the Arts, "State and Regional Program Review: A Report to the National Council for the Arts," February 1993.

26. *Ibid*, p. 3.

27. "Locals Program Review for the National Council for the Arts," August 1992, p. 23.

28. NEA, "State and Regional Program Review," p. 6.

29. NEA, "Locals Program Review," p. 23.

30. For a discussion, see, Paul J. DiMaggio, "Decentralization of Arts Funding from the Federal Government to the States," in *Public Money and the Muse*, edited by Stephen Benedict (New York: W.W. Norton, 1991), pp. 216-256.

31. This point is made by John Urice in his article on "The Future of the State Arts Agency Movement in the 1990's," pp. 21-2.

32. On the evolution of state arts advocacy organizations, see "Dennis Dworkin, "State Advocacy in the Arts: A Historical Overview," *Journal of Arts Management and Law*, Vol. 21, No. 3 (Fall 1991), pp.199-215.

33. For an analysis of changes in states arts funding, see Jeffrey Love, "Sorting Out Our Roles: The State Arts Agencies and the National Endowment for the Arts," *Journal of Arts Management and Law*, Vol. 21, No. 3, (Fall 1991), pp. 215-231.

34. For additional information on state arts funding and activities, see National Assembly of State Arts Agencies, *The State of the State Arts Agencies: 1992* and *State Arts Agencies Legislative Appropriations: Annual Survey* (Washington: NASAA, 1992).

35. "State and Regional Program Review," p. 15.

36. See a chapter in the transition report of the Progressive Policy Institute, reputed to be a policy blueprint for the Clinton Administration. David Osborne, "A New Federal Compact," *Mandate for Change*, edited by Will Marshall and Martin Schram (New York: Berkeley Books, 1993), p.252.

37. For more details on the record of public investments in American artistry, see, National Endowment for the Arts, *The Arts in America 1992* (Washington, D.C.: NEA, 1992).

38. On the idea of an initial survival threshold, see Anthony Downs, *Inside Bureaucracy* (Boston: Little Brown, 1966), p. 9.

39. For recent discussions of issues of cultural diversity and equity in arts policy, see Robert Garfias, "Cultural Equity: Cultural Diversity and the Arts in America," and Gerald D. Yoshitomi, "Cultural Equity: Cultural Democracy," in *Public Money and the Public Muse*, pp.182-194 and 195-215.

40. Quoted in the U.S. House of Representatives, Democratic Study Group, "Special Report: The Stockman Hit List," (Washington, D.C.: mimeograph, 7 February 1981), p. 35.

41. For a discussion of different taste cultures and the aesthetic preferences involved, see Herbert J. Gans, *Popular Culture and High Culture* (New York: Basic Books, 1979). For subsequent thoughts on the subject, see Herbert J. Gans, "American Popular Culture and High Culture in a Changing Class Structure," in Judith H. Balfe and Margaret Jane Wyszomirski, eds., *Art, Ideology and Politics* (New York: Praeger, 1985), pp. 40-57.

42. Paul DiMaggio and Michael Useem, "The Arts and Cultural Participation," *Journal of Aesthetic Education*, Vol. 14 (October 1980), p. 65.

6

Leadership and the NEA: The Roles of the Chairperson and the National Council on the Arts

David B. Pankratz and Carla Hanzal

The National Endowment for the Arts, not unlike the federal government itself, has a three-tiered, overlapping structure for policy development and decision-making. This structure consists of the Chairperson, the National Council on the Arts (NCA), and grant advisory panels, each of which is to further the basic mission and purposes of the Agency as stipulated in the National Foundation on the Arts and Humanities Act of 1965.

This chapter will examine two tiers of this structure -- the Chairperson and the National Council on the Arts. It starts with a description of the relevant statutory language of Congress on their respective roles, turns to policies and practices that have evolved during the Agency's 27-year history, and follows with summary accounts of the initiatives and leadership styles of the five individuals who, to this date, have served as chairpersons of the National Endowment for the Arts. The chapter concludes by acknowledging the shifting contexts which have shaped the administration of the Agency and identifies perennial issues of the roles, authority, and capacities of the National Council and the Endowment Chairperson.

The NEA Chairperson and the National Council: Authorizing Language

The National Foundation on the Arts and the Humanities Act as amended through 1990 defines the responsibilities of the Chairperson and the Council and sets out criteria for their selection and appointment. Members of the 26-person Council are appointed by the President for staggered six-year terms and are subject to Senate confirmation. Since 1965, nearly 150 artists, arts administrators, patrons, trustees, critics, and leaders of state and local arts agencies have served as members of the National Council on the Arts. Nominees are to be selected on the basis of their broad knowledge of or expertise in the arts. Emphasis is also placed on distribution of Council memberships among the major art fields and the representation of women, minorities, and individuals with disabilities. These requirements are intended to ensure broadly diverse composition in Council membership while, at the same time, to encourage fresh perspectives and a sense of institutional memory and continuity in Council operations.

Statutorily, the primary functions of the Council are to advise the Chairperson with respect to policies, programs, and procedures and to review applications for financial assistance and make recommendations on them to the Chairperson. Since 1982, the NCA has been required by legislation to make recommendations to the President on awardees of the National Medal of the Arts. Further, at various points in its history, the Council, acting as a whole or as groups of individuals, has undertaken activities which extend beyond its formal legislative mandate. These include:

- advocacy of legislative and regulatory policies favorable to artists and cultural institutions;
- efforts to draw on the resources of other federal agencies which can assist or make use of the arts;
- encouragement of greater support of the arts by corporations, foundations, state and local governments; and
- contact with the media to increase public awareness of and support for the arts.[1]

The NEA Chairperson is appointed by the President, subject to Senate confirmation, for a term of four years and is eligible for reappointment. The Chairperson also chairs the National Council on the Arts as its 27th member. Extending the programs of the Endowment through partnerships with other public agencies or private groups with interests in the arts is one responsibility of the NEA Chairperson. But the primary role of the Chairperson, at least in statutory terms, is to establish and carry out the Agency's program of grants and contracts to individuals, non-profit organizations, and public agencies at state and local levels. Congress has articulated numerous anticipated benefits of the NEA grants program, such as enabling cultural organizations and institutions to increase private patronage, improve their administration and management, and increase audience participation in their programs. NEA grants are also intended as catalysts for effective state-local cooperation in arts support activities.

This legislation, while offering few operational directions, gives the NEA Chairperson flexibility in making decisions on policy, grants, and the overall operation of the Endowment. This conception of the authority of the Chairperson spurred some debate in the House of Representatives in 1965. Concerns were expressed that the law could permit the Chairperson to act as "cultural czar," subsidizing only artists and organizations he or she likes. An amendment which would have given the power of approval, not just advice, to the National Council was introduced but ultimately defeated.[2] As stated in the 1990 Independent Commission report on the NEA, "...by limiting the National Council to an advisory role, Congress implicitly invested full authority for making awards in the Chairperson who was to be held accountable to the President and to the authorizing and appropriations committees of Congress for the actions of the agency...."[3] The Council's formal relationship to the Chairperson is advisory, and serves as an informal check on any potentially arbitrary actions of the chair.

Council Roles and Procedures

By law, the National Council on the Arts is required to meet at least twice each year, although customarily the practice has been for four three-day meetings annually. A fifth meeting has sometimes been called. All are chaired by the NEA Chairperson. Although the relative emphasis of each meeting agenda changes, most meetings include a combination of:

- application review;
- consideration of program guidelines;
- discussion of policy or program issues;
- annual review of each program's activity;
- reports and discussion of developments in artistic fields; and legislation, and other federal, state or local programs.

Throughout most of the Endowment's history those portions of a Council meeting concerned with policy, planning, program development and review, guidelines, conditions in the field, etc. have been open to the public. The Council would then go into closed session for review of applications or other matters in which confidentiality was considered necessary. Many meetings included an Executive Session, in which the Council would meet alone with the Chairperson and Deputy Chair(s) of the

Endowment. The confidentiality was designed to protect the privacy of individuals and groups whose finances, plans and problems might be discussed and permit Council members to express their views frankly on sensitive matters. In May 1990, the Council, at the urging of Chairman John Frohnmayer, voted to open all sessions to the public.

National Council members are subject to standards of conduct guidelines. A 1987 memorandum by the Endowments's General Counsel notes that these guidelines are intended to avoid conflict of interest situations, especially as they pertain to Council preferences and biases that might have financial implications.[4]

Annually the Council reviews and offers advice on guidelines for each Endowment program. These include information on what the NEA funds, applicant eligibility and legal requirements, and decision criteria used in reviewing grant applications. Each year they are initially reviewed by Endowment program staff and the relevant grant advisory and program overview panels. Proposed changes are sent to the Council for consideration at one of its annual meetings, supplemented when necessary by a brief presentation by program staff or panelists. The Council may recommend changes in the proposed guidelines or recommend them to the Chairperson as proposed. The Chairperson has final approval of all guidelines. Guidelines embody Endowment policy with regard to specific grant categories. Together, they constitute the basic policy regulations of the Agency as a whole.

The National Council may also discuss policy and budgetary issues, significant trends, and general concerns that may encompass a number of specific programs, disciplines or grant categories or that are of interest to the arts in general.

Grants to the arts -- to the individual artists and arts institutions -- are the primary business of the National Endowment for the Arts. Awarding grants is the prime means that the Endowment uses to achieve its mission and purposes. Between 1966 and 1992 more than 95,000 grants have been awarded by the Endowment. While application review was done in closed session for many years, since 1990 it has been done in open session. Council members and the Chairperson may single out specific applications for more information or detailed discussion. However, the Council generally votes its recommendations en banque program by program. Subsequent to Council review and recommendation, the Chairperson makes the final decision on all grant applications, including the amount of the award. Thus, while the National Council is involved in the review of grant applications, it has neither the first nor the final say on award decisions.

Although the original 1965 legislation did not require the use of grant advisory panels, by 1967 the use of panels was common throughout the Endowment. Staff, panelists, Council members, and the NEA Chairperson, often recommended individuals to serve on grant advisory panels. Indeed, many Council members serve as panelists both prior to and after their tenure on the Council.

Perhaps most notably, the Council's role in grant application review has been the subject of internal debate for many years. At first, the Council allocated large blocks of its time to discussing grant applications. But by 1973 as the application workload had increased significantly, the Council sought to streamline its responsibility to free more time to discuss policy issues. Under a new system established in early 1974, the Council was broken into three or four review groups per meeting. Each group was assigned batches of applications and reported on their deliberations to the full Council later in the meeting. Over the next three years, the process evolved so that chairpersons of grant advisory panels met with Council review groups, a Council member was assigned to report to the full Council, and NEA staff attended review group sessions to respond to questions.

Yet in November 1976, the Council voted to disband this system arguing that "...the review groups tended to factionalize the Council between those "in the know" and those "not in the know" on specific grant applications. Also, group discussions sometimes had to be replayed for the full Council, thus, doubling the amount of the time spent on the application...."[5] Furthermore, accommodating varying Council preferences for review group assignments proved difficult since some members preferred to participate in groups matching their own expertise, while others preferred to review applications in disciplines that were new to them.

In 1977, a newly constituted Office of Council and Panel Operations, after analysis of past practice, devised a "yellow sheets" system. In this system, the recommendations of each of the grant advisory panels are forwarded to the Chairperson before going to the Council. In some cases, the Chairperson may "flag" specific applications for special attention by the Council. Materials are sent to Council members two to three weeks prior to each Council meeting. On the yellow sheets, they write questions and concerns they have about applications recommended for award or for rejection. In 1992, this system was combined with a set of informational briefings for Council members on groups of applications on the Thursday preceding each Council meeting. Further, Council members are encouraged to learn more about the workings of grant advisory panels through ex-officio attendance.

The question of how much time the Council as a whole can and should spend on application review remains a focus of debate, as does the issue of the scope and purpose of that review. For example, does NCA application review constitute a separate quality assessment or simply a pro-forma ratification of panel recommendations to the Chair concerning grant amounts? How might the Council most effectively bring its multi-disciplinary expertise to bear on the evaluation of project applications across program categories? Can the Council responsibly fulfill its formal grant review and recommendation functions given the number of applications involved and the limited time commitment of Council members?

The Roles and Records of the NEA Chairman

Six individuals have been confirmed as Chairpersons of the NEA: Roger L. Stevens (1966-69); Nancy Hanks (1969-77); Livingston Biddle (1977-1981); Francis S. M. Hodsoll (1981-89); John Frohnmayer (1989-1992); and Jane Alexander (1993-present). Another four persons have served as Acting Chairpersons on an interim basis: Douglas MacAgy (1968-9); Hugh Southern (1989); Anne-Imelda Radice (1992); and Ana Steele (1993). Each of the Chairpersons has recognized the wisdom and foresight of the framers of the National Foundation on the Arts and Humanities Act of 1965, while also interpreting and building upon the Agency's legislative charge. Initiatives have included:

- identifying new missions and programs;
- nurturing external constituencies and dealing with internal constituencies;
- devising new administrative processes and structures; and
- initiating cooperative programs with other government agencies, state and local governments, and the private sector.

These initiatives have been undertaken in response to changing policy and institutional contexts characterized by varying public funding levels, differing perceptions of the problems and prospects of the arts in America, diverse views of the Agency's accomplishments and record, and shifts in the values and priorities of different political administrations. To a significant degree, these innovations have been achieved through the rhetorical and coalition-building skills of the Chairperson.

The Stevens Years (1966-69)

The first Chairman of the NEA, Roger Stevens, was appointed after having served as a Special Assistant to President Johnson. His tenure was marked by "innovativeness and flexibility,"[6] and constrained by small budgets of less than $10 million a year. Stevens exercised an eclectic, personalistic leadership style that, true to his experience as a Broadway producer, reflected a willingness to gamble on creative ideas.[7] With very few Agency personnel, Stevens paid close attention to the ideas and concerns of the National Council, whose strong opinions and attitudes arose from fame and successful professional experience.

Although Stevens frequently argued for the need to increase the NEA's budget, dramatic increases in funding were not forthcoming from the Johnson Administration, as it became increasingly bogged down in the Vietnam War.

Consequently, and reflecting the NEA's enabling legislation, Stevens stressed that support for the arts was to be a cooperative effort, involving not only federal funds, but also private enterprise, foundations, State and municipal support, regional organizations, and individual contributions. He emphasized that "the arts have not received the broad support from the business community and [private foundations] that they urgently need."[8] Stevens defined the needs of the arts largely in economic terms, noting that the "income gap" was an ever-increasing fact of life for many arts organizations.[9] Yet, American society, he observed, seems "to be doing very little about it aside from dutifully lamenting the sad state of affairs."[10]

The NCA supported this interpretation declaring that: "All Great Societies have been distinguished by a deep devotion to all of the Arts. The National Council on the Arts believes that, with our increased leisure and our widespread education, it is imperative that the Federal Government support the Arts more actively, provide leadership and resources to advance the Arts to a point where our national inner life may be continuously expressed and defined."[11]

In pursuing this belief, Stevens and the Council eschewed the practice of "giving everybody a little money." Instead, they tried to create an impact where a small sum of money could make a significant difference. Program priorities included: (1) the creation of new arts organizations (such as the American Theatre Laboratory, the Association of American Dance Companies, and the Western Opera Theatre; (2) grants to individuals (such as fellowships and sabbaticals for individual creative artists and training for arts students); (3) rescue grants to arts institutions (such as an emergency grant of $100,000 to the American Ballet Theatre as well as an additional $250,000 to promote nationwide tours); (4) experimental and developmental projects (such as the first matching grant for public sculpture, the installation of a Calder sculpture in Grand Rapids, Michigan); and (5) demonstration programs in arts education (such as the Artists-in-the-Schools Program and grants for programming on educational television and radio). Stevens and the Council also sought ways to work cooperatively with other federal agencies, in particular, the then U.S. Office of Education. The Endowment also provided stimulus funding for the states in order, according to Stevens, to "...develop programs, facilities, and services at the community level."[12] In these ways, Stevens cultivated new constituencies to support the mission and programs of the Endowment. In turn, this began the process of building the Agency's constituency base as a hedge against political opponents.

In 1968, Stevens identified as key accomplishments of his tenure the NEA's role in creating The American Film Institute and the role of NEA-funded educational projects in creating arts opportunities for young people and in helping to create future audiences for the arts. He also pointed with pride to NEA "grants to America's creative talents, which have resulted from the National Council on the Arts' deep commitment to providing assistance directly to the individual artist."[13] This commitment stemmed from the fact that the first National Council on the Arts was made up primarily of artists. But whether a primary responsibility of the NEA is to subsidize individuals involved in creating "new art" has been a source of fractious debate throughout the Agency's history.

During Stevens's Chairmanship, since the Agency itself was quite small, the National Council functioned virtually as NEA staff, originating and developing project ideas, carefully reviewing all grant applications, and creating programs in Visual Arts, Architecture and Design, Film, and Music. This discipline program structure, while expanded, remains the predominant organizational framework of the Agency to the present day. The use of grant advisory panels varied from program to program -- some panels became highly structured, others were merely ad hoc. But their use persists. Finally, while the Council of this period contained many influential and famous individuals, in retrospect, at least one critic has questioned its working assumptions, asserting that the Council and Stevens tended to pursue their own personal visions rather than ask "What is appropriate for the United States Government to support?"[14]

The Hanks Years (1969-77)

Appointed by President Nixon, Nancy Hanks came to the NEA from the philanthropic community, having been the Director of the Special Studies Project staff of the Nelson Rockefeller Fund. Under her direction, *The Performing Arts: Problems and Prospectives*, was completed in 1965, a pathbreaking study instrumental in building support for the creation of the NEA.

A brief listing of her most significant achievements would include the following:

- the legitimization of the principle of public funding for the arts, both within Congress and with artists and arts organizations;
- forging a concrete partnership in support of this principle, composed of the public sector, including federal, state, and local agencies and the private sector, i.e., individuals, institutions, corporations, and foundations;
- the coalescing of diverse arts interests into a genuine artistic community and into a mobilized and influential political constituency;
- the establishment of the Endowment as the leader of the arts constituency; and
- the institutionalization of the agency and routinization of its procedures and programs.[15]

In addition, and notably, Hanks's tenure was marked by the dramatic increase in the NEA budget from $8.5 million appropriated in 1969 to $105 million in 1977. As a result, the Agency acquired the resources necessary for it to have a significant national impact upon the arts. Hanks was immeasurably assisted in the budget process by a key member of the

White House staff, Leonard Garment, who served as President Nixon's advisor on the arts. As Garment recounts, NEA budget increases "did not come about just because the powers that be decided it was time to give culture the respect it deserved."[16] Rather because of the Vietnam War, President Nixon "...wanted for his own an issue that would not automatically divide his audience into sympathetic hawks and hostile doves."[17] He was persuaded that the arts presented just such a window of opportunity.

Hanks set Agency goals by linking them to historical trends -- the growth in the number of artists and of arts institutions in America as well as the broadened geographic dispersion of arts activities to communities across the nation. She continually stressed the social and economic benefits of the arts to society, such as their impact on consumer spending, employment, and tourism. Similarly, Hanks touted the role of NEA funds as a catalyst to increase private philanthropy by individuals, corporations, and foundations and as a means for arts organizations "to continue and expand their public service."[18]

Nancy Hanks and the National Council on the Arts set three broad goals for the Endowment: (1) to increase the availability of the arts; (2) to strengthen cultural resources; and (3) to advance the nation's cultural legacy. In 1973 Congressional testimony, Ms. Hanks illustrated how NEA programming was directed toward achievement of these goals. Regarding increased availability, she noted an increase in direct grants to state arts agencies from $36,363 each in 1970 to $127,250 each in 1973; the expansion of the Dance Touring Program to encompass 150 communities in 40 states and 50 American dance companies; and growth of the Artists-in-Schools Program to include over 325 visual artists, 1,200 poets, and 525 schools, more than 7,500 teachers and nearly 175,000 students. Both the Artists-in-Schools program and the Dance Touring Program were operated through the state arts councils, and in Hanks's words, constituted "workable and creatively exciting project[s] for the state art councils to undertake in their regions."[19] In this way, the federal-state partnership extended beyond a block grant arrangement to bolster a key constituency for the growing political base of the Endowment. Hanks seemed to take particular pride in the Endowment's role in making the arts more widely available, frequently noting that nearly 50 percent of the NEA funds went toward achievement of this goal.

The goal of cultural resources development was based on the Endowment's experience, established during the Stevens years, that relatively modest grants seemed to be effective in strengthening established institutions and stabilizing new ones. During the Hanks years, the Endowment institutionalized programs of assistance for the individual arts disciplines, in particular, music, visual arts, architecture, museums, theater, dance, public media, and literature, each with its own NEA program director.

Finally, to help "advance the nations cultural legacy," Ms. Hanks established the Expansion Arts Program, designed to assist community arts groups with professional direction to serve rural and urban areas which could be viewed as culturally disadvantaged. Hanks also considered assistance to individual artists, in the form of fellowships, training programs, and opportunities for experimentation, as means to advance the nations's cultural legacy, as she did the Architecture + Environmental Arts Program, designed to stimulate a broader understanding of architecture as it relates to the physical environment.

Program development during Hanks's tenure also included initiatives which cut across both the three broadly defined goals and the arts disciplines. An Office for Program Information was established to consolidate the informational resources of the agency and disseminate information more widely. Special Projects in Folk Arts were initiated to assist living American traditional artists and support crafts and craftsmen, and the Federal Design Improvement Program was launched, at the urging of the White House, to increase the awareness among federal decision-makers of the importance of design. The National Council supported programs to aid American artists and cultural institutions to take a central place in the 1976 bicentennial celebration. Finally, in 1977, the NEA created the Challenge Grant Program for cultural institutions with national or regional impact. The program required each grantee to match an NEA grant on a ratio of at least 3 to 1, with money acquired from new or increased funding sources. Challenge Grants were designed to help arts organizations to eliminate accumulated debts, to establish or increase an endowment fund, or to acquire more adequate facilities and equipment.

The operational skills that Nancy Hanks acquired during work as coordinator of special projects for the Rockefeller Brothers Fund proved to be useful in piloting the NEA during a period of geometric growth and in her dealings with the National Council. She was thoroughly schooled in the consultative networking style of foundation work. Her leadership style involved forming expert panels, coordinating advisory committee decisions, integrating diverse viewpoints, and distilling information and opinions into acceptable and practical decision options.

She frequently maintained that she never attempted to make statements or decisions that were not based on Council thinking, although NEA legislation did not require her to do so.[20] Under her direction, the NEA came to rely increasingly on grant advisory panels to review applications and to maintain close contact with the artistic community. As the Agency's budget increased, Hanks also expanded the NEA staff nearly 600 percent in order to deal with the increase of applications (from 2,000 to 20,000) and of grants (from 584 to 4000).

With the increased reliance on advisory panels to review grant applications and the expansion of staff responsibilities for both ongoing administration and initiative development, the role and concerns of the National Council shifted. As a result, grant application review occurred during panel review sessions, while the Council came to be seen as merely rubber stamping these panel recommendations.[21] At the same time, the Council felt it should give more attention to policy, including the development of program guidelines. Thus, it initiated a practice of devoting one full meeting a year to policy matters and experimented with review groups. During the last year of Hanks's tenure, a policy and planning committee of the Council was formed. However, Hanks's Deputy Chairman Michael Straight questioned the effectiveness of such redirected activity. He contends that "Council meetings were seen as promotional opportunities.... Confrontations and controversies were avoided whenever possible. Bad news was rarely brought to the attention of Council members; serious debate was not encouraged. Many members were chosen for lustre rather than insight; others were seen as means of increasing political leverage, in increasing appropriations, and adding constituencies. Astute Council members...were compelled in private sessions to tell Ms. Hanks that their time was being wasted and misspent."[22]

Thus, amidst the successful institutionalization and growth of the NEA, the role of the National Council remained unclear and its own expectations unsettled.

The Biddle Years (1977-81)

Appointed by President Carter, Livingston Biddle served as the third Chairman of the Arts Endowment. He had both political and artistic credentials, having served as Senator Claiborne Pell's staff director at the Subcommittee for Education, Arts and Humanities, drafting the original 1965 legislation creating the Endowments, and having served briefly as NEA Deputy under Roger Stevens and later, starting in 1974, as the first Congressional Liaison under Nancy Hanks. Before coming to Washington, he had established a career as a novelist in his native Philadelphia.

Still, Biddle's appointment as Chairman was greeted with dismay in some quarters. His ties to a prominent Senator were seen as evidence of political intrusion in the Endowment by the Carter Administration. According to Hilton Kramer, it was the beginning of "...a new era marked by an aggressive politicization of federal cultural policy,"[23] an era, in his view, ...to entail the increased influence of "pressure groups" and "vested interests" dedicated to imposing funding quotas on the NEA." Whatever the merits of this viewpoint, Biddle's appointment did set the political stage for public awareness over subsequent appointments of the NEA chair.

Biddle also confronted an emerging elitism-populism debate. In this debate, defenders of elitism stressed that artistic quality should be the sole criterion in grant decisions and that artistic quality is most consistently found in established high culture institutions. Defenders of populism stressed the need for wide public availability of the arts and a more pluralistic concept of artistic excellence.

Biddle responded directly to both the "politicization" and "elitism-populism" issues in his nomination hearing before the Senate. He stressed that safeguards against politicalization, i.e., inappropriate governmental pressures were written into the 1965 law that created the NEA. He also envisioned "...a lasting and developing partnership between the federal government and private community, and between the federal government and state and local governments...."[24] Regarding the elitism-populism issue, Biddle testified that words like 'elitism' and 'populism' lead to a polarization of the arts, where battle lines are drawn and alternatives chosen. He saw no need for either/or choices, proposing "access to the best" as a defensible cultural goal for the nation.

In a fashion similar to Nancy Hanks, Biddle often spoke of the many benefits of the arts to society as a whole, touting them as magnets for tourism, as special educators, as vital elements in reviving urban areas, and as sources of economic activity. He spoke of their intangible values as well. Still, Mr. Biddle viewed the arts world, at the time, as beset by serious problems. Specifically, he cited the danger of fragmentation, that many in the arts "concentrate too narrowly on their own particular interests ...[and] bicker over resources and relative status."[25]

Biddle established five basic priorities for the NEA during his tenure:

- individual creativity and excellence;
- institutional creativity and excellence;
- living heritage;
- making the arts available; and
- leadership in the arts.

Several new programs and offices were created during Biddle's Administration to help achieve these goals. The Opera-Musical Theatre Program and an Office of Minority Affairs and an Office of Special Constituencies were established, while Folk Arts, for several years a part of the Special Projects office, was formalized as a separate program. In addition, the Federal-State Partnership was revised to contain a "funding formula that takes account of a state's need (based on population) and effort (based on the state legislature's arts appropriations) factored by the state's per capita income."[26] Further, a Livable Cities Program, jointly administered by the Department of Housing and Urban Development in cooperation with the Endowment, marked "the first time the Endowment [had] been legislatively joined to another federal agency in a cooperative endeavor."[27] These program development activities were facilitated by significant NEA budget increases -- from $105 million in FY 1977 to $149 million in FY 1979.

Biddle also initiated a number of structural changes at the Endowment to improve Agency efficiency and accountability. He reorganized Endowment administration by naming three deputy chairs -- for Programs; for Policy and Planning; and for Intergovernmental Activities -- and by placing a five-year limit on the tenure of all staff program directors. He also elaborated the policy role of the National Council on the Arts, and formalized its work in smaller committees for the first time.

Despite Biddle's ability to implement new programs and procedures for the Agency, his tenure was hardly immune from criticism. For example, Biddle drew criticism from members of the arts community when he withdrew a controversial grant approved by a panel and the National Council. While charged with censorship by some, Mr. Biddle has expressed no regret subsequently arguing that "when an emergency arises, I believe emphatic action should be taken. This is a Chairman's important responsibility."[28] At the same time, Mr. Biddle has warned against unilateral decisions by the Chairperson. He regarded the Council "more as a board of directors than a council of advisors,"[29] and felt Council deliberations of controversial issues afforded, "the very best protection of our essential freedoms."[30]

The Hodsoll Years (1981-89)

Francis S. M. Hodsoll was appointed by President Reagan as the fourth Chairman of the NEA. A career bureaucrat and former Foreign Service Officer, Hodsoll was bureaucratically seasoned but lacked experience in the arts. Indeed, his limited experience in the area had been acquired when, as Deputy Assistant to White House Chief of Staff James Baker in 1981, he had helped organize the Presidential Task Force on the Arts and Humanities. Hodsoll himself told a Senate confirmation panel that he was fully cognizant of his lack of experience in arts administration.

But by the time Hodsoll assumed office in mid-October 1981, the Reagan Administration had already articulated its political philosophy of limited government, including stress on reduction in the size, scope, and spending of the federal government. Specifically, it sought to reduce governmental activities perceived as *not* being in the public domain, including the arts, preferring to rely to a far greater degree on private sector support. Further, the Reagan Administration, fueled by a report issued by the Heritage Foundation, criticized what was seen as the politicalization of the federal arts policy during the Carter presidency.[31] Although not successful in substantially reducing federal spending for the arts, as originally intended, Administration budgetary tactics did spur two unintended political developments: the organization of Congressional advocates of the arts and further mobilization of arts interest groups. It was thus a particularly challenging environment which Frank Hodsoll inherited upon his assumption of the NEA Chairmanship. Hodsoll acknowledged this in 1982 by stating "I think it is fair to say that my first real job was to rebuild a sense of confidence about the Endowment."[32]

Hodsoll's early policy statements stressed the importance of a public-private partnership in support of the arts. He argued that "the arts in our country have always depended on a pluralistic system of support in which no one sector dominates."[33]

Hodsoll saw the Endowment's mission as fostering excellence, diversity and vitality. To pursue this mission amidst significant social, demographic, technological, and artistic changes, Chairman Hodsoll adopted a six-part strategy:

- emphasizing longer-term institutional support;
- encouraging projects that advance the art forms or bring a diversity of art to a broader audience;
- encouraging better management and planning by arts institutions;
- developing partnership among public sectors of the arts;
- encouraging greater private support; and
- initiating development of arts information systems

The public-private partnership policy informed program development strategies during Hodsoll's tenure. New programs encouraged partnerships between the Endowment and local arts agencies (e.g., the Local Tests Program) and between the NEA and other federal agencies (e.g., the National Arts Education Research Center, co-sponsored by the NEA and the U.S. Department of Education). To facilitate public-private partnerships, Hodsoll created a new position -- Director of Private Partnerships -- and supported the development of Endowment-private sector collaborations such as an invigorated Challenge Grant Program for established institutions, the Advancement Program for developing organizations, the Community Foundation Initiative of the Expansion Arts Program, and the Dance Program collaboration with the Rockefeller and Exxon foundations to assist new choreographers.

Significant administrative features of Hodsoll's tenure were changes which effected greater centralization of authority in the Chairman's office, closer scrutiny for individual grant recommendations, and more attention to long-range planning and program evaluation. For example, Hodsoll took a very active role in overseeing the recommendations of the peer review panels. During his first year in office, Hodsoll personally reviewed approximately 5,000 grants that had already secured panel recommendations and National Council approval. Also, during his first term, Hodsoll took twenty-eight applications to the Council for direct consideration. Of these, he turned down fifteen with Council concurrence, rejected another five despite Council endorsement, and approved eight after discussion. Chairman Hodsoll, by his own account, reversed panel or Council recommendations primarily because of three reasons: (1) a lack of substantial evidence of quality in a grant application as revealed in the record of the panel meeting; (2) evidence, in the record, of improper panel process; and (3) in a few instances, inappropriateness for public funding. Hodsoll's willingness to actively exercise his decision authority reflected his view of the NEA's legislative directives. "The Arts Endowment's authorizing statute specifically places authority to run the programs in the Chairman; all the other players (panels, council, staff) are advisory to the Chairman."[34]

This concern for administrative centralization probably played a role in the increase of planning and evaluation activities at the NEA. During Hodsoll's tenure, the Agency prepared five, five-year plans for Congress, initiated research projects to study public participation in the arts,[35] and, at the request of Congress, prepared three major reports: *The Arts in America*,[36] an analysis of the state of the arts in the late 1980's, a "Panel Study Report" on the grant review panel system, and *Toward Civilization*, the first national study of the state of arts education over a decade. Indeed, arts education was a major NEA policy priority during the Hodsoll years, one that tested his rhetorical and coalition-building skills perhaps more than any other issue before the Endowment.

Chairman Hodsoll, early in his tenure, also implemented several revisions in the grant advisory panel system, including: (1) staff documentation of panel's decision to approve or reject grants; and (2) staff communication to the Chairman about panel recommendations on potentially "controversial" grants.

During Hodsoll's term, the Endowment was able to resist Congressional attempts to legislate restrictions on NEA grant support for work which, for example, might denigrate any ethnic, racial, religious, or minority group. Mr. Hodsoll, in reflecting on these Congressional critics, agreed with the proposition that those who provide the money -- the President and Congress -- can and should exert appropriate control over Agency funding. "This represents appropriate democratic control of the public purse, not censorship."[37] But he further argued that "specific judgements on grants to artists and arts institutions should be left to Endowment policy level officials; these actions cannot easily be legislated."[38] In cases where art works go beyond limits of tolerance and are inappropriate for public funding, "...it is the duty of the Arts Endowment Chairman", he has concluded, "to turn down grants that in his judgment would go beyond these limits...."[39]

Frank Hodsoll was widely considered an effective Chairman. Cuts in the NEA budget in 1981 and 1982 were restored by 1984. More broadly, as someone with credibility within the Reagan White House, Hodsoll served as a buffer to those in the Administration who would have diminished the status and autonomy of the NEA. Yet his tenure spawned considerable tension with the National Council. At various points, individual Council members resisted Hodsoll's centralization of authority, his willingness to override panel and Council grant recommendations, and, ultimately, his literal reading of the NEA's authorizing legislation on the advisory role of the Council. These tensions came to a head in 1987 when Hodsoll proposed use of a computer program system to review the monetary amounts of agency grants. It would have addressed a problem Hodsoll perceived, namely, that projects and organizations of similar artistic quality received widely dissimilar grant monies during a granting period. Before the proposal could be reviewed, Council members denounced it as a recipe for "formula funding" and an attack on the indispensable role of the panel system. Hodsoll, after an initial defense, withdrew the proposal.

But the incident was noteworthy as a public disagreement between the Chairperson and the Council over their respective roles and responsibilities.

On February 15, 1989, Hodsoll stepped down as NEA Chairman to assume a senior position at the Office of Management and Budget. His Deputy Director, Hugh Southern, served as Interim Chairman for six months.

The Frohnmayer Years (1989-92)

John Frohnmayer was nominated by President Bush on July 6, 1989, and confirmed by the Senate on September 29, 1989, as the fifth chairperson of the National Endowment for the Arts. Because of the controversy surrounding the Endowment's funding of the work of Robert Mapplethorpe and Andres Serrano as well as the Congressional imposition of content restrictions that Summer, the usual private lobbying that precedes such a Presidential nomination was the focus of much media attention.

A lawyer in Portland, Oregon, Frohnmayer had served as Chairman of the Oregon Arts Commission from 1980 to 1984, as a director of the Western States Arts Foundation, and was a Bush presidential campaign supporter. He is also a singer. His particular qualifications for the chairmanship, however, were not the focus of concern either for vocal advocates in the arts community or for Endowment detractors. Rather, advocates were interested in the new chairman's dedication to artistic freedom and opposition to content restrictions on NEA funding, while Endowment critics wanted assurance that he would uphold Congressional intent and improve the accountability of the Agency to the American taxpayer.

A decision by Mr. Frohnmayer, early in his tenure, served to polarize these groups further. On November 8, 1989, he suspended a $10,000 grant to Artists Space, a nonprofit art gallery in New York, for "Witnesses: Against our Vanishing," a show about AIDS. A grant advisory panel, in February, and the National Council in May, had recommended funding for the exhibit. At first, Frohnmayer defended his suspension of the grant by saying the show has become too political. Then, one week after his original announcement, Mr. Frohnmayer visited the exhibit at Artists Space and met with concerned artists. While not reversing his position on the grant, Frohnmayer did promise to work for the removal of the legislation restricting Endowment grants for art works considered obscene.[40]

The Artists Space episode served to diminish the goodwill of many arts advocates for Mr. Frohnmayer and the NEA and, at the same time, antagonized Endowment critics who expected Frohnmayer to uphold the new laws passed by Congress. Subsequent actions over the next several months further eroded Mr. Frohnmayer's position with both constituencies. Al Feltzenberg, the NEA Deputy Chairman with close connections to the White House, engaged in public disputes with the Chairman and was subsequently fired by him. Also, in Spring 1990, the NEA issued a statement of policy and guidance declaring that: "grant recipients, in order to receive funds, must agree that they will not use those grant funds to promote, disseminate or produce materials that are "obscene" under the well-settled legal definition employed by the Supreme Court in Miller v. California". This statement seemed to satisfy no one. Endowment critics felt the statement subverted the intent of Congress in instituting content restrictions. Nearly 20 organizations and individuals rejected their NEA grants in protest of what they perceived as the NEA "anti-obscenity pledge," often accompanied, as in the case of Joseph Papp of the New York Shakespeare Festival, by extended statements to the press and television appearances.

Further, arguing that the "anti-obscenity pledge" was unconstitutional, lawyers for three NEA applicants filed lawsuits against the NEA. Throughout this period, the Government Accounting Office was monitoring the Endowment's compliance with Congressionally-passed content restrictions at the request of a skeptical Senator Jesse Helms. Finally, Frohnmayer canceled grants to four performance artists in early 1991, further antagonizing many arts advocates.[41]

In response to these contending constituencies, Chairman Frohnmayer adopted a strategy of portraying the Endowment, not as a passive Agency caught in the crossfire, but an organization capable of vigorous internal reform. This strategy, he hoped, would reassure Congressional critics that if Endowment procedures for reviewing grants were improved, accountability of the Agency to the public would be assured, thus eliminating the need for content restrictions.

A focal point of Frohnmayer's internal reform proposals was the grant review process. He sought to institute numerous changes in panel processes, ranging from a broadening of panel memberships to include wider geographic, ethnic, and lay person representation as well as an opening of policy panel deliberations and careful recording of all panel deliberations, to highlighting anti-obscenity measures in panel background materials and grant applicant guidelines and seeking an increased Council role in attendance at panel meetings and review of grant recommendations.

Mr. Frohnmayer also attempted to articulate a new sense of mission for the Agency -- one which stressed access of the American people to the arts, in order to rebuild the bridge between the arts and the public, a bridge damaged during the year-long controversy. He outlined a set of program initiatives to serve the American people: (1) emphasis on arts education; (2) promotion of broad access to the arts through emphasis on delivery of the arts to multicultural and rural communities; (3) emphasis on the Endowment's international activities; and (4) strengthening of America's core arts institutions.[42]

Implementation of these proposed reforms and hence fulfillment of a new mission would require careful, consistent attention from Chairman Frohnmayer and his executive staff, make more demands on the time and attention of National Council members, and necessitate considerable administrative follow-through. However, the succession of grant controversies, Congressional criticism, and personal turnover at the Endowment left inadequate time, focus or policy memory to fully realize these reforms. Instead, the centralized administrative system of Frohnmayer's predecessor Frank Hodsoll was abandoned for an ad hoc crisis management mode. Meanwhile, the National Council grew increasingly restive at the Chairman's public efforts to secure Council endorsement for his shifting political judgments. Exposed to criticism from their own arts community while seeking to defuse Congressional and conservative criticism of the Agency, the Council wavered between wanting to control (not just advise) the Chairman and urging the Chairman to exercise stronger executive leadership. Council frustration was further exacerbated by budgetary stagnation -- as year after year, amidst controversy, the Agency saw no increases in its total budget. Instead, it was subject to a mandated redistribution of funds from discipline programs to state arts agencies, to arts education activities, to underserved rural and inner-city communities, and to growing administrative costs incurred by procedural reforms.

Frohnmayer's tenure as NEA chairman, from the start, was conditioned by unprecedented public scrutiny and Congressional oversight of the Agency. The degree to which the events which plunged the Agency into such controversy were beyond or within Frohnmayer's control is a matter of debate. Less debatable, however, is the conclusion that Frohnmayer's attempts to recast the Endowment as a builder of bridges between the arts and the American people failed. What he left is a legacy of leadership which vacillated between attempts to appease Congressional critics and to appeal to the amorphous "arts community." As a consequence, several key assumptions about relationships between the

Chairperson and the National Council, assumptions embodied both in the Agency's enabling legislation and in the practices of previous chairpersons, no longer possess a ring of certitude.

John Frohnmayer's chairmanship may have served to bring out many dilemmas of leadership at the NEA, but any opportunity to resolve them was forestalled when, once more, external events overwhelmed his leadership. It came in the form of frequent Endowment critic Patrick Buchanan's primary challenges to President Bush which, in turn, led to Frohnmayer's forced resignation by the Bush Administration in April 1992. Anne-Imelda Radice, who actively sought to address Congress' concerns, often to the dismay of Council members, served as Acting Chairperson until the end of the Bush Administration.

Leadership and the NEA

Doig and Hargrove, as students of entrepreneurial leadership in government agencies, argue that leaders can "make a difference" in a variety of ways. They can, for example: (1) identify new missions and programs for their organizations; (2) develop and nourish external constituencies; (3) create internal constituencies; and (4) enhance the organization's technical expertise. Both external factors and the personality and skill of individual leaders, including rhetorical and coalition-building skills, condition the capacity for organizational stability, growth, and innovation. Success is most likely achieved when, according to Doig and Hargrove, there is a good match of individual skill and organizational tasks, a match that is further reinforced by historical conditions.[43]

This chapter has, in many ways, illustrated the validity of the Doig-Hargrove typology. Nancy Hanks, through use of networking skills learned during her work in the foundation sector, was able to capitalize on the Nixon Administration's influx of monies to the Endowment to both identify new programs and build a broad constituency base. Frank Hodsoll, through his rhetorical skills, was able to increase the research and technical expertise of the Endowment, highlight arts education as a program area, and build enough internal constituencies among skeptical Reagan Administration officials to ward off overt political intrusion in the Agency.

That said, leadership at the NEA cannot be wholly understood with reference to this particular typology, in large part, because of the leadership structure of the Endowment, i.e., a structure which apportions leadership responsibilities to both the Chairperson and the National Council. The National Foundation on the Arts and Humanities Act, as was seen, outlines the responsibilities of the Chairperson and the Council. But, as was also seen, this legislation offers few operational directives. Hence, there exists considerable flexibility in making decisions on policy, grants, and the overall operation of the Endowment. The historical record, as reviewed in this chapter, revealed how the authorizing legislation has been interpreted in diverse ways in different historical and political contexts. What emerges is a set of recurring, perennial dilemmas over the respective roles and responsibilities of the Chairperson and the National Council.

A key dilemma surrounding the Chairperson's role has been debated since the Agency's creation. It centers on the formal authority of the Chairperson to set policy and make all final decisions, including those on grants. To some, this authority raises the specter of a "cultural czar" able to make arbitrary, capricious decisions beyond any form of citizen control. To others, such authority is necessary if the accountability of the Agency to the President and the American people is to be upheld.

Dilemmas confronting the National Council have to do with its role and capacities vis-a-vis the Chairperson, panels, the arts community, and the general public. For example, is the Council to be free to pursue its own visions or to provide support for the Chairperson? Is the Council to serve as a Board of Directors deliberating over controversial issues or as advisors to a Chairperson who makes all final decisions? Regarding its relationship to grant advisory panels, to what extent should the Council review all grant recommendations of panels? What level of review is feasible? How should attention to grant recommendation review be balanced against a Council role in agency policy development? Finally, what purposes can and should the Council legitimately serve -- advocate for the arts to external constituencies, internal promoter of the interests of artists and arts organizations, or as servant of a general public interest? Are these purposes mutually exclusive or complementary?

All of these dilemmas are, to some degree, inherent in the structure and context of the Endowment, i.e., they are perennial issues. But perennial issues are not unresolvable. Indeed, it can be argued that throughout the Endowment's history, these dilemmas, while surely not to the satisfaction of all, have been sufficiently resolved to at least permit innovation and growth in the Agency. The same cannot be said with confidence after the recent years of controversy surrounding the Agency. It appears that the terms of Chairperson-Council relations have changed. No longer can it be assumed that the Council will help to support and legitimize decisions of the Chairperson. Nor is it clear that the Council can be counted on as a buffer to insulate the Agency from political intrusion rather than a magnifier of political interests. Further, given these changes in the terms of Council-Chairperson relations, a new dilemma has emerged -- is a Council that acts independently best seen as an antidote to unilateral decisions of the Chairperson or an obstacle to the Chair's ability to exercise political judgment and leadership?

The extent to which these and other questions will be addressed and perhaps resolved by vigorous public debate, by Congressional legislation, or become grist for the mill of interest groups, depends on the next Chairperson's success in rebuilding public confidence in the Endowment and the broad coalition that has supported the Agency's work for twenty-five years. The decidedly changed environment of the recent past will require leadership to devise new strategies to develop new constituency relations both internally and externally. The process of turning formal authority into effective influence, admittedly, will involve many complex, mysterious connections and a fresh infusion of wisdom and vision. But without these developments, the future of the Endowment and the idea of public support for the arts will be in doubt.

Notes

1. For further discussion of these activities, see *The National Council on the Arts and the National Endowment for the Arts* (Washington, DC: National Endowment for the Arts, 1978).

2. For a fuller discussion of legislative intent, see Jason Hall, *NFAH Act of 1965 -- Legislative Intent*, a study prepared for the Independent Commission, Washington, DC, August 1990.

3. The Independent Commission, *A Report to Congress on the National Endowment for the Arts* (Washington, DC: The Independent Commission, September 1990), p. 22.

4. Frederic R. Kellogg, "Standards of Conduct for Council Members and Arts Endowment Panelists," Memorandum issued by the NEA General Counsel, February 17, 1987.

5. Ana Steele, "Council Role in Application Review," a report for discussion to the National Council on the Arts, August 1989, p. 10.

6. C. Richard Swaim, "The National Endowment for the Arts: 1965-80," in Kevin V. Mulcahy and C. Richard Swaim, eds., *Public Policy and the Arts* (Boulder, CO: Westview Press, 1982), p. 180.

7. This point is made in Fannie Taylor and Anthony C. Barresi, *The Arts at a*

New Frontier: The National Endowment for the Arts (New York: Plenum Press, 1984), p. 56.

8. Roger Stevens, "Chairman's Statement," *Annual Report: 1967* (Washington, DC: National Endowment for the Arts, 1967), p. 1.

9. The "income gap" argument was first introduced in William J. Baumol and William G. Bowen, *The Performing Arts: The Economic Dilemma* (New York: Twentieth Century Fund, 1966).

10. Roger Stevens, "Chairman's Statement," *Annual Report: 1968* (Washington, DC: National Endowment for the Arts, 1968), p. 3.

11. Roger Stevens, "Chairman's Statement," *Annual Report: 1965* (Washington, DC: National Endowment for the Arts, 1965), p. 1.

12. Roger Stevens, "Chairman's Statement," *Annual Report: 1967* (Washington, DC: National Endowment for the Arts, 1967), p. 5.

13. Roger Stevens, in *Annual Report: 1968*, p. 2.

14. Michael Straight, written testimony submitted to The Independent Commission, July 24, 1990, p. 2.

15. For a more detailed account of Nancy Hanks's tenure and her accomplishments, see Margaret J. Wyszomirski, "The Politics of Art: Nancy Hanks and the National Endowment for the Arts," in Jameson P. Doig and Erwin C. Hargrove, eds., *Leadership and Innovation: A Biographical Perspective on Entrepreneurs in Government* (Baltimore: Johns Hopkins University Press, 1987).

16. Leonard Garment, "Education and the Future of the Arts: The Second Annual Nancy Hanks Lecture on the Arts and Public Policy," in David B. Pankratz and Valerie B. Morris, eds., *The Future of the Arts: Public Policy and Arts Research* (New York: Praeger, 1990), p. 17.

17. Ibid., p. 17.

18. Nancy Hanks, "Chairman's Statement," in *Annual Report: 1973* (Washington, DC: National Endowment for the Arts, 1973), p. 10.

19. Ibid., p. 16.

20. Michael Straight disputes this account of Nancy Hanks's relationship with the Council. "Ms. Hanks was emphatic in insisting that she never overrode Council recommendations. This was a bit disingenuous since she managed on several occasions to persuade the Council to reverse positions which it had taken." Michael Straight, written testimony submitted to The Independent Commission, July 24, 1990, p. 4.

21. See C. Richard Swaim, "The National Endowment for the Arts: 1965-80."

22. Michael Straight, written testimony submitted to The Independent Commission, July 24, 1990, pp. 2-3.

23. Hilton Kramer, "The Threat of Politicization of Federal Arts Programs," *New York Times*, October 16, 1977, sec. 2, 36.

24. Livingston Biddle, "Chairman's Statement," in *Annual Report: 1977* (Washington, DC: National Endowment for the Arts, 1977), p. 7.

25. Livingston Biddle, "Chairman's Statement," in *Annual Report: 1979* (Washington, DC: National Endowment for the Arts, 1979), p. 2.

26. Livingston Biddle, "Chairman's Statement," in *Annual Report: 1978* (Washington, DC: National Endowment for the Arts, 1978), pp. 9-10.

27. Ibid., p. 10.

28. Livingston Biddle, written testimony submitted to The Independent Commission, July 24, 1990, p. 5.

29. Ibid., p. 6.

30. Ibid., p. 6.

31. For further discussion of the early years of Hodsoll's chairmanship, see Margaret J. Wyszomirski, "The Reagan Administration and the Arts: 1981-83," Paper presented at the Annual Conference of the American Political Association, Chicago, IL, Sept 1983.

32. Frank Hodsoll, "Chairman's Statement," in *Annual Report: 1982* (Washington, DC: National Endowment for the Arts, 1982), p. 4.

33. Ibid., p. 4.

34. Frank Hodsoll, written testimony submitted to the Independent Commission, July 25, 1990, p. 3.

35. See John P. Robinson, et al., *Survey of Public Participation in the Arts: 1985, Volume 1, Project Report* (Washington, DC: University of Maryland and the National Endowment for the Arts, 1987).

36. For a critical discussion of this report, see Margaret J. Wyszomirski, Monnie Peters, and Kevin V. Mulcahy, "The Policy Utility of the NEA's Report on the State of the Arts," in David B. Pankratz and Valerie B. Morris, eds., *The Future of the Arts: Public Policy and Arts Research* (New York: Praeger, 1990).

37. Frank Hodsoll, written testimony submitted to The Independent Commission, p. 2.

38. Ibid., p. 14.

39. Ibid., pp. 14-15.

40. See William H. Honan, "Frohnmayer Says He'll Seek End of Art-Grant Law," *New York Times*, November 16, 1989, C27.

41. See Kim Masters, "Arts Chief Ignores Advice, Vetoes Grant," *Washington Post*, November 22, 1990, C4.

42. For greater detail on these initiatives, see John Frohnmayer, "Talking Points," Newsmakers Breakfast, National Press Club, September 17, 1990.

43. For further discussion of this typology, see Jameson P. Doig and Erwin C. Hargrove, op cit.

7

The NEA and the Reauthorization Process: Congress and Arts Policy Issues

Kevin V. Mulcahy

The National Endowment for the Arts (NEA) is the legislative ward of the House Committee on Education and Labor working through subcommittees variously entitled Select Education, Post-secondary Education, Labor-Management Relations and the Subcommittee on Education, Arts, and Humanities of the Senate Committee on Labor and Human Resources. From its creation in 1965 until 1985, the NEA has had six sets of hearings before these Senate and House authorizing subcommittees.[1] Succinctly defined, "an authorization is a statement of legislative policy, while an appropriation is the funding of that policy."[2] The legislative process, then, is a two-step procedure whereby programs must be authorized before funds can be appropriated for their implementation.[3] Furthermore, an authorization may or may not be permanent. If a program is not permanently authorized, the legislative committee, after some specified time period, must reauthorize it.[4] The time period for such authorization may be annually; more commonly it is two to five years. About 40 percent of the federal budget involves annual or periodic extensions of legislative authority.[5]

While the appropriations decisions are crucial to the survival of an agency, reauthorizations provide occasions to review a public program, re-evaluate its operations and impact, and reassess the amount of funding made available.[6] Reauthorizations also present opportunities for the substantive committees to influence budgetary outcomes through their spending recommendations.[7] However, it should be noted that over the past twenty years there has been a decided rise in the importance of the appropriations subcommittees which often affect authorization through funding recommendations. Regardless, these periodic reviews allow the authorizing committees, the agencies under their oversight, and the relevant organized interest groups to gather for the purpose of examining the implementation of a public policy. The committees -- or, more typically, specialized subcommittees -- can use reauthorization hearings as a vehicle for increasing their influence over the agencies under their statutory supervision.[8]

During its entire administrative history, the NEA has been the legislative preserve of one Senate subcommittee (the Subcommittee on Education, Arts, and Humanities) and two chairmen -- Senator Claiborne Pell (D-RI) and, for a briefer time, Senator Robert Stafford (R-VT). In the House, the cultural subcommittee has been less stable, although for ten years there existed what may be called the "Brademas subcommittee." This subcommittee -- under its various sequence of names -- was either chaired or strongly influenced by Representative John Brademas (D-IN) until his electoral defeat in 1980.

Authority over the NEA and the related cultural agencies is shared by the Subcommittee on Select Education, chaired by Representative Pat Williams (D-MT) and the Subcommittee on Postsecondary Education, chaired by Representative William Ford (D-MI). The cultural subcommittees have had many distinguished members over the years -- for example, Senator Paul Simon (D-IL), Representative Frank Thompson (D-NJ), and Senators Walter Mondale (D-MN) and Edward Kennedy (D-MA) -- and a tradition of bipartisan support, particularly from the late Senator Jacob Javits (R-NY) and Representatives Ogden Reid (R-NY) and Peter Peyser (R-NY). Subcommittee membership is small: six in the Senate until 1985, 11 at present, 13 in the House until 1985, 21 at present. A disproportionate number of members have come from urban areas and the Northeast in particular.[9]

In the course of the NEA's reauthorization hearings before the cultural subcommittees, during the period 1967-85, 222 days were spent in public session. Testimony was provided by NEA staff members, representatives of cultural institutions and arts service organizations, artists, members of the general public, representatives, and senators. The number of witnesses averaged 17 for each hearing. This discussion is based almost exclusively on that written record of hearings -- a total of approximately 7,800 pages. It does not deal, except in passing, with the Appropriations Committee, floor debates, and final legislative disposition, or with White House or NEA officials acting in arenas other than these hearings. The printed record is not necessarily a verbatim account of the proceedings and does not provide the invaluable information that would be gained from preauthorization activities, direct observation or from interviewing the principals. The reauthorization hearings over the NEA's administrative lifetime, however, are a valuable source of insight into the politics and administration of public arts policy.

The occasions for contact between a subcommittee and the agency it oversees are many. There are numerous year-round contacts in the form of telephone calls and personal visits between subcommittee members and staff and agency personnel as information is sought or inquiries made on behalf of constituents. Hearings, however, are the principal point of public contact and are taken very seriously both in Congress and in the bureaucracy.

The witnesses at the NEA reauthorization hearings have typically represented the best organized and most politically self-conscious segments of the cultural constituency: 30 percent were from state and local arts agencies; 25 percent, cultural institutions; 12 percent, arts service organizations; 13 percent, were self-identified as artists; and the remaining 20 percent included university professors, labor union officials, and corporate executives. Congressional scholar Ralph Huitt explains how the hearings worked:

> Thousands of questions were asked and answered. Out of a welter of facts and opinions, what did the Committee learn about the problems? ...What kinds of questions did its members ask? What picture of the factual situation emerged from the answers they got?

As Huitt concluded, "There were questions which, because of their persistence, were raised again and again" by the witnesses and the committee members.[10]

The NEA's enabling legislation contains little guidance on purpose and policies (save admonitions like "foster the arts") and no guidance on programs, standards for grant allocations, methods of grant decisionmaking.[11] In the absence of statutory specifics, the NEA has developed policies and programs deemed compatible with the legislative intent of P.L. 89-209 and Congress has reacted to these over two decades with fairly persistent concerns. The NEA's reauthorization hearings reveal six perennial questions that, although frequently asked, were variously and inconclusively answered. These questions are: first, do advisory panels provide an impartial system for awarding grants?

second, is the geographic distribution of grants equitable? third, who should receive public support? fourth, what is the government's responsibility to promote good art? fifth, should public arts policy be elitist or populist? sixth, what is the record of the Arts Endowment?

At root, these questions reflect two basic political issues involving any public policy: what is the nature of the distribution of the public benefits, and which public's values are furthered by a government program? Resolving such issues is never an easy political determination. In arts policy-making, deference to the strong traditions of cultural "autonomy" and artistic "excellence" have tended to insulate public arts programs from political evaluation. Yet, as examination of the following questions will reveal, considerations of politics and of governance have arisen with regard to arts policy-making from different actors in the cultural subgovernment.

Do Advisory Panels Provide an Impartial System for Awarding Grants?

The most persistent issue at reauthorization hearings has been the matter of NEA advisory panels. At the first joint hearings in 1967, Senator Pell asked Chairman Roger Stevens to "enlarge a bit on the grant process" and the role played by the advisory panels. In 1973, the subcommittee urged the NEA chairman to ensure that panels had "broad geographic representation."[12] Panels arose again as an issue in the 1980 hearings. Judging by the nature of his questions, Senator Pell seemed extremely upset about an Appropriations Committee report that had criticized the NEA as being a "closed circle of advisors."[13] NEA Chairman Livingston Biddle denied such a characterization. He pointed out that over half the panel members that year were new and pledged to make the panel (and staff) advisory systems more responsive to their cultural constituents.[14]

> ...I have sought to make our panels, which make recommendations on the various activities of the Endowment, more responsive to the fields they serve. We have been criticized by the report that Senator Pell referred to a little while ago, but we have made a very great effort to avoid any such thing, and 56 percent of those who serve . . . on our panels . . . are new members this year.[15]

The panel issue emerged again in 1985 in a sharp attack by Representative Steve Bartlett (R-TX) on "cronyism" among panel members, NEA staff, and grantees. He noted an "imbalance" in the makeup of the panels in philosophy, geography, and aesthetic judgement, among other things. Furthermore, several allegations of conflict of interest among NEA panel members led the subcommittee chairman, Representative Williams, to respond, "I want to say for the record that in the normal course of our reauthorization we, of course, were concerned to review this matter even before it became public today. We determined that cronyism could not be demonstrated."[16] Chairman Frank Hodsoll reaffirmed the centrality of "representative" panels for grant decision making.[17] Nonetheless, the 1985 reauthorization asked for a full report from both the NEA (and the NEH) on panel operations. The NEA complied and forwarded a report in 1987 that detailed panelist selection, panel operations, and possible conflicts-of-interest.

Panels have been the administrative bedrock on which the NEA has rested. These advisory bodies were meant to insure that the NEA would not use its grant-making process as a cultural pork barrel or as an opportunity for artistic logrolling. The criterion for a grant was to be artistic merit, not political expediency. Moreover, given the sensitivity over the issue of artistic freedom and the political controversies associated with the Works Progress Administration (WPA) arts projects of the 1930s, advisory panels were supposed to ensure a high degree of independence from political and bureaucratic interference. Instead of an "official culture," with a national ministry of the arts imposing aesthetic preferences, panels were designed to foster pluralism in grant awards.

Panels, in sum, have been seen as making two contributions to the NEA's performance. As a symbolic commitment to the principle that government support for the arts was not "politics as usual," panels composed of members of the arts world would legitimize grant decisions by evaluating proposals and offering recommendations about their artistic merit. Historically, panels have also served as an important administrative buffer in shielding the NEA from untoward political pressures.[18] Diverse panels are more likely to provide such protection than are unrepresentative ones. The NEA, however, has never clearly articulated what dimensions of diversity were relevant or legitimate. It should also be noted that the NEA's panel system has never been completely insulated from arts politics and has not acted in isolation from political norms as witnessed by the early introduction of geographic representativeness in panelist selection.

Is the Geographic Distribution of Grants Equitable?

The question of what constitutes a desirable formula for the allocation of grants also emerged frequently as a divisive issue in the NEA reauthorization hearings. In 1970, Representative Ogden Reid (R-NY) asked Chairman Nancy Hanks and Deputy Chairman Michael Straight the following question (which seems to have elicited a prepared response):

> MR. REID: Do you have any material showing the grants across the United States, how they have been given or chosen in distribution?
> MISS HANKS: I am glad you asked. This is our visual aid...
> MR. STRAIGHT: We have one chart for each program, Mr. Chairman. The wide distribution of dots on these charts is intended to indicate that, in fact, the distribution of the program follows quite closely the population of the United States.[19]

In 1973, Representative Albert Quie (R-MN) quizzed Chairman Hanks about why so many of the little dots on her program charts were concentrated in the Northeast.[20] In the 1976 reauthorization process, the issue of "proper" geographic distribution in grant allocations focussed on the imbalance alleged to exist in grant receipts between New York and the rest of the nation. As economist Dick Netzer put it, "In congressional committee hearings on NEA authorizations and appropriations, the Endowment's area of greatest vulnerability is its support of established artistic institutions and of activities concentrated in New York."[21] Representative William Lehman (D-FL), for example, described his district as a "have-not cultural area" and asked what the NEA was doing to promote greater cultural diversification.[22]

During the 1980 hearings, an unsuccessful effort was made to earmark NEA funds to establish and maintain municipal arts programs. Criticisms by Representative Mario Biaggi (R-NY) stated that the greatest cultural institutions of his city were being shortchanged for reasons of "political necessity and geographical distribution," causing Subcommittee Chairman Ford to retort that localities are being shortchanged "because New York is so big and draws so much weight."[23]

Neither Hanks nor Biddle needed to be reminded that members of Congress are more supportive of funding programs that they know have an impact, however modest, in their districts. Chairman Hanks reaffirmed the NEA's commitment to make the arts more available; in the reauthorization of 1976, she pointed out that approximately half of the NEA's spending was to promote the greater availability of the arts, particularly "where there are geographic or economic barriers to access as mandated in 1973."[24] Congress had also mandated in 1973 that 20 percent of NEA funds be allocated to state arts agencies to institutionalize geographic dispersion. (This allocation was raised to 35 percent in 1990.)

Chairman Biddle also defended the policy of including geographic distribution among the criteria for grant making as recognition of the tremendous growth of the arts outside traditional areas.

> In the beginning of this program, when it first started out, the arts were primarily concentrated in New York City, in the middle of the country, and the Far West. Now, so much of the activity is on a broader base. It is all across the country. I think we have to recognize that the arts are growing at a dramatic rate, not only in the traditional roots but all across the Nation. We have to take this into consideration in our funding.[25]

Economist Dick Netzer argues that inevitably "the political price of large-scale federal support of the arts in the United States would be an overriding emphasis on wider availability."[26] Game theorist Douglas Arnold has demonstrated that building successful coalitions in the House of Representatives for allocating benefits depends upon geographic distribution.[27] Overall, the political realities of congressional support added to the case for equalizing access and promoting cultural egalitarianism suggest that public culture has an important public mission. In fact, the NEA has strongly supported the nation's major cultural organizations -- and has been criticized for this -- both through regular project grants and through challenge grants that are essentially general support funds -- in effect, subsidies that run counter to the NEA's general policy of not underwriting operating costs.[28] The debate is essentially over whether NEA grants should be awarded on the basis of artistic excellence alone, as defined by the professional arts world, or whether NEA grants should seek to develop the social and political values of cultural democratization, greater access by people of different cultures, ethnicities, and greater accessibility in all geographic locations.

In sum, the question has been perceived as a choice between a metropolitan or community emphasis. Should public funds be used to subsidize cultural institutions with a national orientation or those with a more localized appeal? The metropolitan emphasis is popular with established cultural institutions and organized art groups. The localistic emphasis is popular with grass-roots cultural groups and their congressional representatives. There is also a question of multiculturalism involving the claims of a dominant culture and a plurality of cultures. What remains unanswered is what are the best cultural policy objectives for a national public arts agency. This would require specifying the relationship between the social and aesthetic goals of arts policy.[29] It would also require a determination of whether the proper standard of judgment in public culture is artistic professionalism or political accountability or a combination.

Who Should Receive Public Support?

Inherent in any public policy undertaking is the question of who is to be the recipient of funding and what form that funding will take. With specific reference to government support for the arts, the funding issue has posed the following: should the beneficiary be the individual artist or an arts institution; if an arts institution, is it to be a private-not-for-profit or state and local arts agencies; should any institutional assistance support general operating costs or provide specific project assistance? Clearly, the funding policies of the NEA need not necessarily be all one way or the other; indeed, they have not been so.

This issue of the type of grantee and the form of the support has surfaced periodically during the reauthorization hearings. In 1970, the NEA was questioned about the percentage of grants -- then between 6 and 7 percent -- to individual artists ("with exceptional talent," as added to the authorizing legislation in 1968) and about why the performing arts were generally favored over the visual arts.[30] Similarly, the proposal for an Institute of Museum Services (IMS) engendered considerable debate (like that concerning the American Film Institute) over whether this program violated a prohibition against subsidizing the operating costs of cultural institutions. It was feared the IMS might create a precedent leading to the "fragmentation" of the NEA and the "line itemization" of the cultural budget.[31]

These questions about the intended recipients of NEA grants are not unimportant in shaping a public culture. They are, however, distinctly subordinated questions in shaping American arts policy. It has been essentially resolved that the NEA's resources would be spent in making program grants rather than subsidizing institutional expenses or directly providing cultural services. According to Nancy Hanks, the policy of the National Council on the Arts "is basically not support for bricks and mortar except under exceptional circumstances. . . . In other words, it is my interpretation of congressional feeling that the priorities be set in programming for the arts rather than building facilities."[32]

As a limited partner in cultural enterprises, the NEA sought to avoid the political consequences of direct responsibility for specific cultural products, as had been the case with certain controversial WPA programs. The NEA decided to be cautious and to guard its bureaucratic credibility. Institutions, with their financial resources and strong community ties, have been judged to be safer than individuals. Arts organizations, such as orchestras and museums, are strong institutional allies and represent a stable long-term investment for the NEA.

Individual artists, by contrast, can be troublesome and unpredictable for a public arts agency dependent upon the sufferance of the electorate and its representatives because inevitably the agency becomes involved both with the expressive process and the aesthetic outcome. (By contrast, the NEA's authorization prohibits it from exercising any direction or control over the operations of an organizational grantee.) Moreover, the NEA has had several bad experiences of political fallout from grants that proved controversial. Visual arts fellowships have created problems because of the often esoteric or confrontational nature of the works.[33] Michael Straight advised abolishing the fellowship program to eliminate possible battles between artists and taxpayers, with the NEA caught in the middle: "For as long as the Endowment attempts to take predominant financial responsibility for work which seems offensive, frivolous, or simply incomprehensible to the majority of Americans, it is largely vulnerable to criticism."[34] On the other hand, the NEA's wariness in funding individuals (unless of "exceptional" talent) has arguably caused it to forego opportunities for supporting artist-training and arts-development programs.

What is the Government's Responsibility to Promote Good Art?

In one way or another, criticism has been endemic of many aspects of the NEA's administration of culture as well as the aesthetics, and content of the culture supported. Indeed, these criticisms have emerged in some form in every reauthorization, providing sensational incidents of clashes over cultural values. In the first reauthorization hearings in 1968, a flap developed over an NEA grant to study comic strips. As Representative Frank Thompson observed,

> One of our colleagues on the House side chose to make that the major thrust of an effort to kill not only the appropriation in its entirety but indeed to kill the principles of this legislation. . . . I would expect continued attacks, particularly where grants are made to persons whose political views do not conform to those of the majority.[35]

Representative Thompson might also have noted that the artists most likely to be attacked were those whose aesthetic views did not conform to those of the legislative majority.

Much of this activism was of a relatively benign nature, such as Senator Pell's "perennial question" about the stylistic mix for the visual arts. These questions gave the NEA's founding father and legislative protector the opportunity to stress the greater value of representational art for the reasons of both aesthetic superiority and greater popular comprehensibility.[36] The following exchanges in 1970 provide insights into Senator Pell's aesthetic values and NEA's efforts to accommodate them.

> SENATOR PELL: Another question here with regard to the kind of grants. I think most people in the United States like -- maybe it is in poor taste, but they do like paintings that they can understand and comprehend. There is a great tendency, I think, to turn up one's nose at what might be called Saturday Evening Post art, but many people do enjoy it.
> I was disturbed several years ago to learn that of the individual grants made by the Endowment, out of the sixty grants in painting, forty-eight were made to so-called abstract artists while the other twelve went to representational comprehendible artists.
> What would you say the present ratio is?...
> MISS HANKS: You will have to ask Mr. O'Doherty.
> MR. O'DOHERTY: I am program director for visual arts...The overall figure is 119 grants, including painting and sculpture.... With respect to your question, how many realistic, and how many are not...I can identify half a dozen that are frankly realistic, and then I can identify about thirty or forty in which recognizable elements appear. [Laughter]
> I think that the others fall into the category of what is described as abstract painting....
> SENATOR PELL: Right, this is to my mind an improvement. The ratio instead of being 5 to 1 is now about 4 to 1. But I still believe that it is a little more in balance, so that painters of recognizable form, which would have included I guess, Michelangelo and Leonardo, would have had the same chance of receiving a grant as would others, and I would just make a point that I will continue to press in this direction, as the original sponsor of the legislation....[37]

Senator Pell again asked in 1973 what he described as his "perennial question" on the breakdown of grants to painters and sculptors who were representational or non-representational. Brian O'Doherty gave what was described as a "masterful" response:

> "We happen to have some notes on ------------------------that here, Senator. The sixty-five awards given in the past three years can be broken down in terms of realism and nonrealistic or abstract modes of painting and making sculpture in a number of ways...." twelve grants were of the 'frankly realistic' school, in which there is 'no

doubt' of what is being seen; fourteen grants to 'recognizable subject matter', with ten grants to modifications of fantasy and four to 'metaphorical', 'elusive', and 'very indirect' interpretations; and nine grants to subject matter from everyday life -- rapes, street salvage, and the like.[38]

In 1985, Senator Pell again quizzed Chairman Frank Hodsoll on this issue.

SENATOR PELL: I would be interested, too, in your view as to why more public money has usually gone for abstract, avant garde art, which is really not understood by the majority of the general public. . . .
MR. HODSOLL: In the 1970's, I do not think there was any question that the abstract aspects of arts were the most heavily represented. . . . There has been a change in the last several years toward more representational kinds of art....
SENATOR PELL: So roughly, the percentage would be...
MR. HODSOLL: Over half is now representational in terms of the latest figures I have.
SENATOR PELL: Well, that is a very real step in the correct direction, particularly in view of the fact that-I do not recall a poll ever taken -- 90 percent of our people prefer representational art. It would be a very interesting thought if you could have the funds to get some king of public poll on this matter, and we would know if my theories are correct or if they are incorrect.[39]

The 1985 attacks of Representative Bartlett and his allies from the Texas delegation represented a less than benign effort to create content-sensitive standards for NEA-sponsored grants. Much of the criticism was related to the recurrent issue of peer review. The process was seen as one in which grants were evaluated by a "closed circle" of panelists and were awarded to projects of dubious cultural value, generating derisive publicity unrelated to the principle of artistic excellence. Clearly, the grant for tape recording sound from beneath the Brooklyn Bridge, which Representative Bartlett singled out, did not measure up to the Congressman's aesthetic standards.

How does your peer review system operate in a way that ends up funding the tape recording of noise from under the Brooklyn Bridge, or the picture of the woman kissing the dog, and other things that make the newspapers? Are there ways that this committee could improve it, to have more of a 100-percent commitment to excellence in art?[40]

Even more threatening were the Congressman's attacks on the NEA for supporting pornographic, subversive, and generally "offensive" art and a proposal to establish a panel that would screen out any grants awarded to art "potentially offensive to the average person." Chairman Hodsoll agreed that the NEA should not fund pornography. "The issue is, What is pornography? And that, I would strongly urge, should be decided at the community level."[41]

> MR. HODSOLL: I don't see any way...for a federal panel...expert in the arts, not expert in the community standards but experts in artistic excellence, to make determinations for the entire nation as to what is acceptable, or what is not going to be patently offensive, or some other formulation.[42]

Here in the form of an attack on pornography was the threat of official censorship that so worried the early advocates of government support for the arts. While the NEA weathered this storm in 1985 without much political damage, the events associated with the Mapplethorpe affair a few years later would demonstrate the dangers involved with seeming to give offense to congressional standards of artistic appropriateness.

Should Public Arts Policy Be Populist or Elitist?

In a nation professing egalitarian political values with no history of deference to the claims of a superior cultural tradition, public arts programs were bound to be the subject of controversy. In nations with a commonly-accepted artistic heritage, cultural politics may not experience the deep fissures that have characterized government support for the arts in the United States.[43] American arts policy-making has revealed a sharp cleavage between populist and elitist conceptions of public culture. For the elitist, the arts have an intrinsic worth that merits support independent of their social value; this support is also expected to be given without conditions in order to protect the integrity and independence of artistic expression. For the populist, the arts have an aesthetic and social value as the manifestation for artistic excellence and innovation is to be balanced against the claims of cultural preservation, enhanced access for different social groups and geographic areas, and the dissemination and promotion of the arts among the culturally underserved.

NEA reauthorization hearings, in 1975 and 1979 in particular, engaged the elitism/populism debate. Senator Pell in 1975 sharply rebuked the chairman of the National Endowment for the Humanities, Ronald Berman, for failing to develop "diversified, popularly supported constructive programs at a grass-roots level."[44] Although the NEA was not included in the criticism, the populist expectation (at least of Senator Pell) should have been lost on no one. Similarly, Senator Pell in 1979 made it clear that there was to be no privileged circle of NEA program directors, arts organization officers, and favored artists. Chairman Biddle quickly assured him that he had sought to make the NEA more responsive to its various constituencies.[45]

Public arts policy has sought to accommodate both of these ideological positions, although not always with complete success. Essentially, the NEA has sought a "balanced" cultural policy -- both maintaining the major urban cultural institutions (largely those in New York) and assisting community artistic development; both supporting excellent artistic production and promoting public awareness and accessibility. This political strategy has not been without a cost. In accepting Caesar's embrace, the muses have become publicly dependent and accountable. The value of the arts has to be justified to the taxpayers, for example, by demonstrating the beneficial impact of the arts on the local economy.[46] The "hand" doing the "feeding" requires assurances that the benefits are needed and widely appreciated. For some, this obligation constitutes politicization of the arts; for others, it is a cost of doing public business.[47] Historically, this political strategy has been an important ingredient in the NEA's bureaucratic success.

What is the Record of the Arts Agency?

How good a job has the NEA done of enhancing the nation's cultural life? An answer to that question can be difficult because there are no commonly agreed-upon gauges of performance. From the preponderance of testimony in the reauthorization hearings, however, public culture was judged to be an unqualified success during its first twenty years for three reasons.

First, the NEA had as its chairman an administrative advocate like Nancy Hanks. Less concerned about the fate of high culture (or what Senator Pell would deride as "mandarin culture"), Hanks, in classic advocacy fashion, built a public arts agency supporting a wide range of artistic activities and having broad political support from the arts community and the culturally-conscious citizenry.

Second, Senator Pell never had to admonish the NEA, as the NEH was admonished, to spread its grants more widely beyond academia -- both quantitatively and qualitatively.[48] Under Chairman Hanks, half of NEA funds went to increasing the availability of the arts.[49]

Third, unlike the NEH, under which state councils were slow to come into being, and whose directors were politically uninvolved,[50] the NEA had fostered a nationwide network of state arts agencies to contribute political support to its programs.[51] In Representative Brademas's judgment, "These state arts councils represent one of the most imaginative and successful components of federal support for the arts..."[52]

The 1976 hearings contained a series of exchanges about the need for grass-roots programming and local networking and for greater diversification in NEA programs to assist in the development of "have-not" cultural areas. In Senator Pell's judgement, "...the state arts programs, supported by the Endowment, have greatly strengthened our national understanding and appreciation of the values and meaning of the arts."[53]

The Senator was particularly disturbed by the lack of "balanced progress" between the two "cultural twins," especially with the NEH's failure to develop humanities councils in the states in a structure similar to that of the NEA. This criticism echoed the themes of the 1970 hearings, stressing the importance of geographically dispersed grants to foster public awareness of the arts and the role state arts councils play in ensuring that cultural programs operate in a "socially tolerant" manner. State arts councils were cited for relating to the cultural needs of the economically deprived in the cities and, perhaps most important, to the geographically deprived living in rural areas.[54]

In the 1980 hearings, on the other hand, Senator Pell and the NEA were on the defensive, having to respond to the Appropriations Committee's charges of relying on a "closed circle of panelists." Panel representation had long been an awkward issue whether discussion focussed on geography, race, occupation, accomplishments, or the aesthetic preferences of the panelists. Yet, the panels survived as a mechanism for evaluating a growing number of applications involving the politics of taste if only for the lack of an acceptable alternative. The panel imprimatur was also supposed to provide the NEA some latitude in making potentially "offensive" grants. By 1990, however, the panels had ceased to provide political insulation and had become lightning rods during a full-scale storm over public culture's content and mode of administration.

One great success story emerging from these hearings is the partnership forged by the NEA with the "little NEAs" in the states and localities. The mutually beneficial nature of this relationship -- politically and administratively was cited repeatedly; so, too, was the value of the state programs in spreading the benefits of the arts to diverse constituents.

Fostering the growth of state arts agencies may have been the NEA's most important achievement. This movement gave the arts a strong local visibility and elicited the ongoing commitment of state governments. The state arts agencies have also benefited (if unwittingly) from the troubles of the NEA when Congress increased the basic state grant from 20 percent to roughly 35 percent of the Agency's budget in 1990.

The events leading up to the 1990 reauthorization hearings saw much of what had been praise for the NEA turn into condemnation. What had been a celebratory record of support for artistic excellence was criticized as too avant-garde if not pornographic. Despite the NEA's efforts at geographic dispersion, grant allocations were labeled elitist and biased toward metropolitan culture. Where the Arts Endowment had been judged the premier culture agency, the Humanities Endowment was now found superior for having avoided cultural confrontation and political controversy. While the NEA had consciously chosen to largely support cultural institutions, a few performance-artist grants threatened to undermine the foundations of public support for the arts. Above all, the legitimacy and efficacy of the panel system for reviewing and recommending grants was severely compromised. An advisory process that had been designed to insulate the administration of public culture from political interference became the symbol for many critics of what was wrong with the NEA as a public agency.

Concluding Observations

As budgetary scholar Allen Schick sees it, periodic reauthorizations are sought by legislative committees for two distinct reasons. "One is to enhance Congressional oversight and control of executive agencies; the other is to enable the committee to serve as advocate for favored programs."[55] The House Select Education and Postsecondary Education Subcommittees and the Senate Subcommittee on Education, Arts, and Humanities are almost unabashedly advocacy committees. This is not to say that the subcommittees have not been critical or that significant administrative changes have not been realized. The record of the NEA reauthorization hearings contains many examples that would testify to this. Still, these committees are almost synonymous with the legislators (Pell and Brademas) who made reputations for themselves as champions of public support for the arts.

Some question the utility of any legislative committees spending "time reviewing the behavior of agencies and programs that they are almost surely not going to question seriously, given their commitment to them."[56]

Congressional scholar Roger Davidson, among others, has argued that the most effective oversight comes during the yearly review of the appropriations committees, "precisely because it is addressed to specific problems where the committee has to say 'up' or 'down' on specific sums of money."[57] The concrete proposals of appropriations require closer attention to specific problems than is required of the authorizing committees. When one considers, however, the basic unanswered questions facing public culture, it is clear that these are not highly specific, but are rather broad issues of arts policy-making. The cultural subcommittee should be commended because their hearings have searched for answers to the following questions:

- Does the panel system work as effectively as it might for guaranteeing informed and fair recommendations?
- Which criterion should apply in grant-making -- artistic excellence or geographic distribution (or, put another way, cultural consolidation or cultural development)?
- What are the proper emphases in funding in the arts: institutions or individuals, the performing or fine arts, project or operating support?
- To what extent is the government responsible for defining "good" art (for example, should the NEA support arts whose content is "inoffensive" and whose style is "popular" with the public at large)?
- What is the appropriate balance in public support between the "high" culture of established arts organizations that preserve and maintain the classical European heritage and more popular culture of emerging arts organizations with avant-garde and experimental artistic expressions?
- How should public culture be administered in terms of available funding, organizational structure, and degree of direct responsibility for the nation's cultural condition?

These questions arose in various guises during the first twenty years of hearings with no clear resolution. All were unresolved in the lengthy debate over the 1990 reauthorization. Throughout this period, the effort has been concentrated on reconciling many contradictory positions which might be termed a "cultural latitudinarianism" that has sought to accommodate the variety of doctrinal formulations about what should best characterize public culture. Unfortunately, the effort to construct such a broad-church cultural policy may have only papered over deep fissures about the role of the arts in American society and the public's responsibility, if any, for the diverse activities that make up American culture. It seems there has been a policy of cultural pluralism -- if only by default. Whether this pluralism is adequate to meet the needs of public culture itself will necessarily be a matter for continued debate in future reauthorizations.

Perhaps the greatest value of the reauthorization hearings has been as a forum for debating the nature of public arts policy. As is so often observed, although the dollar amount in support of the arts is low in relation to other parts of the budget, the level of controversy is often extremely high. At root, this may be because the purposes and programs for public culture are not clear-cut. The NEA's advocates and adversaries have articulated beliefs about what should, and should not, constitute a national arts policy. Most public policies are controversial. Some, however -- such as foreign affairs, national defense and, to a lesser degree, arts policy -- seem to elicit more intense value clashes. This cannot be the occasion for analyzing the ideological divisions that run through arts policy-making.[58] However, it must be clear that these disputes emerge in the hearings as voiced by committee members, NEA officials and the various witnesses from the arts community. The nature of a legislative hearing facilitates these kind of exchanges, allowing for some measure of public accountability in making and administering policy. The NEA reauthorization hearings are admittedly a rough approximation of comprehensive systematic oversight. Nevertheless, the review of the NEA's programs and the exchanges recorded about their desirability represent a significant forum for assessing the political standing of public culture.

Notes

1. For the original hearings, see *National Arts and Humanities Foundation*, Joint Hearings before the Special Subcommittee on Arts and Humanities of the Committee on Labor and Public Welfare, United States Senate, and the Special Subcommittee on Labor of the Committee on Education and Labor, United States House, 89th Cong., 1st sess., 1965, parts 1 and 2. For an administrative history of the NEA's early years, see Fannie Taylor and Anthony Barresi, *The Arts at the New Frontier* (New York: Plenum Press, 1984).

2. Lance T. Leloup, *Budgetary Politics: Dollars, Deficits, Decisions* (Brunswick, OH: King's Court Communications, Inc., 1977), p. 152.

3. Louis Fisher, "The Authorization/Appropriation Process in Congress: Formal Rules and Informal Practices," *Catholic University Law Review*, 29 (1979), p. 52.

4. Allen Schick, *Congress and Money* (Washington, DC: The Urban Institute, 1980), p. 152.

5. Lance T. LeLoup, *The Fiscal Congress: Legislative Control of the Budget* (Westport, CT: Greenwood Press, 1980), pp. 113-15.

6. *Ibid.*, 113.

7. Schick, *Congress and money*, p. 175.

8. Randall B. Ripley, *Congress: Process and Policy* (New York: W. W. Norton, 1983), p. 178; see also Roger H. Davidson, "Subcommittee Government: New Channels for Policy-Making," in Thomas E. Mann and Norman J. Ornstein, eds., *The New Congress* (Washington, DC: The American Enterprise Institute, 1981), chapter 4.

9. Mary Weaver, "The Politics of Congressional Arts Policy," in Margaret J. Wyszomirski, ed., *Congress and the Arts* (New York: American Council on the Arts, 1988), pp. 47-50.

10. Ralph K. Huitt, "The Congressional Committee: A Case Study," in Ralph K. Huitt and Robert L. Peabody, eds., *Congress: Two Decades of Analysis* (New York: Harper and Row, 1969), p. 95.

11. See Gary O. Larson, *The Reluctant Patron: The United States Government and the Arts, 1943-1965* (Philadelphia: University of Pennsylvania Press, 1983), pp. 181-218.

12. *Arts and Humanities Amendments of 1967*, Hearings before the Special Subcommittee on Arts and Humanities of the Committee on Labor and Public Welfare, United States Senate, 90th Cong., 1st sess., pt. 2, hearings of August 15 and 16, 1967, 365. Cited hereafter as *1967 Senate Subcommittee Hearings*; see also M. Straight, *Twigs for an Eagle's Nest* (New York: Devon Press, 1979), p. 79.

13. *Arts, Humanities, and Museum Services Act of 1979*, Hearings before the Subcommittee on Education, Arts, and Humanities of the Committee on Labor and Human Resources, United States Senate, 96th Cong., 1st sess., hearings of June 26, 27, and 29, 1979, 2. Cited hereafter as *1979 Senate Subcommittee Hearings*; see also *Report on the National Endowment for the Arts and Humanities*, Committee on Appropriations, United States House, 96th Cong., 1st sess., vol. 1, 865-1041.

14. *Ibid.*, 22, 59-60.

15. *Ibid.*

16. *Reauthorization of Foundation on the Arts and the Humanities Act of 1985*, Joint Hearings before the Subcommittee on Postsecondary Education of the Committee on Education and Labor, United States House, 99th Cong., 1st sess., Hearings held in Washington, DC, May 2, June 19, and September 10; New York, NY, June 3; and Philadelphia, PA, July 22, 1985, 573-74, 597. Cited hereafter as *1985 House Joint Subcommittee Hearings*.

17. *National Foundation on the Arts and Humanities Amendments of 1985*, Hearings before the Subcommittee on Education, Arts, and Humanities of the Committee on Labor and Human Resources, United States Senate, 99th Cong., 1st sess., hearings of June 19 and 20, 1985, 15-16. Cited hereafter as *1985 Senate Subcommittee Hearings*.

18. Kevin V. Mulcahy, "The NEA as Public Patron of the Arts," in Judith H. Balfe and Margaret J. Wyszomirski, eds., *Art, Ideology, and Politics* (New York: Praeger, 1985), pp. 318-22.

19. *Amendments to the National Foundation on the Arts and Humanities Act of 1970*, Joint Hearings before the Select Subcommittee on Education of the Committee on Education and Labor, United States House, and the Special

Subcommittee on Arts and Humanities of the Committee on Labor and Public Welfare, United States Senate, 91st Cong., 2d sess., hearings of January 26, 28, February 3, 1970, 148. Cited hereafter as *1970 Joint Hearings*.

20. *National Foundation on the Arts and the Humanities Amendments of 1973*, Joint Hearings before the Special Subcommittee on the Arts and Humanities of the Committee on Labor and Public Welfare, United States Senate, and the Select Subcommittee on Education of the Committee on Education and Labor, United States House, 93rd Cong., 1st sess., pt. 1, hearings of March 6, 7, and 8, 1973, 89. Cited hereafter as *1970 Joint Hearings*.

21. Dick Netzer, *The Subsidized Muse: Public Support for the Arts in the United States* (New York: Cambridge University Press, 1978), p. 73.

22. *Arts, Humanities, and Cultural Affairs Act of 1975*, Joint Hearings before the Subcommittee on Select Education of the Committee on Education and Labor, United States House, and the Special Subcommittee on Arts and Humanities of the Committee on Labor and Public Welfare, United States Senate, 94th Cong., 1st sess., hearings of November 12, 13, and 14, 1975, 33-35. Cited hereafter as *1975 Joint Hearings*.

23. *Reauthorization of the National Foundation for the Arts and the Humanities Act and the Museum Services Act*, Hearings before the Subcommittee on Postsecondary Education of the Committee on Education and Labor, United States House, 96th Cong., 2d sess., hearings of February 6, 21, March 5, and April 2, 1980, pp. 319-22. Cited hereafter as *1980 House Subcommittee Hearings*.

24. *1975 Joint Hearings*, p. 53; Straight, *Twigs for an eagle's nest*, p. 79.

25. *1980 House Subcommittee Hearings*, p. 322.

26. Netzer, *Subsidized Muse*, p. 73. Percentages calculated from the dollar amounts in tables 4-7.

27. R.Douglas Arnold, *Congress and the Bureaucracy: A Theory of Influence* (New Haven: Yale University Press, 1979).

28. Netzer, *Subsidized Muse*, pp. 63, 246.

29. Mulcahy, "NEA as Public Patron," p. 330.

30. *1970 Joint Hearings*, pp. 130, 189.

31. *Ibid.*, p. 89; see also *National Foundation on the Arts and Humanities*, Hearings before the Subcommittee on Select Education of the Committee on Education and Labor, United States House, 94th Cong., 1st sess., hearings held in Washington, DC, September 24, 25, 26, and October 31; Fort Worth, TX, September 27; Brooklyn, NY, November 8; and New York, NY, November 10, 1975, 223. Cited hereafter as *1975 House Subcommittee Hearings*.

32. *1975 Joint Hearings*, p. 28.

33. Straight, *Twigs for an Eagle's Nest*, p. 28.

34. *Ibid.*, p. 171.

35. *Arts and Humanities Amendments of 1967*, Joint Hearings before the Special Subcommittee on Arts and Humanities of the Committee on Labor and Public Welfare, United States Senate, and the Special Subcommittee on Labor of the Committee on Education and Labor, United States House, 90th Cong., 1st sess., pt. 1, hearings of July 12 and 13, 1967, p. 97. Cited hereafter as *1967 Joint Hearings*.

36. See, for example, the "perennial question" in *1970 Joint Hearings*, 136-38; *1973 Joint Hearings*, 190-91; and *1985 Senate Subcommittee Hearings*, pp. 55-56, 58.

37. *1970 Joint Hearings*, pp. 136-38.

38. *1973 Joint Hearings*, p. 190. The "masterful response" description is by Taylor and Barresi, *Arts at a New Frontier*, p. 167.

39. *1985 Senate Subcommittee Hearings*, pp. 55-56, 58.

40. *1985 House Joint Subcommittee Hearings*, p. 26.

41. *Ibid.*, p. 605.

42. *Ibid.*, p. 552.

43. See Milton C. Cummings and Richard S. Katz, *The Patron State: Government and the Arts in Western Europe, North America, and Japan* (New York: Oxford University Press, 1987).

44. *1975 Joint Hearings*, p. 124.

45. *1979 Senate Subcommittee Hearings*, p. 21.

46. See Kevin V. Mulcahy, "The Arts and Their Economic Impact: The Values of Utility," *The Journal of Arts Management and Law*, 16 (1986), pp. 33-48.

47. See Margaret J. Wyszomirski, "Controversies in Arts and Policy-making," in Kevin V. Mulcahy and C. Richard Swaim, eds., *Public Policy and the Arts* (Boulder, CO: Westview Press, 1981), pp. 11-31.

48. *1975 Joint Hearings*, p. 205.

49. *Ibid.*, p. 53.

50. *Ibid.*, p. 124.

51. *1970 Joint Hearings*, p. 197.

52. *Ibid.*, p. 198.

53. *1975 Joint Hearings*, p. 13.

54. *1970 Joint Hearings*, p. 264.

55. Schick, *Congress and Money*, p. 173.

56. Lawrence C. Dodd and Richard L. Schott, *Congress and the Administrative State* (New York: John Wiley and Sons, 1979), pp. 239-40.

57. Quoted in Morris S. Ogul, *Congress Oversees the Bureaucracy* (Pittsburg: University of Pittsburg Press, 1976), p. 180.

58. For a discussion of these divisions from different perspectives, see Edward Banfield, *The Democratic Muse: Visual Arts and the Public Interest* (New York: Basic Books, 1984) and Kevin V. Mulcahy, "Ideology and Public Culture," *Journal of Aesthetic Education 16* (Summer 1982), pp. 11-24.

8

The Process of Commissioning Public Sculpture: "Due" or "Duel"

Judith Huggins Balfe

American towns and cities have long been studded with public art -- most of which is commemorative statuary honoring the heroic dead, or an historic event, or personifying some abstract ideal such as "Truth." Typically, the subject and purpose of the commissioned work has been as much a matter of prior public agreement as has been the intended style of its execution. Artists were favored if -- and because -- they could express the common will and taste. In those cases where controversy has erupted -- e.g. over a statue of George Washington clad in a toga or an expressionistic portrait of John F. Kennedy -- the dispute has focused on the style, rather than the subject of the commission itself or on the artist who carried it out. Otherwise, art commissions, like art patronage generally, have been considered to be a private matter between individuals: the state's role was as mediator to preserve the public peace.

In recent years, however, as government arts programs have become more extensive, not only have they supported established (hence traditional) art forms and institutions but increasingly they have funded the creation of new works, with increasing public acceptance of this role.[1] Frank Hodsoll, when he was NEA Chairman in 1988, stated the Endowment's rationale for taking the attendant risks:

> Though the vast amount of our money still goes toward supporting traditional areas of the arts, we have increased our spending in the experimental area...we have an obligation similar to the National Science Foundation in assisting experimental work. For out of that work will come the art that is seen as traditional 50 years from now.[2]

Yet questions remain concerning how such assistance is to be provided, and for which "experimental" works. Any new work is an experiment: even if created by a recognized master, few such works will stand the test of time.

The case for public support for commissioning new works of visual art differs from that for new work in the performing arts. In the latter case, the commissioning agency can fund works in a variety of styles, thereby fostering a pluralistic aesthetic because the works are both inherently reproducible and impermanent. While only one work might be performed at any given time and place, any performance site can be shared on other occasions and the work itself can be performed both again and elsewhere, or never. Thus, the stage is available for other "experiments," however controversial some of them may be.[3]

Public funding of the temporary display of visual artworks whose subject matter some have found offensive has led to demands for "content restrictions" similar to those demanded of certain performance pieces. But even when the work is abstract, with no specific content, controversy can be provoked. This is particularly the case in the public commissioning of sculpture which is unique, often permanent, and intentionally situated in a public forum of limited dimensions, rather than in a voluntarily attended (and sharable) performance site. Accordingly, only a few works can be publicly commissioned for any given space, and once in place, they are difficult to move. Seen from a national, state, or even city-wide perspective, a pluralistic aesthetic may prevail across the totality of commissioned works.[4] However, this pluralism is seldom experienced by those who live or work in the locality in which any single piece is sited.

Furthermore, given the trends of contemporary art (combined with the desire to avoid disputes over potentially offensive content), many of the new commissions will be abstract, in styles still incomprehensible to much of the public. The many stylistic varieties of abstraction seem to afford free reign both to creative expression and to individual interpretation. Yet speaking from and to individual uniqueness, such works inevitably elude easy consensus concerning their purpose and the effectiveness of its realization. Thus, unlike traditional commemorative public art, contemporary visual art commissions are likely to lack public consensus about their style, subject, purpose and expected response. Consequently, such public artworks are likely to prompt public disagreement about their aesthetic merits.

It is not surprising, then, that controversies over public support for the arts in general have been particularly virulent when they focus on sculpture that has been commissioned and thus, newly created for a permanent installation in a particular site. The risks of artistic or social failure are greater, even as the need for success is increased: the total aesthetic effect and public acceptance of the new piece cannot be altogether anticipated prior to its installation. Yet at that point, whoever encounters it must come to terms with its intrusive and permanent presence -- on turf to which each member of the public may have felt prior claim.

As a result, the installation of such pieces of "plop art" have provoked debates over their style and purpose. Such debates tend to question *how* -- with so many important ideas or events for commemoration or public expression, so many different artists and types of creativity worthy of support, so many public sites in need of beautification, so many alternative styles and media which are generally acceptable to wide publics -- *how did that thing get here*?

Such debate is as healthy as it is legitimate in any public art commission, and is not confined to the current period. Public support for artists and their art, during the Depression, aroused controversies which did not cease with the end of the various projects, but have continued to haunt even contemporary commissioners of public art. In oversimplified form, the central problem has always been to achieve a balance between the rights of the contemporary artist and those of the present and future publics -- with the artwork itself and the commissioning agency in the middle. My purpose here is to compare past and current commissioning processes and the resultant artwork, and to consider their respective degrees of success -- political as well as artistic. What can be learned from these precedents?

Public Arts Commissioning During the New Deal

The several public arts programs of the Depression varied in their primary purposes and resultant practices.[5] The Federal Arts Project of the WPA (FAP/WPA) distributed about 90 percent of the total government arts funding during the entire period. Its major purpose was to provide work relief for unemployed artists by paying them for practical projects such as teaching and data collection as well as for producing art. As directed by Holger Cahill, a follower of John Dewey's philosophy that art should be integrated into everyday life, the FAP/WPA involved local advisory committees in the various projects. However, these worked under the

191

guidelines of appointed district supervisors who themselves were directed by state and national FAP/WPA officers. These officials required that low-income artists be hired regardless of the style of their work or their political views. To be sure, while some artistically and/or politically radical work was thus produced and given regional outlets, the majority of such arts production was concentrated in the more sophisticated cities. But even here, it was subject to much criticism from conservative factions who objected vehemently to political avant gardes (and hence to artistic ones) while also opposing any government support for the "frills" of the arts.

In contrast to this "top down" and centralized approach to expanding the reach of the arts was the Section on Fine Arts under the Treasury Department, which in time allocated about 10 percent of the total arts funding. Here the primary rationale was the aesthetic enhancement of public buildings, such as new post offices, through the innovative provision that one percent of construction costs be allocated for art.[6] In the Section, decision-making was altogether delegated to local judging panels. These chose among competing artists without regard to their financial need, and without pressure from sophisticates in Washington. In practice, giving such power to local elites meant that commissions were awarded -- almost without exception -- to stylistically conservative "American scene" painters rather than to the avant garde. With the Section, then, criticism came from the progressives, and focused on issues of artistic control.[7]

In any case, very little public sculpture was created under FAP/WPA programs and none under the Section.[8] Sculpture was largely undeveloped as an independent art in America at the time; its functions were understood by artists as well as the public to be either decorative (in low relief like a mural on a building wall) or commemorative. Thus, many of the artistic challenges posed by recent commissions of public sculpture simply did not arise.

Nonetheless, there was much controversy concerning the structure of the New Deal arts programs, and the resultant processes and consequences. Debates over aesthetic matters were understood by both sides to be grounded in political disagreements between conservatives and liberals. Subject to attack by both sides, when the programs ended with World War II they were remembered as both artistic and political failures, which had resulted in more controversy than benefit to all the parties involved.

Thereafter, in the highly politicized atmosphere during and immediately following the war, the only direct government support for the arts came through cultural exchange programs. Even here, in 1947 when the State

Department bought works by contemporary painters for display in Europe, controversy erupted over the propriety of such public ownership of avant garde works, as well as over the political philosophies of their creators. The works were sold and the program ended: again, the lesson seemed to be that government arts support could succeed only if it could avoid making political and aesthetic decisions![9]

Alternative Contemporary Models: the NEA and GSA

With the revival of governmental programs supporting the arts in the mid-1960's, there was still enormous caution about direct commissioning of new works. Among the original low-budget programs that did give direct support to individual creative artists were the GSA Art-in-Architecture program (AiA), started in 1963 to incorporate fine art into newly designed federal buildings under a formula of one-half of one percent of the allocated construction budget [10] and the NEA Art-in-Public Places program (AiPP), started in 1967 to enhance public places and assist "communities in their efforts to increase public awareness of contemporary art."[11] In different ways, these respective programs built upon the lessons of the New Deal arts programs. They combined the earlier rationales and commissioning procedures in new ways to meet the increased public acceptance of innovative and abstract art, even as they recognized that the views of artworld experts and cognescente were not universal and that there was still widespread public resistance to "modern art." But by insisting that their entire purpose was the aesthetic enrichment of American communities, they hoped to avoid the earlier battles about the use of art to express political views.

Let us consider the NEA's AiPP program. From the beginning the NEA has disclaimed the espousal of either a political or an aesthetic ideology. In order to remain "at arm's length" from such controversies, most NEA arts funding of individual grant proposals channeled through independent, appointed panels of artworld experts. These are deliberately selected with an eye toward diversity in composition and presumably without regard to political persuasion. In addition to making recommendations for the award decisions (the final decisions rest with the Endowment chairman), their collective purpose is ostensibly to protect the NEA from both political and artworld pressures.[12] Procedurally, such pressures are further diluted by the mechanism of the matching grant: the recipient of an NEA grant must still raise the bulk of the funds from local individual, corporation, or foundation supporters. These requirements have generally insulated the NEA from public (hence congressional) criticism. As the granting procedures were successively refined, they helped to dampen the chronic debates over aesthetic standards vs social utility; artistic freedom vs public understanding; elite metropolitan institutions vs grass roots local ones.

In any event, in its AiPP program the NEA has always played only a supportive role.[13] Initiatives for the commission of a particular work for a particular site begin at the local level: a community sponsor -- whether an ad hoc citizens committee, a town council, a private institution like a college -- establishes its own selection procedure and decides on site, artist, and work. The entire project is then presented to the NEA for partial funding. Through the award of a matching grant -- usually for less than one-third of the total proposed cost -- the NEA does provide an often crucial imprimatur of the project's aesthetic value, but otherwise the project must receive widespread acceptance in the community in which it will be housed if it is to match (and thus receive) government funds.[14] In any case, after the commission is completed, the NEA has no further responsibility for the new work or its site: ownership, maintenance, and disposition reside in the original community sponsors.

Here, then, are recombined elements of the different New Deal arts programs. Like the FAP/WPA, there is informed control from the top, in that the NEA grants panels (which determine the funding of different AiPP projects) are composed of national artworld professionals. Yet given their diversity, presumably, pluralistic aesthetic standards are applied, and projects in a "democratic" variety of styles -- both abstract and representational -- have received "official approval" through NEA funding. Like the Section, the original choices are made by local elites, who must be responsive to community taste if they are to raise the bulk of the funds themselves. But today, the artists selected are not necessarily conservative in style or politics, nor even from the state or region. Rather, local elites often want to demonstrate their own sophistication by commissioning nationally and even internationally-known artists. (This means that a small number of top-ranked artists have received several different commissions through the AiPP program.) Indeed, the choice of abstract works, whether by local artists or by artworld "stars," is so frequent that one component of the application for NEA funding of local public art projects is a description of the information and education campaign that is planned "to encourage an informed response to the project in the community."[15] Even if its involvement is "at arms length," the NEA seeks to prevent negative reactions to the artwork for which it has granted public funds.

Certainly this model has been a success. Between 1967 and 1992, AiPP has awarded approximately $12 million in support of more than 600 projects from virtually every state, involving over 900 artists. This example has helped stimulate the establishment of at least 135 state and local funding programs for public art, further decentralizing the process.[16]

GSA's Art-in-Architecture (AiA) was established through administrative order three years before the NEA itself came into being, and it inherently follows a more centralized model, as AiA commissioned works are owned and maintained as federal property. The AiA program is underwritten by percent-for-art funds but otherwise has no direct congressional oversight and funding, just as had been the Treasury Section. Again like the Section, it was plagued from the outset with controversies about the aesthetic quality of its commissions -- to the point that it was suspended altogether in 1966. Reactivated in 1973, its commissioning procedures were revised to draw upon the now-accepted expertise of NEA panels. Subsequently, for each project an NEA-appointed advisory panel nominates three to five artists for the specific site, itself predetermined by prior GSA decisions on construction. Controversy over several AiA commissions in the late-1970's led to a change in the composition of the artist-nominating panels: local government officials now nominate candidates to serve as the representative of the community on the NEA selection panel. Presumably this greater community involvement leads to greater acceptance of the work. In any event, the final choice of artist and artwork to be commissioned resides with the GSA administrator. While this is clearly a "top-down" process of commissioning, it is in accord with those of the federal building projects which provide both funds and sites.

GSA sees its mandate in AiA as the establishment of a geographically dispersed, national collection of works by living American artists.[17] To insure a democratic pluralism of taste, only one work may be commissioned from a single artist, regardless of artworld status. In practice, then, artists with only regional or local reputations may be awarded these federal commissions. However, given the advisory role played by the NEA-appointed panels, it is not surprising that AiPP and AiA "collections" overlap considerably in terms of artists whose work is included, and especially in terms of the abstract styles and media of those works. Like AiPP, AiA mandates an educational program to increase public understanding of the work out of the same recognition that contemporary work is difficult for many to understand regardless of who commissions and installs it.

Unlike AiPP projects which are owned and maintained by their community sponsors, artworks in the AiA program belong solely to the federal government. Even with the recent addition of a community nominee to the artist-selection panel, there is no local buffer between the artist and the commissioning agent, no existing "support group" with any incentive or standing to defend the work at its site. On the other hand, once the commission is decided upon, GSA can protect the artist from local detractors, and provide a federal guarantee of "artistic freedom" which not even local supporters could ensure.

Thus AiA combines elements of the various New Deal arts programs in different ways than does the NEA's AiPP. It is like the Section in funding, but closer to FAP/WPA in its "top-down" commissioning process and its general support for an "art-for-arts-sake" ideology. Lacking community initiative reflecting particular local concerns, AiA commissions can have only aesthetic purposes. Not surprisingly, then, the AiA program receives strong artworld support as a matter of principle. But while AiA allies artists and the commissioning federal agency, it has been a target of criticism from other interests who feel their concerns are not being served, indeed not even acknowledged, by the national government.

"Tilted Arc" and the Vietnam Memorial

Regardless of the commissioning process, most AiA projects have been as enthusiastically welcomed by local audiences as those installed with AiPP support. But when this has not been the case, with no local buffer or means of arbitration, GSA has found itself in the midst of difficult, if not unresolvable, controversies. These can be better understood if we contrast the problems resulting from the absence of community participation in the process of commissioning public art with those resulting from a great deal of public involvement. (NEA's AiPP would fall between these two poles.) Recently and respectively problematic have been Richard Serra's "Tilted Arc," commissioned under AiA and installed in 1981 in the small plaza in front of the Javits Federal Office Building in Foley Square, New York City, and Maya Yang Lin's design for the Vietnam Memorial in Washington, D.C., installed on the Mall in 1984.[18] The resultant controversies have received such publicity that they need not be detailed here. Let us compare their respective commissioning processes, and the ways in which those procedures afforded a response to public outcry against their similarly minimalist aesthetics.

"Tilted Arc" was commissioned according to the original AiA process outlined above, with a rationale of purely aesthetic enrichment. A world-renowned sculptor, Serra was nominated by a panel of three New York arts experts and selected by GSA to create a piece for the specific site of Javits Plaza in 1979, with percent-for-art funding when an addition to the original office building was being constructed. (As the requirement of a community representative on the nominating panel was not yet in place, no such person was involved in the selection process.) Some efforts were made to inform the 10,000 office workers who enter the building daily of the nature of the contracted piece: 120 feet long, 12 feet high, a sloping arc of corten (rusty) steel. But its reality was not clear until its installation in 1981, by which time the Administration in Washington had changed hands. Given the resultant changes in personnel and policies in other government agencies, it was not surprising that GSA's own AiA guidelines were not followed in every particular here, and no specific educational efforts were made to help the public understand "Tilted Arc."

Early complaints were ignored to allow time for such understanding to develop. As dissatisfaction continued to be expressed, in 1984 a newly appointed local GSA Administrator (whose offices were housed in the Javits Building) instigated a removal petition that resulted in a 3-day hearing to consider the issue. The artworld almost unanimously agreed with Serra that his work was site-specific and would be aesthetically "destroyed" if moved. GSA itself was somewhat embarrassed at the evident disagreement among past and present members of its staff; in any case, the office workers in whose interest the removal was supposedly being considered stayed away from the hearing en masse (perhaps intimidated by the expertise of Serra's numerous supporters). Nonetheless, the hearing recommended that "Tilted Arc" be removed, a decision that was accepted by top GSA officials.

Thereupon Serra filed suit against GSA for $30 million in damages for harm to his reputation and career, as well as for violation of his freedom of expression. In August 1987 that suit was denied, and GSA's legal right to remove the piece was upheld.[19] A few months later, a special advisory panel appointed by the NEA to find an alternative site unanimously agreed that the work's artistic integrity would be destroyed if it were to be moved. Meanwhile the only two institutions that had publicly appeared willing to accept it withdrew under the threat of further legal action from Serra. In May 1988, the U.S. Court of Appeals upheld the original decision affirming GSA's right to remove the piece, declaring that due process had been served according to contract and legal precedent, and that none of Serra's rights had been violated. Finally, avoiding any last-minute protesters by having the work done in the middle of the night, GSA had "Tilted Arc" removed in March 1989, eight years after its installation. It now rests in sections in a warehouse in Brooklyn. In retrospect, the furor over "Tilted Arc" may be seen as a precursor of the 1990 controversies that plagued the NEA. Whether or not there is any specific content that may be offensive (clearly, "Tilted Arc" has very little "content"), in both instances the artworld was perceived as arrogant in its disregard for community aesthetic standards.

Despite the apparent "victory" for those publics who detested "Tilted Arc" and the commissioning process which prompted its installation, in the long run this must be seen as a duel resulting in a "lose-lose" stalemate for all concerned. Recognizing that its commissioning process contributed to the difficulties, GSA changed its procedures: since 1985 artists working under its commission must be involved with the architects and community representatives from the beginning of the project to ensure that the work is fully suited to its site, seen both as architecture and as public space. But public input is not necessarily a guarantee against controversy.

For example, in contrast to the simple and purely aesthetic rationale for "Tilted Arc," consider the diverse and conflicting political purposes that determined the process by which the Vietnam Memorial was commissioned. Here the initiatives came totally from the "grass roots," with all funds being raised privately. Following congressional authorization of the Memorial in 1980, the main involvement of the federal government was limited to donation of the site and a guarantee of maintenance. Instead, the privately established Vietnam Veterans Memorial Fund announced a nation-wide competition, with the only limitation put on the design being that the names of all the American war dead were to be included. (NEA's involvement was limited to partial funding of the design competition.) The final decision was made by an independently appointed federal agency, the generally conservative seven-person Fine Arts Commission (established in 1910 to judge the aesthetic merits of proposals for public monuments erected in Washington).

There was a public uproar when, out of more than 1400 entries, the winning design was for twin black granite walls, each 200 feet long and sunk 10 feet into the ground at the apex to form a wide V. Additionally controversial was the fact that its designer, Maya Yang Lin, was an unknown 21 year old female architecture student (who incidentally acknowledged Serra's influence upon her work). As with the disliked minimalism of "Tilted Arc," the abstraction which permits countless individual meanings was here seen as a denial of the war's reality as it had been experienced by the Vietnam veterans most insistent upon public legitimation of their war service, and most involved in raising funds for the commission in the first place. Selection of the design was further attacked on the grounds that neither the Fine Arts Commissioners nor the winning designer had served in Vietnam, so they knew only the "civilian reality" of the war -- however complex that certainly was.

Despite wide support for the design from official Washington and the architectural community, criticism from Vietnam veterans (including organizers of the original Memorial Fund) reached such a pitch that in 1983, the Fine Arts Commission held public hearings to consider its revision even though construction of the Memorial had already begun. The final compromise was to include Frederick E. Hart's realistic bronze statue of three combat soldiers and a pole for the United States flag, installed 100 feet away from the abstract wall so as to complement and not compete with its integrity.[20] The result appears to have been a complete success, with honor and dignity affirmed for both the survivors of the war and those who died -- and also for the two artists who designed the respective parts of the Memorial itself.

Whatever the problems, here is a near total contrast to "Tilted Arc," in both commissioning process and result. At outset, this project was as unique as it was publicly important: it was not the product of institutionalized entities with established interests and procedures designed to serve other ends as well. Nor was it merely an attractive but socially purpose-free adornment of public space. It could not have come into existence without the welcome involvement of many individuals and groups with many conflicting experiences and interests. However they differed, all recognized that aesthetics were here to serve non-aesthetic, political and social ends of overwhelming importance. There was further agreement that this memorial was to be an expression of public feeling rather than a governmental statement. The conflicts and compromises that were inherent in the process of the Memorial's commission and construction became part of the public meaning of the work. As testimony of and for reconciliation, the Vietnam Memorial appears to have achieved the highest purposes of public art -- that it be "revelation as well as inspiration."[21]

Why has the Vietnam Memorial succeeded despite public involvement in its final total design? One intervening variable here may be that of scale: it can be argued that the Vietnam Memorial embodied such political importance that public participation in its commissioning was part of its aesthetic function of social reconciliation. If so, its lessons may not be fully applicable to less politicized art commissions, operating according to traditional assumptions that creativity and connoisseurship are inherently "undemocratic." These norms allow for little public consultation in advance of the commissioning and creation of public art.

However, after several decades of increased arts activity and, indeed, public art patronage, the public may well be less philistine and more understanding of varying aesthetics than artworld professionals would concede. With the Vietnam Memorial, Frederick E. Hart, sculptor of the realistic statue of three soldiers determined its strategic distance from the "the Wall" out of his great respect for its abstract design, and the artistic quality of that statue has accommodated those of conservative taste without offending advocates of abstraction. Indeed, by seeming to "embody" each name inscribed on the polished wall face, it undergirds the aesthetic power of "the Wall"'s minimalism. It has surely contributed to the universal acknowledgement of the Memorial's total affect. In contrast, neither GSA nor Serra himself facilitated any compromise over "Tilted Arc." Perhaps, a realistic bronze statue could also have been installed to establish the "Arc" as a piece of sculpture, rather than the piece of sculpture on a site whose social utility was neither recognized nor enhanced until after the costly "duel" was over.

Indeed, once it is considered that the public might understand very well its own aesthetic (as well as political, economic, and social) interest, other models of commissioning public art can be -- and have been -- developed.

Art in Transit

In 1977, the federal Department of Transportation initiated a policy granting up to two percent of total costs of new or rehabilatory construction for design and art. A year later, guidelines were developed by the Urban Mass Transportation Administration to facilitate use of these funds.

The first group to take advantage of this new opportunity was the Cambridge (MA) Arts Council, capitalizing on a $574 million, 3.2 mile subway extension northwest of Boston and a subsequent 4.7 mile subway relocation project to the southwest, under the Massachusetts Bay Transit Authority. The federal government provided 80 percent of the financing, with the rest coming from state and local funds. The Arts Council developed guidelines for the commissioning and installation of artworks at each of the new stations, some 30 pieces in all. The public had already been much involved in the project: to start with, the Massachusetts electorate had voted to redirect federal highway funds for use in mass transit. Once the MBTA could tap these funds to modernize and extend its lines, representatives of 110 agencies, community groups, and businesses met in over 650 public meetings to consider issues of the environmental, economic, and social impact of several alternative routes for the subway construction. Given this degree of public involvement, no arts project could presume to operate according to AiA precedent, with all decisions made by arts experts in the absence of public participation. As with the Vietnam Memorial, the commissioned artworks needed to serve more than aesthetic purposes: without disrupting mass-transit operations, they are intended to affirm community identities and enhance public participation in what is, after all, its own transit system. Thus mandated education programs focused here on community history rather than on explaining the selected artworks, which have had community acceptance from the outset.

To be sure, initiative for the commissions did not come from the public as it did for the Vietnam Memorial. However, along with MBTA and Arts Council officials, members of the community around each subway station were included on the decision-making site committees from the beginning. This public involvement, as well as the stylistic variety of the resulting commissions, precluded any implication that this was "official" art. The commissioning process evolved further with experience: understandable difficulties in coordination in the first stage of subway construction led to selection of an independent agency, Urbanarts Inc, to serve as administrator, coordinator, and mediator among all involved parties in the second stage. While total project expenses were proportionately lower on a per-station basis, thereby reducing the arts budgets allocated for each station, public input was increased as site committees determined the theme of each commission. In addition, the site committees had a voice in the final decision among several proposals submitted by artists, themselves selected from a national registry of those willing to work under the social and engineering constraints of such projects.[22] Thus, while funding, ownership, and maintenance was based upon the GSA model (in that the MBTA fully owns the works), the process of commissioning and management followed the NEA model of the initiative coming from a local agency. Given the degree of public involvement in that process, the MBTA model also included elements that contributed to the success of the Vietnam Memorial.

The Future of Public Art Commissions

Given its obvious success, the MBTA commissioning process has been adapted and widely used elsewhere. Expertise and experience in the field has developed as well, so that, for example, guidelines for funding, siting, and implementation often allow pooling of resources to fit community needs.[23] Accordingly, it is unlikely that mistakes such as those that characterized the "Tilted Arc" controversy will recur. For one thing, public artists are now more willing to work for community approval, not just for that of the elite artworld. It is now common practice for public artists to work with other professionals on design teams to fully integrate the artworks into the site.[24] Despite these procedural improvements intended to engage public participation to inform the commission, there is no such participation in the prior selection of the artist to be included in the team. Decisions will still be made from the top, by experts.

To be sure, some projects make impractical public involvement such as that for MBTA stations, for example a newly announced design competition for a massive highway interchange in Houston. Here, as in other cases where funding is for the development of new infrastructure, there is no "community" in existence until construction on the site is completed, so no prior consultation can occur. Alternately, the bulk of public money for construction -- hence for public art -- will go to projects such as transportation facilities or prisons, whose publics do not constitute a community in the ordinary sense of the word. The challenges of commissioning excellent art for such sites will only increase in the future. Accordingly, increased attention must be paid to guarantee due process in the commissioning so that all interests may find adequate expression. The response of future publics must be anticipated as well, through contractual provision for maintenance and even "de-accessioning" of works whose surrounding contexts are no longer supportive.[25]

Over the last 25 years of public art commissions, each of the three parties involved has acquired greater sophistication. First, officials in the commissioning agencies and legislators who enact and administer the guidelines have refined the "due process" according to which such commissions will be carried out. Second, artists who choose to submit proposals for public commissions have developed a keener awareness of the role of the public in public art. Finally, the lay public has acquired greater familiarity and acceptance of public artwork styles and functions. As the Vietnam Memorial and MBTA examples attest, when all have worked together, the result is affirmation: public art can both address current concerns and help its audience to transcend them.

Notes

1. Not all are so accepting, however: among those who strongly disagree is Edward Banfield, in *The Democratic Muse* (New York: Basic Books, 1984). See also William D. Grampp, *Pricing the Priceless: Art, Artists, and Economics* (New York: Basic Books, 1989). Widespread support for their views, resurfacing in the 1990 NEA controversy, has been countered by the growth of regional and national competitions for public art commissions and scholarly work examining the field. Concerning the former, see *Going Public: A Field Guide to Developments in Art in Public Places*, Pam Korza, ed. (Amherst: Arts Extension Service of the University of Massachusetts and the National Endowment for the Arts, 1988). Otherwise, see David B. Pankratz and Valerie B. Morris, eds: *The Future of the Arts: Public Policy and Arts Research* (New York: Praeger, 1990) and Stephen Benedict, ed.: *Public Money and the Muse: Essays on Government Funding for the Arts* (New York: Norton, 1991).

2. *The New York Times*, July 28, 1987, C16.

3. Stephen C. Dubin focuses on both visual artwork and performance artists in his book *Arresting Images: Impolitic Art and Uncivil Actions* (New York: Routledge, 1992).

4. For example, see the "catalogs" of the "NEA Collection": Andy Leon Harvey, ed.; John Beardsley, "Introduction": *Art in Public Places* (Washington: Partners for Livable Places, 1981); and that of the "GSA Collection": Donald W. Thalacker: *The Place of Art in the World of Architecture* (New York: Chelsea House, 1980). In addition, *Art for the Public: The Collection of the Port Authority of New York and New Jersey* (New York: Port Authority of New York and New Jersey, 1985) and Margot Gayle and Michele Cohen: *Guide to Manhattan's Outdoor Sculpture* (New York: Prentice Hall, 1988).

5. Lawrence D. Mankin, "Government Patronage: an Historical Overview," in *Public Policy and the Arts*, 111-140; Helen Townsend, "The Social Origins of the Federal Arts Project," in *Art, Ideology, & Politics*, Judith H. Balfe and Margaret J. Wyszomirski, eds. (New York: Praeger, 1984), 264-292.

6. Karal Ann Marling, *Wall-to-Wall America* (Minneapolis: University of Minnesota Press, 1982); Marlene Park and Gerald E. Markowitz, *Democratic Vistas: Post Offices and Public Art in the New Deal* (Philadelphia: Temple University Press, 1984).

7. Townsend, "Social Origins of the Federal Arts Project."

8. Francis V. O'Connor, ed., *Art for the Millions* (Boston: New York Graphic Society, 1973).

9. Gary Larson, *The Reluctant Patron* (Philadelphia: University of Pennsylvania Press, 1983). See also Jane deHart Mathews, "Art and Politics in Cold War America," *American Historical Review* 81 (Oct. 1976), 762-787.

10. Donald W. Thalacker, *The Place of Art in the World of Architecture*.

11. John Beardsley, *Art in Public Places*, p. 10.

12. Ann M. Galligan, "The Politicization of Peer-Review Panels at the NEA" in *Paying the Piper: Causes and Consequences of Art Patronage*, Judith Huggins Balfe, ed. (Champaign-Urbana, IL: University of Illinois Press, 1993).

13. John Beardsley, *Art in Public Places*, pp. 12, 13.

14. When such acceptance is lacking, the project is withdrawn. See *The New York Times*, March 6, 1981, C42 re: the rejection by the Peoria Civic Center Authority of a Richard Serra sculpture commissioned by the local Junior League, applying for NEA matching funds.

15. Arthur Beale, President of the National Institute for Conservation, at the Appropriation Hearings for the NEA, March 19, 1985, Washington.

16. John Beardsley, *Art in Public Places*, p. 13. Update on information via telephone with NEA Office of Planning, Research, and Budget Coordination, 1 February 1993.

17. Donald W. Thalacker, *The Place of Art in the World of Architecture*, pp. xii-xiii.

18. Judith H. Balfe and Margaret J. Wyszomirski, "Public Art and Public Policy," *Journal of Arts Management and Law* 15:4 (Winter 1986), 5-30; "The Commissioning of a Work of Public Sculpture," *Public Art, Public Controversy: The Tilted Arc on Trial* (New York: American Council for the Arts, 1988), 18-27.

19. Barbara Hoffman, "'Tilted Arc'": the Legal Angle" and "Epilogue," *Public Art, Public Controversy: The Tilted Arc on Trial*, 28-46; 179-184.

20. A subsequent effort to add a statue commemorating women Vietnam veterans has been a matter of controversy because of a proposed memorial to women veterans of all wars.

21. Robin Wagner-Pacifici and Barry Schwartz, "The Vietnam Memorial: Ambivalence as a Genre Problem" (Chicago: Annual Meeting of the American Sociological Association, 1987), 10.

22. *Red Line Northwest Extension* (Boston: Metropolitan Boston Transit Authority, 1985); Richard Wolkomir, "Art Goes Underground in Boston," *Smithsonian* 18:1 (April 1987), 114-127. Interviews with Mary Jane O'Meara and Arlene Sanders, MBTA Arts Coordinators, and with Pamela Worden, Executive Director of Urban Arts Inc; on April 16 and July 14, 1987.

23. Pam Korza, *Going Public*.

24. In the words of one such artist, Siah Armajani: "Public art should not intimidate or assault or control the public. It should be neighborly. It should enhance a given place. The word 'art' in public art is not a genteel art. It is a missionary art. The public artist is citizen first. There is no room for self expression." *The New York Times*, Sept. 22, 1985, p. 19.

25. Barbara Hoffman, 'Tilted Arc': the Legal Angle," describes the New York City Bar Association's Model Agreement for such commissions, and advocates that such contracts include provisions regarding maintenance, alteration, or deaccessioning of the work.

9

The Public Interest and Arts Policy

Kevin V. Mulcahy

The political *cause celebre* involving the National Endowment for the Arts and its support for exhibits of photography by Robert Mapplethorpe and Andres Serrano has called into question the fundamental assumptions underlying public support for the arts in the United States. The degree of public scrutiny is ludicrous for two reasons: first, given the magnitude of the public expenditure (approximately one-hundredth of one percent of the federal budget) and the rarity of controversial grants from among the total awarded, there was little reason for a great public scandal. Second, what should have been a political side show that the NEA could have routinely survived developed into a "kulturkampf" -- used here to mean a struggle over the legitimacy of public support for the arts and the NEA as a public arts agency.[1] After previous congressional reauthorizations and a relatively noncontroversial political record, the NEA should have already passed its "threshold of survival"[2] and been assured of a secure federal government commitment. That this proved not to be the case speaks very clearly about a consequence of the NEA's ambiguity in articulating a public interest in government support of the arts. It also suggests that allegations of supporting pornography are not the sum total of the problems facing the NEA.

The "Kulturkampf" in Political Perspective

Public cultural policy has four reference points that suggest the broader political and administrative context in which the NEA's policies and programs operate.[3] Each of these reference points underscores the publicness of the NEA. First, the NEA's status as a public arts agency; second, the public need to be served by the NEA; third, the nature of political accountability in the public sector; and fourth, decisionmaking processes in the public sector.

To begin, one needs to recognize the implications of the fact that the NEA is a public arts agency not a private, third-party agent of government.[4] In particular, this requires recognition of the NEA's status as a politically accountable governmental entity entrusted with the promotion of a socially desirable goal. Like schools, libraries and universities, the arts are supported because of their generalized, not particularized, value. In other words, it is not just teachers, librarians and professors who benefit from these programs, but society in general or the public-at-large (or, at least, large numbers of the public).

Second, just as every government program must in some way address an identifiable public need, so too must the NEA address a legitimate public need. While this will properly include needs specific to the arts community, the fundamental policy questions must be framed more broadly. How are national cultural objectives to be promoted by the NEA? How does a specific grant enhance the public's artistic awareness, understanding, or productivity. Indeed, even more fundamentally, how are national cultural objectives to be ascertained? Finding the answers to such questions is by no means a simple undertaking; certainly it is more complicated than simply ratifying the demands of the Agency's claimants and constituents. Seemingly, however, this axiom of American public policy-making has not been fully appreciated by cultural institutions and arts advocacy organizations. Other domestic policy areas similar to the arts like higher education, public medicine, and scientific research are long accustomed to justifying their funding in terms of identifiable public goods while also furthering their own interests. By contrast, the various arts interest groups, which lobby the NEA and benefit from its largesse have seemed to assert a special status for their claims while virtually assuming that their self-interest equates to a public benefit. Put perhaps too simply, the cultural community needs to understand that the NEA is not a "national endowment just for artists" -- that would merely be special interest politics. Rather the NEA must address the aesthetic needs of the American public as well as of American artists and promote the cultural welfare of the general citizenry as well as the artistic resources of the nation.

A third observation is a corollary of the above. As a public agency, the NEA is subject to the same kind of political accountability as its administrative counterparts elsewhere in the federal bureaucracy. That this may at times entail a degree of scrutiny and criticism judged by some to be intrusive and perhaps even philistine is an unpleasant fact of political life in a democracy. A lack of a full understanding of public accountability is further betrayed in the description of the NEA as "America's Medici."

Not only is a democratic concept of patronage different from one based on aristocratic rule, but the operative criteria for deciding what should be patronized are radically different as well. The Medici princes were free to indulge their personal taste; the NEA must decide which expenditures of public funds are most likely to realize a greater level of artistic activity and awareness than would be the case under private patronage alone. Like it or not, the infusion of public funds into cultural enterprises empowers the taxpayers and their elected representatives to exercise their aesthetic judgment and not to serve simply as paymasters of the arts. In sum, the democratization of support for culture brings with it the oversight of a democratic political system.

If the NEA and cultural policy are recognized as sharing certain general similarities with other public agencies and policies, a fourth characteristic of cultural policy-making that must be recognized is the nature of the decisionmaking process in the public sector. Along with the censorship issue, the NEA's grant-making procedures have been at the center of the most recent reauthorization debate and both issues have persistently arisen in past NEA reauthorization hearings.[5] Indeed one of the ironies of this "kulturkampf" is that the advisory panels, which were designed to insulate the NEA from political interference, have become the focus of much of the debate. Both adversaries and advocates of the NEA have vested the panels with an importance that was never intended by the enabling legislation of P.L. 89-209. The proper role of panels in the grant-making process as well as their structure, composition and relationship to the National Council on the Arts and the NEA Chairman needs detailed discussion. However, it can be observed here that, if the panels are not a closed-circle of cultural conspirators as has been sometimes averred, neither are they a choir of angels rendering disinterested decisions. Public decisions cannot simply be the preserve of professionals within arts disciplines. To assert the inviolability of such a peer-review process is to profoundly misunderstand how public policies are formulated, implemented and evaluated. In the last analysis, arts funding, like all public funding in a democracy, is a political determination preferably well informed by expert opinion, but subject to public debate, congressional review, and electoral approval.

Finally, without seeming to give aid and comfort to NEA detractors such as Senator Helms and the Reverend Wildmon, it would be a serious mistake to dismiss criticisms of the NEA as simply atavistic. The range, intensity, credibility and impact of such criticism has been too great to be regarded solely as a manifestation on the political fringes. In the minds of many moderate citizens and their elected representatives, the NEA has become labelled as the nation's chief promoter of pornography. Such a characterization is not only outrageous, but, to the degree to which it is given popular credence, it threatens to undermine public support for the arts, to discredit the NEA's past successes, and to endanger the future of public support for the arts.

In sum, what is at issue in this "kulturkampf" is the future of public support for the arts. For its first twenty-five years, the NEA has functioned largely without an explicit national cultural policy. Indeed, many have argued that any articulated national cultural policy would be inimical to the American system of artistic and expressive freedom and would turn the NEA into a repressive "Ministry of Culture." Instead, the NEA appears to have accepted as public culture what were the interests of private culture as defined by the discipline-based panels. The political consequences of not having a concept of public culture, whatever the risks of an "official culture," were manifest in the events associated with the 1990 reauthorization process. When necessary, so specialized a policy as government support for the arts (as with the humanities and higher education) must be especially able to justify its funding to the general public and to demonstrate how its programs contribute to the general welfare.

Clearly, each of these characteristics provides a context for understanding public cultural policy-making and warrants a developed analysis. However, the purpose of this discussion is to delineate how the public's interest in public support for the arts might best be served. Therefore, the focus will be on the National Endowment for the Arts as an administrative agency and on the arts policy-making and implementation processes, rather than on the content of the art forms supported. Arguably, the Arts Endowment might have distanced itself from the Mapplethorpe affair if it could have retained public confidence in its policy-making processes. At root, this would entail compliance with democratic decision-making norms such as equity, fairness, due process, representativeness, accountability.[6] However, a clear understanding of proper administrative procedures seemed not to have been explicitly defined or well explained. Ultimately, serious questions were raised (and not just from implacable foes of the principle of public support of the arts) about whether the NEA had a public mission to serve as distinct from servicing its constituent publics. From that perspective, the NEA itself was the problem that needed to be addressed if its many reluctant critics were to be reassured.

Recalling the general political context in which cultural policy-making has been cast, there are five aspects of the NEA's policy-making process that merit serious evaluation if an explicit public cultural interest is to be articulated.

1. How is the public cultural interest distinguished from the interests of private culture?
2. What organizational structures would best serve the NEA as a public arts agency?
3. How can a representative decision-making process be insured?
4. What will adequately assure public accountability in NEA policy-making?
5. How can public cultural needs be ascertained and which of these needs can best be addressed by the NEA?

Each of the above will be considered as part of an overall effort to define the public interest in public culture.

Public Culture and Private Culture

Public culture is not synonymous with private culture. Put another way, public culture is not simply the summation of the interests of the various private cultural activities. As a tax-supported activity with discretionary authority, a public arts agency represents a cultural purpose that is necessarily distinct from that of a private cultural institution. In other words, an appropriate question to ask of a publicly-supported arts program is not only does it measure up to private standards of artistic excellence, but how does it promote the cultural commonwealth?

In my judgment, this central distinction for making public arts policy has not enjoyed the recognition it deserves among members of the NEA's constituency. It cannot suffice for public arts policy-making to legitimize its grant decisions only with reference to a reputed aesthetic hierarchy that certifies "the best." Rather, grants should be awarded to those among the best that best address a public cultural need. The real issue with the grant for the Mapplethorpe exhibition was not whether some of the photographs were obscene, but what public purpose was the NEA promoting in awarding the grant in the first place?

Government involvement in the arts may be awkward as can be seen in the case of "blacklisting" and House Un-American Activities Committee investigations in the late 1940's and early 1950's. Alternatively, well-intentioned public cultural policies can become controversial as witnessed, for example, by the experience of the General Services Administration with its artistic commissions for federal buildings. Here, as in the case of Richard Serra's sculpture "Tilted Arc," the issue involved the question of who or what community should have a say in art for public places and how these decisions should be made.[7] It was not a case of proscribing an artistic style.

The denial of grants to some performance artists has raised deeply felt fears about official censorship. Receiving a NEA grant is not a seal of official approval (despite misleading claims by both the Agency and grant recipients). Conversely, denial of a grant is not a seal of disapproval or official repression, but merely the exercise of administrative judgment. No one is entitled to a grant; awards are discretionary. Most of the more exaggerated anxieties about government involvement with the arts really involve concerns about imposing an official culture, not fostering public support for the arts.

An "official culture" is a body of artistic work produced wholly or largely with public funds and subject to varying degrees of scrutiny for correctness by the state or the ruling party. Usually, cultural correctness is determined by its faithfulness to a dominant ideology that defines the regime's political and social goals. "Cultural repression" is official action in which certain forms of artistic expression are censored, certain subject matter forbidden, and certain thematic material favored. The stringency with which a political system may enforce its official culture can vary, as can be seen in Stalinist and post-Stalinist Russia; but regardless of such variation, the demands for conformity to the dominant ideology remain very high.[8]

By contrast, government support for the arts in the United States follows a model of public culture. Public support for the arts is neither art for arts sake, nor art for politics sake. Rather, public support seeks to link artistic excellence to the service of the public. The artistic excellence supported should reflect the diversity of cultures in the American heritage and the public served should be both from the arts community and the general community.

In fact, there is very little in the record or in government policy in the United States -- either under the contemporary NEA or the Section on Fine Arts and the Works Progress Administration during the New Deal -- to suggest the workings of an official culture.[9] Seemingly however, the NEA has been so fearful of its official embrace that it has neglected responsibility for fostering public support for the arts in favor of a laissez-faire administration in which the agency effectively ratifies the private culture consensus exhibited within each of its art disciplinary sub-divisions. This description may appear more critical than is warranted or intended. In the Endowment's early years, it was reasonable to enlist a coalition of artistic interests in support of the nascent agency. However, as the NEA enjoyed large budgetary growth in the 1970's and its grants became an important "seal of approval" in the arts world, its devolution of policy-making responsibility to the art disciplines (through the advisory panels) came to look like a "closed circle of cultural cognoscente" practicing "cronyism" in the distribution of the "cultural porkbarrel." More recently this perceived state of affairs was compounded by a prevailing adversarial aesthetic within some arts disciplines that seems to border on political propaganda or seeks to shock through the provocative use of sexually explicit or religious imagery. While these allegations are grossly overstated, such perceptions coupled with the fact that the NEA's administrative procedures were also under fire, made it extremely difficult for the Agency to refute criticism of its processes or decisions. Furthermore the NEA's attempts to deflect criticism did little to reassure the broad center of public officials or a public that was disturbed by deliberately inflammatory images.

The lesson to be learned is that, even after 25 years of operation, the NEA must adapt to changes in the arts policy environment to justify its claim to be a continuing recipient of public funding. It may seem unfair to require the NEA to have to rationalize its public purpose when one can think of any number of other government undertakings or programs that are more suspect and less scrutinized. Perhaps the subjective nature of artistic achievements makes it difficult for the NEA to explain convincingly its public contributions to those outside of the cultural community. Regardless, the NEA's political problems are not likely to go away until it defines what role public support can play as a complement to, catalyst for, and collaborator with the broader private culture.

The public interest that is served by arts policy cannot be determined solely by the recipients of public funding. Many argue that it should be otherwise because of the specialized nature of cultural decisions. However, this is analogous to arguing that defense policy is too complex to be decided by elected representatives and the electorate, but should instead be the exclusive prerogative of military officers and defense contractors. If military spending is too important to leave solely to the users and suppliers of the weapons, then equally, government support for the arts cannot be decided exclusively by the artists and cultural institutions that are its beneficiaries. Similarly, the priorities for public support cannot be simply the ratification of whatever consensus emits from the private arts community. There is a public interest involved in how much gets spent and for what purpose.[10] On a national scale, Congress deals with these issues in the annual appropriations process and in periodic reauthorizations.[11]

While the arts community is part of the public, one cannot assume that its interests and preferences are synonymous with a broader and more general public interest. Certainly, there is reason for wariness about improper government intrusions into any area of individual expression or values. During the 1930s there is some evidence of artists contriving to "paint Section" in order to win public commissions -- that is, conforming to an American regionalist aesthetic and avoiding offensive political subjects.[12] Most recently, it was the NEA's "seal of approval" as awarded by the advisory panels that caused such a furor over the Mapplethorpe and Serrano photographs. Segments of the public became very vocal in their opposition to what they perceived as official sanction for a public art that was they felt pornographic and sacrilegious or, at least, not an acceptable use of their tax money. Some extreme critics would argue that to win a grant it is necessary to "photograph NEA," that is to subscribe to an adversarial aesthetic and to choose subjects deliberately designed to outrage the public. Others have argued that the NEA's preference for the artistic "cutting edge" may discriminate against arts activities found to be insufficiently "avant garde."

NEA panels were expected to avoid the problems associated with some New Deal arts programs by offering advice informed by "neutral competence," rather than politics or ideology. Instead of insulating public funding for the arts from partisan or ideological interference, however, the panels system stands accused of imposing its minoritarian cultural values on the American public. If the NEA is to avoid a future "kulturkampf" it must chart a political and administrative course that avoids the appearance of either imposing a repressive aesthetic on the cultural community or of allowing an unrepresentative culture to be imposed on the American public.

Reorganizing the NEA by Goal

One basic criticism of the process by which the NEA makes its decisions on grants is that the determination is made largely by discipline-related panels. Given the duration of this practice and the role in which the NEA has been cast by many of the most interested arts groups, there is a logic to the evolution of this administrative practice. After all, the major art forms detailed in P.L. 89-209 -- among these: music, the visual arts, ballet and modern dance, theater, opera -- have been the principal beneficiaries of the NEA's sponsorship. Similarly, the growth in arts organizations -- especially orchestras, opera companies, dance groups, and repertory theaters -- is often cited by the NEA as evidence of its success as a public arts agency. However, administration by the various disciplines does not necessarily constitute an ideal system of organization, nor is a summation of these disciplinary interests equivalent to the public's cultural interest or the fatality of the cultural constituency.

By way of administrative contrast, the NEA's twin agency, the National Endowment for the Humanities (NEH), is organized in a very different manner. In particular, the NEH is not structured around its constituent disciplines such as history, philosophy, art history, English, foreign languages, linguistics, jurisprudence. Rather, the administrative structure of the NEH reflects the programs by which it seeks to promote humanistic activities: research fellowships, summer seminars, public programs, humanities education. Similarly, the Los Angeles City Plan for Year 2000 argues that decision-making by art disciplines is inconsistent with the public interest of a multicultural society.[13]

The organization of the NEA is a matter of legitimate debate since reorganization can affect policy processes and outcomes. Organizational structure is not preordained and administrative procedures are not neutral. There is a logic and validity to a variety of various administrative schemes -- geography, goal, discipline -- but each has consequences which must be considered. Thus the organization of the NEA may be a matter of political feasibility, constituency preference, or administrative rationality.[14]

The disciplinary programs, their directors, and the advisory panels have been the bureaucratic bedrock on which the NEA has rested and to which much of its early success can be credited. In essence, this organizational form embodied the NEA's alliance with the nation's institutionalized arts community. During the NEA's early years, it was necessary to allay the initial skepticism of some artists and arts organizations about possible governmental interference with artistic creativity. Later, the value of having a artistic constituency that could lobby on behalf of continued public support for the arts became clear. Reliance upon interest group politics only became manifest during the 1990 NEA reauthorization process.

After initial sparring over the appropriateness of a few grants, the struggle escalated into a full-scale debate over who was the interested public in government support of the arts -- the arts community exclusively or the general public as well. In other words, should public culture be responsive solely to the demands of the creators, performers, and the institutions professionally involved with the arts or is there also a more generalized responsibility to serve the needs of the public-at-large. If the NEA is to avoid being stigmatized as an agency "captured" by the interests that are its clientele,[15] it must be able to demonstrate that it also serves the interest of the general citizenry.

What this point of view reflects is the assumption that public support for the arts must be calculated with reference to the concerns of both interested publics and the public interest. Accordingly, one might want to consider a shift from administration by art discipline to administration by cultural objective. Rather than making funding decisions by a calculus of disciplinary needs or interest group influence, the arts budget might be formulated according to functional objectives that are determined -- through combined artistic, political and public discourse -- to be principal components of a public cultural policy.

At the start, it should be noted that organization by goal is a common administrative practice.[16] The goals proposed here are one possible set that might be used to organize arts policy-making. For example, the New York City Department of Cultural Affairs uses the following funding categories: cultural institutions, facilities services, program services, real estate, percent for art, community arts development, and services to the fields. Alternatively, the Los Angeles plan calls for awarding support for creators, distributors, educators, and institutional advancement.[17] Each of these organizational focusses on broad areas where public support for the arts can have an impact, and elicits questions that can be addressed by both members of the arts community and the culturally-interested public. It can also be argued that such an organization allows for broad public appreciation of and participation in the arts while promoting excellence among arts institutions and individual artists.

While the goals of a national cultural policy are rightly the subject of public debate, basic funding categories, other than those currently employed, might be more appropriate. The 2 I's -- support for arts Institutions and for Individual artists -- and the 2 A's -- Arts development and Arts education -- are outlined below. They represent four general goals that could direct the NEA's present disciplinary programs toward a more general cultural interest.

Institutional Support

The first goal would be to provide institutional support for the basic operational and maintenance costs of selected cultural institutions. This would entail a dramatic change from past NEA practices in two ways: for the first time, direct subsidy to institutions would be generally provided as distinct from project assistance, and there would necessarily have to be some criteria established to determine which institutions would be eligible. As a general rule, eligibility criteria should favor institutions whose activities contribute to some publicly defined good such as the promotion of artistic diversity, participation by underrepresented cultural groups, the preservation of a unique cultural heritage or of a recognized center of artistic excellence. On the one hand, a commitment to broad institutional support would inevitably lead to the need to make choices among worthy institutions. On the other hand, the NEA would be less involved in controversies about the merit or appropriateness of specific artistic decisions. The emphasis would be on broad programmatic assistance in support of the public mission of an arts organization and its contributions to the cultural commonwealth rather than the current focus on specific projects of arts institutions judged primarily in terms of their professional interest rather than their public merit.

Arts Development

A second, and related, NEA goal might be concerned with arts development; that is, a comprehensive strategy for investment in cultural resources. Traditionally, arts development has been associated with specific programs, such as expansion arts, which are designed to foster minority cultural activities. However, a concern with such cultural underdevelopment is only part of what could be entailed with a focus on arts development. The NEA could approximate the evaluation of a comprehensive cultural strategy designed to achieve a complementary relationship between arts centers and their environs and between national and regional cultures. This would necessitate: first, a program of regional planning, whereby major arts institutions in metropolitan areas develop regularized arrangements with suburban and rural communities; second, a policy of cultural symbiosis that would connect high culture (whether established or avant garde) and indigenous cultures (whether minoritarian or regional). Administratively, certain regional centers of artistic excellence could be designated as conduits for technical and capital assistance required by community-based organizations to energize local arts activities and, in turn, broaden the audience base and public support for the cultural centers. The goal would be to provide greater public access to the diversity of cultural heritages in the United States and to the highest standards of artistic excellence within these different aesthetics.

Arts Education

A third possible goal that follows from the aforementioned emphasis on comprehensive strategies for institutional support and arts development is the need for increased arts education. As a cultural objective, for most of its history, the NEA has seemed to have relegated K-12 education in the arts to the periphery of its concerns and to have little interest in continuing or adult arts education.[18] Given the NEA's close working ties with the professional, nonprofit arts world, educational programs may have appeared as an unaffordable luxury or an unnecessary diversion -- in either case, something that was properly the responsibility of the Department of Education. On the other hand, the NEA's allocation of 3.3 percent of its budget for arts education is dramatically less than the 12.8 percent of the NEH budget that it allocates for humanities education or just over 5% which the National Science Foundation allocates to science education.[19] For a start, greater budgetary parity may be advisable. More importantly, the NEA should place arts education within the context of its public cultural mission. In particular, given the importance of early exposure to the arts for adult appreciation,[20] art education may be one of the best, long-term means for realizing the goals of broad access and wide support associated with cultural democracy.

Furthermore, K-12 arts education could offer the means for achieving greater "cultural equity," that is, the right of every citizen to participate as producer or consumer at some basic level of cultural activity and to be exposed to diversity of expressions that is part of the American cultural heritage.[21] In effect, a heightened emphasis on arts education could provide cultural opportunities on a basis that is less related to socio-economic background than is usual with performing arts organizations and even museums. Schools, with their local roots, may also be well suited to relate to minority and community cultures that are typically underrepresented in the professional arts world. A policy of cultural democracy that sought to broaden public appreciation of and participation in the arts could also broaden public understanding of and support for the NEA. Indeed, as a consequence of receiving an expanded mandate for arts education in the 1990 reauthorization, the NEA for a time, became more interested in this area.[22]

Individual Artist Support

The promotion of artistic excellence is certainly one of the most important commitments of public arts policy. The NEA should continue to develop programs that assist the professional development of the arts disciplines and the personal growth of creative individuals through fellowships, project assistance administered by organizations, and artist residencies. However, the question that needs to be asked with regard to individual artist programs is the same as for other cultural objectives: what public purpose is to be served? The NEA cannot function as a general employment or income maintenance program for artists; however deserving and/or economically distressed. Not even the most utopian of budgetary hopes could support such an undertaking and Public Law 89-209 provides no such legislative mandate. Nor can the NEA seem to be exclusively concerned with funding art that appeals to a narrow "cultural cognoscente" in the capitals of the arts world; a National Endowment for the Arts must also be responsive to the need for artistic growth and recognition in culturally lesser-developed areas.

Urging an appreciation of grassroots arts activities is not an endorsement of a policy of cultural populism or for an aesthetic of provincial philistinism.[23] In essence, it is the best that should be supported; wherever it originates. The complexities of such a decisionmaking process strongly suggest that the NEA might want to consider a substantial delegation of this responsibility to the state and/or regional arts agencies. At the national level, the volume of individual artist applications consumes an inordinate amount of staff time relative to the funds to be allocated, the incidence of disappointment is necessarily high, and the potential repercussions of a controversial grant are alarming. State (and local) arts agencies are close to indigenous cultures and emerging talent. Given the past record of these "little NEA's" in administering other public arts programs, such an enhanced role for state arts agencies has a strong potential of success.[24] Not unimportantly, the political fallout of an ill-advised grant would be localized and, consequently, less threatening to the national objectives of public support for the arts.

Panels, Representativeness, and Public Support for the Arts

Discussion of the relation between the organizational structure of the NEA and the accomplishments of its policy goals also gives rise to consideration of the relationship between panel representativeness and the public's cultural interests. Panels, along with censorship, were the focus of major attacks during the 1990 reauthorization hearings. Moreover, as has been discussed earlier, panels (and censorship) have been the subject of persistent attention in reauthorization hearings during the previous twenty years.[25] The root criticism, whatever the particular objections, is that the NEA maintains a system of advisory panels that is exclusive and incestuous, that is, composed of individuals from a small number of cultural centers who share similar aesthetic values and who promote each others artistic interests and careers.[26] Such a characterization of the panels is exaggerated especially since the NEA has after 1990 corrected obvious breaches of conflict-of-interest standards. Nonetheless, it is a criticism with an element of truth and one that is frequently leveled at the peer review process more generally -- whether in the arts and humanities or science and health research. In sum, the charge that the panel system is unrepresentative is not entirely unjustified in the case of the NEA even though not for the reasons that are usually suggested.[27]

If panel members constitute a "cultural coterie," it is directly related to the administrative structure of the NEA by arts disciplines. If there is "cronyism," it is not by conspiratorial design, it is because of the restricted pool from which disciplinary panelists must necessarily be drawn when one is seeking only professional excellence. If there is "decisional bias," it is largely the unintentional, if inevitable, consequence of restricting panels to members of the same art discipline and sometimes even more narrowly to the same art form within a discipline. What needs to be recognized, despite the foregoing exculpations, is that the NEA seems to have been operating on the faulty assumption that its grant-making procedures were analogous to those of a juried art show or a trial jury. Further, as The Independent Commission has further noted, these panels have become more than merely advisory and are in fact, the dominant and authoritative factor in grant decisions.[28] As such, the panels constitute a de facto delegation of government decision-making authority to private and therefore, publically unaccountable, individuals.

Such an interpretation admittedly runs counter to the received wisdom about what has been right with the NEA's decisionmaking; principally, the inviolability of panel determinations about artistic excellence. While an understandable attempt to safeguard the autonomy of culture against "politicization," such a characterization of the decisional process has had the unanticipated and incapacitating result of devolving cultural decisionmaking to unaccountable panels and, consequently, of embroiling the NEA in political controversy. By allowing one (somewhat misunderstood) aspect of its mission -- promoting artistic excellence -- to preempt all other legitimate goals, the NEA has allowed arts policy to be usurped by its advisory panels. That these panels are discipline-based, conduct their deliberations in closed sessions, and have been plagued in the past by apparent conflicts-of-interests, further limits the scope and openness of the grant-making process. That this state of administrative affairs is politically problematic will be elaborated below. The point being argued here is that policy-making by panel has distorted the mission of the NEA as a public arts agency by substituting expert definitions of individual artistic excellence for a public policy that places artistic excellence in the service of the nation's perceived cultural needs.

Peer review is a procedure developed for judging the merits of complex scientific research and technical proposals. In such situations, the only peers available to review are necessarily from within disciplinary subdivisions because the methodologies employed would be inexplicable to anyone outside of that specialty. This is an inappropriate protocol for judging subjective public policies such as public support for the arts where a jury of one's peers must include the concerned public as well as technical experts. It should also allow for appellate political review as well as disciplinary due process.

The juried art show model of decisionmaking is also inappropriate for public arts agencies because its criteria for choice are exclusively artistic excellence and aesthetic innovation. This is how it should be for private cultural institutions whose judgments usually rely exclusively on a consensus of disciplinary experts. The NEA's enabling legislation, on the other hand, has the following criteria for evaluating grants: "substantial artistic and cultural significance, giving emphasis to American creativity and cultural diversity and the maintenance and encouragement of professional excellence." In other words, the claims of artistic excellence should be consequential, but not controlling. Properly, a proposed grant must be evaluated within the context of legitimate public-cultural considerations such as geographic dispersion, aesthetic representativeness, opportunities for public participation, development of requisite cultural infrastructure.

Overall, the NEA, as a public arts agency, might be better served by a system of inter-disciplinary advisory panels, which would bring together a variety of artistic perspectives on a broad cultural objective, and broadly representative panelists, who would ensure some approximation of a public perspective in public support for the arts. Such a panel system would be a natural consequence of goal-oriented reorganization of the NEA's administrative structure.

The recent practice of appointing "informed lay people" to the advisory panels is a step toward a more representative and responsible advisory process. However, the independent lay person should not be cast in the role of a "token" or a "devil's advocate." A truly interdisciplinary panel would have artists from different disciplines, members of arts service organizations, community arts leaders, culturally-concerned members of the public. The goal is a mix of specialist and generalist perspective, interested and disinterested advice, and art professionals and amateurs, artists and arts administrators, arts advocates, art lovers, and art critics. In such an open and competitive process, a more representative cultural policy is likely to emerge. More representative panels would also be an antidote for any tendency toward what political theorist Robert Dahl has called a "guardianship government," that is, one with an over-reliance in policy-making on knowledgeable, but elite, minorities because ordinary citizens are judged unqualified to govern themselves.[29]

In sum, it is not the personal qualities or professional qualifications of NEA panelists (either their judgment or integrity) that is the issue. It is the decisional context and the proper mix of members that is really at issue. The public interest in public support for the arts is best approximated by a decisionmaking process whose members are broadly representative of artists, the arts community, and the public-at-large. Arts policy as a public policy will be most successful as it addresses both, the general cultural interests of the American public as well as particular needs of the various art disciplines.

Arts Policy and Public Accountability

In democratizing the panels and providing for a more representative public culture, the NEA might also enjoy a greater degree of insulation from political controversy than has been the case in recent years. Proposals that may seem laudatory within a specific art discipline may appear less meritorious in the light of an inter-disciplinary perspective or when measured against the public cultural need to be served. Furthermore, lay panelists are more likely than expert/peer panelists to apply something like a "reasonableness test" in evaluating grant proposals. *Pour epater la bourgeoisie* is one of the time-honored rights of an artist in the free marketplace of culture. However, the interests of public support for the arts cannot be well served when public arts agencies appear to support aesthetic values that are seen to be deeply at odds with the moral and religious beliefs of a significant proportion of the public.

In their thirteen-nation study of governmental arts policies, Milton C. Cummings, Jr. and Richard Katz observed that few democratic governments are immune from pressures to control some forms of reputedly artistic expression. "Should governments try to control pornography, which often is presented as a form of 'art'? And how is government to define where valid artistic expression ends and pornography begins?"[30] The authors conclude as follows:

> These are just some of the issues involving questions of taste, judgment, or political censorship and control that governments that support the arts have actually wrestled with. The practice in the countries in our survey has been to give a wide latitude to free artistic expression. But, at some point on a continuum between complete government control of artistic expression and complete freedom for anything which is claimed to be artistic expression, most governments are likely to intervene.[31]

This is not to argue for a publicly supported culture that is constricted or derivative; cultural experimentation will continue as a vital artistic activity. The difficult decisions will involve distinguishing which applicants possessing artistic excellence are also appropriate beneficiaries of public support.

This is admittedly a sensitive issue and a difficult distinction, but it can be argued that it is an obligation that is incumbent upon an agency accountable to the public. Whether an artist receives a grant is a public determination, not a personal right. Nor is the denial of a grant *ipso facto* evidence of censorship or "fascism." Frankly, there is something disingenuous about the creators of confrontational or (in Arthur Danto's phrase) "disturbatory" art expressing shock that the taxpayers being offended may themselves be shocked at such an expenditure of public money. The most culturally radical might take a certain pride in having so outraged the bourgeoisie as to be rejected for public funding.

Excellence is, of course, a prerequisite for any public-supported artistic endeavor. Selecting among excellent applications is related to the priorities and goals of a national arts policy. It is the responsibility of the NEA, pursuant to its legislative mandate, with guidance from elected officials and in consultation with the interested publics, to articulate such policy.[32] In the absence of a general arts policy, each grant decision becomes tantamount to a new policy rather than the implementation of an established policy. For many members of the arts community this basic tenet of public administration has been the cause of some surprise. Yet, Public Law 89-209 is very clear that the ultimate arbiter of grant-making is the Chairman and that authority over NEA policies and programs is vested in the Chairman acting in consultation with the National Council as the statutory advisory body. The panels are informal administrative conveniences created by the NEA for programmatic, not policy, advice and are not legally mandated. Their recommendations on the merits of grant applications are designed to ensure that any grant that will be approved has artistic merit. This is very different from claiming that the panel's task is to define what is artistic excellence and which applications qualify. One simple remedy would be to have the panels present a slate of approved applications from which the Council and Chairman could make final choices.

That very few NEA chairmen have disagreed with panel recommendations has given the impression that any such action is administratively improper and politically censorious.[33] Nothing could be less correct. NEA chairmen are not only within their rights, as the politically accountable executive, when rejecting a grant, they are fundamentally responsible for every grant decision made by the Agency. Nor does rejection of a grant constitute some form of cultural repression: not every applicant qualifies, panel recommendations are not binding, and legitimate public interests can prompt the questioning of a panel's judgment. In terms of formal authority, it is the purview of the chairperson to render final award judgments. Such determinations would possess even greater legitimacy, if they are seen to emanate from an established set of guidelines or principles rather than as *ad hoc* matters of personal pique, private preference, or political opportunism.

In the last analysis, of course, the resolution of value conflicts in the public sector is a political decision. While public and private cultural interests are largely complementary, they are not identical. The adjustment of conflicting interests, which is the essence of public policy-making, is a political activity that requires the leadership of the NEA chairman. As the recent cultural controversies have made manifest, attempting to address the public's cultural interest can generate dissension within the arts community and between the NEA and its cultural constituency.

> Is the primary goal of cultural policy to be of service to the community? Or is it to be of service to the artists? The former conception implies emphasis on expanding access to the arts for the public and providing those artistic services that the public wants and would directly benefit from. It may also entail a capacious conception of the government's role in shaping the development of the arts. On the other hand, if programs are designed primarily to benefit the artists, emphasis will be placed on freeing artists from

the restraints of the box office and mass taste and allowing them to do what they want with fewer budgetary strings attached.[34]

These contending viewpoints point up the NEA chairman's role as mediator between the interests of the arts world and of the public-at-large. That this may not be the most enviable of roles has doubtless been apparent to the recent chairmen. Regardless, it is the essential challenge to be addressed by any one who would assume responsibility for the formulation and administration of American public support for the arts.

Toward A Latitudinarian Arts Policy

Underlying much of the foregoing arguments is an assumption that the NEA would be well advised to reaffirm the legislative intent of Public Law 89-209 which, in my judgement, mandates a latitudinarian approach to public support for the arts. Such an approach would seek to increase the public's access to and appreciation of the diversity of artistic excellence in American society. Put another way, the public interest in the arts requires a public culture that is "elitist" in composition and "populist" in accessibility. By this, I mean to suggest a public arts policy that will remain faithful to the highest standards of artistic excellence while providing the broadest possible access to people from different geographic locales, socioeconomic strata, aesthetic preferences, and cultural heritages.

In conceiving of public policy as an opportunity to provide alternatives not readily available in the private arts world, public support for the arts would be better positioned to complement the efforts of private arts institutions -- rather than duplicate, preempt, challenge, or dictate their activities. Structuring the NEA according to the goals suggested earlier -- the 2 I's, support for arts Institutions and Individual artists: and the 2 A's, Arts education and Arts development -- would require the NEA to consider proposed grants in terms of their contributions to a public cultural interest. Similarly, a reorganized panel system, as has been proposed, would, in its inclusion of a broader array of culturally-concerned citizens, better approximate a representative arts policy reflecting public-cultural goals as well as art-disciplinary interests.

In sum, the goal of a latitudinarian culture would suggest that a public arts agency should be guided in its grant-making by P.L. 89-209's principle of "artistic excellence that is broadly accessible." What constitutes excellence in the arts is primarily a determination of its creators, conveyors, critics, and consumers in the private sector. On the other hand, the promotion of public access -- involving conservation availability, approachability, and appropriateness -- is the responsibility of the administrators of public arts agencies whose decisions (made following consultation with advisory panels and independent councils) are subject to oversight by elected officials and the electorate.

While the term "latitudinarian public culture" is a new formulation, it reflects the original mission of government support for the arts rooted in the bi-partisan consensus of Public Law 89-209. Public subsidy can enable cultural institutions to do what they otherwise could not afford and can encourage them to engage in activities that they might not otherwise consider. Public funds can, for example, make possible low-cost concerts for groups outside of the usual cultural clientele; bring the arts to regions and locales with little cultural infrastructure and to atypical facilities (such as work places, hospitals, custodial institutions); encourage and develop younger artists and art developments outside of cultural centers; educate new arts audiences (both youth and adult) in aesthetic standards and appreciation for the varieties of cultural expression. The realization of such comprehensive goals is a proper undertaking for the NEA which, as an accountable agency, is best suited to provide for a representative procedure in the distribution of public cultural resources.

The balance sought is to have a public culture that is not an official culture. The solution would seem to rest with basing public support for the arts on a policy of cultural pluralism that recognizes the diversity of expressions of artistic excellence and respects the autonomy of artists and the art world, while also respecting the diverse beliefs and traditions of the American people. For the government to sanction a particular artistic style or mode of expression, even with only a "seal of approval," is to risk the official establishment of that form. By contrast, government support for programs that encourage both cultural democracy and the democratization of culture seeks to broaden the scope of cultural activities and the incidence of cultural participation, but does not formulate a cultural ideology. The essential goal of such a public arts policy is procedural not substantive; the government acts as a catalyst to create greater equality of cultural access and participation.[35]

This is not to say that a policy of cultural pluralism is without problems. One of the most fundamental is the question of group representation that has been discussed herein.[36] What publics are to be included in shaping public support for the arts? Also, just how far in advance of community values can publicly supported culture be? Or, for that matter, how offensive can a cultural activity be of the public and the government that provides its funding? In effect, these political questions were involved in the Mapplethorpe and related controversies. Despite these problems an explicitly pluralistic public culture can seek to insure that the broad range of artistic heritages in the United States receive public recognition and funding.

The NEA might want to undertake as its cultural mission the task of persuading the public that there is a societal obligation to ensure that what has come to be regarded as the best of its cultural accomplishments should be passed on from one generation to the next and that a democratic culture would seek to provide opportunities for artistic participation by as large a number of people and in as many different ways as feasible. Dick Netzer voices one aspect of this cultural mission when he argues that "government intervention is necessary to assure more and better artistic production and consumption than would result from unaided pursuit of narrower commercial purposes by artists and artistic organizations."[37] A complementary mission for public support for the arts might be to intervene to guarantee a more varied and accessible range of cultural expressions than would be the case under private patronage and the box office alone. An eventual outcome of such a mission might be also to mitigate the political parochialism that has failed to appreciate the central role that the National Endowment for the Arts has played, and should continue to play, in fostering the country's cultural condition.

Notes

1. Kevin V. Mulcahy, "Government and the Arts: A Symposium," *Journal of Aesthetic Education*, 14 (October, 1980): pp. 48-53.

2. Anthony Downs, *Inside Bureaucracy* (Boston: Little Brown, 1967), p. 9.

3. For well-known treatments of public agencies in the public administration literature, see Frank Rourke, *Bureaucracy, Politics, and Public Policy* (Boston: Little Brown, 1984); Harold Seidman and Robert Gilmour, *Politics, Position, and Power* (New York: Oxford University Press, 1986); James W. Fesler and Donald F. Kettl, *The Politics of the Administrative Process* (Chatham, NJ: Chatham House, 1991).

4. Margaret J. Wyszomirski, "Administrative Agents, Policy Partners and Political Catalysts: Structural Perspective on the Interactions of Governmental and Nonprofit Organizations," *Teaching Political Science* 16 (Spring, 1989), pp. 122-30.

5. Kevin V. Mulcahy, "The Politics of Cultural Oversight: The Reauthorization Process and the National Endowment for the Arts," in Margaret J. Wyszomirski, ed., *Congress and the Arts: A Precarious Alliance* (New York: American Council for the Arts, 1988), p. 69.

6. For a classic discussion of the democratic foundations of public administration, see Paul Appleby, *Big Democracy* (New York: Knopf, 1945).

7. Judith H. Balfe and Margaret J. Wyszomirski, *Art, Ideology and Politics* (New York: Preager, 1985), pp. 5-29.

8. Kevin V. Mulcahy, "The NEA as Public Patron of the Arts," in Judith Huggins Balfe and Margaret Jane Wyszomirski, eds., *Arts, Ideology and Politics* (New York: Praeger, 1985), pp. 69-83.

9. Lawrence D. Mankin, "Government Patronage: A Historical Overview," in Kevin V. Mulcahy and C. Richard Swaim, eds., *Public Policy and the Arts* (Boulder, CO: Westview, 1982), pp. 117-36.

10. On public budgeting, see Aaron Wildavsky, *The New Politics of the Budgetary* Process (Glenview, IL: Scott, Foresman, 1988).

11. Margaret J. Wyszomirski, "Budgetary Politics and Legislative Support: the Arts in Congress," in *Congress and the Arts*, pp. 9-17.

12. For a discussion of ideology and government support of the arts during the New Deal, see Helen Townsend, "The Social Origin of the Federal Art Project" in Judith H. Balfe and Margaret J. Wyszomirski, eds., *Art, Ideology and Politics* (New York: Praeger, 1985): 264-92. For a cultural analysis of Post Office murals during the 1930s, see Karal Ann Marling, *Wall to Wall America* (Minneapolis: University of Minnesota Press, 1982). See also Richard D. McKinzie, *The New Deal for Artists* (Princeton: Princeton University Press, 1972) and Francis V. O'Connor, *Federal Support for the Visual Arts: The New Deal and Now* (Greenwich, CT: New York Graphic Society, 1971).

13. See the report of the Multicultural Arts Working Group, *Our Many Voices: A New Composition* (Los Angeles: The 2000 Partnership, 1991), pp. 13-15.

14. On the politics of administrative organization, see James G. March and Johan P. Olson, "What Administrative Reorganization Tells Us About Governing," *American Political Science Review*, 77 (June, 1983): 281-96 and Lester M. Salamon, "The Question of Goals" in Peter Szanton, editor, *Federal Reorganization: What Have We Learned?* (Chatham, NJ: Chatham House Publishers, 1981); 58-84.

15. On the concept of a "captured agency," see Marver H. Bernstein, *Regulating Business by Independent Commission* (Princeton: Princeton University Press, 1955); Glendon Schubert, "The Public Interest in Administrative Decisionmaking," *American Political Science Review*, 51 (June, 1957): 346-68; Barry Mitnick, "A Typology of Conceptions of the Public Interest," *Administration and Society*, 9 (May, 1976): 5-28.

16. On the different purposes and forms of administrative organization, see the classic study by John C. March and Herbert Simon, *Organizations* (New York: Wiley, 1958).

17. Judith H. Balfe and Joanie Cherbo Heine, *Arts Education Beyond the Classroom* (New York: American Council for the Arts, 1988).

18. Multicultural Arts Working Group, *Our Many Voices*, pp. 23-25.

19. National Endowment for the Arts, *Toward Civilization: A Report on Arts Education* (Washington, DC: National Endowment for the Arts, 1988), pp. 32-33.

20. Paul Dimaggio, Michael Useem and Paula Brown, *Audience Studies of the Performing Arts and Museums: A Critical Review* (Washington, DC: National Endowment for the Arts, 1978).

21. David B. Pankratz, "Toward an Integrated Study of Cultural and Educational Policy," *Design for Arts and Education* 17 (November/December, 1987): p. 17; David B. Pankratz and Kevin V. Mulcahy, *Arts Education: What Role Can Research Play* (New York: American Council for the Arts, 1988).

22. See *The Arts in America 1992: A Report to the President and to the Congress* (Washington, DC: National Endowment for the Arts, 1992), pp. III 1 to 11.

23. See Margaret J. Wyszomirski, "Arts Policy-making and Interest-Group Politics," *Journal of Aesthetic Education*, 14 (October, 1980): 28-34.

24. Kevin V. Mulcahy, "Government and the Arts in the United States," in Milton C. Cummings and Richard S. Katz, eds., *The Patron State: Government and the Arts in Europe, North America and Japan* (New York: Oxford University Press, 1987), pp. 316-20.

25. Kevin V. Mulcahy, "The Politics of Cultural Oversight," pp. 83-86.

26. On the NEA panels, see "Report on the National Endowment for the Arts and Humanities, "Committee on Appropriations, U.S. House of Representatives, 96th Congress, 1st session, Vol. 1, pp. 865-1041; National Endowment for the Arts, *Panel Study Report to Congress* (Washington, D.C., October, 1987); Ann Galligan, "The Politicization of Peer Review Panels" in Judith H. Balfe, ed., *Paying the Piper: Causes and Consequences of Arts Patronage* (Chicago: University of Illinois Press, 1993); Margaret J. Wyszomirski, "The Art and Politics of Peer Review" *Vantage Point*, No. 25 (Spring 1990), pp. 12-13. On panels more generally, see Ruston Roy, "Funding Science: The Real Defects of Peer Review and Alternatives To It," *Science Technology and Human Values*, 10 (Summer, 1985): 74; Daryl E. Chubin and Edward J. Hackett, *Peerless Science: Peer Review and U.S. Science Policy* (Albany: State University of New York Press, 1988).

27. Panels have their advantages and disadvantages. "On the plus side, panels with rotating membership increase the possibility that decision-makers will be in touch with new developments in the arts. They offer a way to bring experts on particular art forms to the service of government....On the minus side, however, panels of artists can act as a kind of mutual admiration society. They share the notable unwillingness of most professional groups to make negative judgments about their peers. The community of leading artists, the pool from which panelists are commonly drawn, may develop their own inbred standards of taste. "Cummings and Katz, *The Patron State*, pp. 361-62.

28. Independent Commission, A Report to the Congress on the National Endowment for the Arts, Washington, DC: Sept. 1990) p.71.

29. Robert H. Dahl, *Democracy and Its Critics* (New Haven: Yale University Press, 1989).

30. Cummings and Katz, *The Patron State*, p. 363.

31. Arthur C. Danto, *Encounters and Reflections; Art in the Historical Present* (New York: Farrar Straus Giroux, 1990).

32. For a classic study of political executives and administrative agencies, see Norton Long, "Power and Administration," *Public Administration Review*, 9 (Autumn, 1949): 257-64.

33. In his first year as NEA chairman, Frank Hodsoll exercised a chairman's veto on 20 of a total of nearly 6,000 panel endorsed applications. This was considered highly unusual. Hodsoll's predecessor, Livingston Biddle could not recollect a single occasion of his having overruled a panel recommendation. See Margaret J. Wyszomirski, "The Reagan Administration and the Arts," paper presented at the 1983 Annual Meeting of the American Political Science Association, Chicago, Illinois.

34. Cummings and Katz, *The Patron State*, p. 366.

35. Kevin V. Mulcahy, "The Attack on Public Culture and the Rationale for Public Culture," in Kevin V. Mulcahy and C. Richard Swaim, eds., *Public Policy and the Arts* (Boulder, CO: Westview, 1982), pp. 52-53; Kevin V. Mulcahy, "The NEA as Public Patron of the Arts," pp. 332-38.

36. Judith H. Balfe and Margaret J. Wyszomirski, "Public Art and a Public Policy," *Journal of Arts Management and Law* Vol 15, No 4 (Winter, 1986), pp. 5-29.

37. Dick Netzer, *The Subsidized Muse: Public Support for the Arts in the United States* (New York: Cambridge University Press, 1978), p. 16.

Index

accessibility 33, 123, 127, 133, 138, 156, 163, 175, 180, 181, 216, 220, 224
accountability 53, 65, 66, 68, 131, 136, 146, 157, 161, 162, 165, 176, 181, 185, 205-206, 208-209, 218, 220-224
Actors Equity 97, 110
advocacy and lobbying 6, 14, 19, 25, 54, 57, 58, 62, 63, 69, 113, 133, 135, 145, 161, 181, 206, 213
  see Arts Advocacy Day
Alexander, Jane 18, 31, 149
American Arts Alliance 16, 58
American Association of Museums 16
American Civil Liberties Union 10
American Council for the Arts 45, 62
American Council of Graduate Schools 113
American Council of Learned Societies 113
American Family Association 2, 69
  see Wildmon, Donald
American Federation of Musicians 89, 103, 110
American Film Institute 151, 156
American Symphony Orchestra League 110
Anderson, Clinton (Senator) 97
architecture 54, 106, 117, 121, 151, 153, 154, 198
Armey, Richard (Representative) 3, 41, 64
Art-in-Architecture Program (GSA) 20, 125, 193, 195
Art Institute of Chicago 3
Artist Trust of Seattle 15
artistic excellence 8, 13, 24, 26, 28, 29, 30, 33, 121, 123, 129, 132, 139, 156, 158, 172, 175, 179, 180, 183-184, 209-210, 214-217, 224
Arts Advocacy Day 62
arts audiences 21, 28, 35, 39, 85, 115, 132, 139, 146, 151, 152, 158, 196, 202, 215, 224
arts controversies (non-NEA)
  Cobb County Georgia, County Commission 18
  GSA Art-in-Architecture 20, 125, 193, 195
  Tilted Arc 64, 196-200, 202, 210
  see New Deal
  see Vietnam Veterans Memorial
arts education 8, 19-22, 26, 29, 34, 27, 38, 48, 69, 114, 126, 132, 134, 139, 151, 159-160, 163-164, 201, 214-216, 223
arts organizations 15-16, 21, 24, 26, 28, 31, 35, 36, 39, 80, 107, 110, 115-116, 121, 123-124, 126-127, 132,133-134, 138, 145-146
Athey, Ron 18

Barrie, Dennis 7, 9
Bartlett, Steve (Representative) 65, 172, 179
Baker, James 158
Bella Lewitsky Dance Company 8
Bellow, Saul 189
Berman, Ronald 180
Bernstein, Leonard 6, 42
Biaggi, Mario (Representative) 174
Biddle, Livingston 23, 56-58, 61, 128, 134, 149, 155-157
  as NEA Chairman 172-175,181
  see NEA, Chairman
Brademas, John (former Representative) 7, 21, 55-56, 60, 63, 68, 170, 182-183
Buchanan, Patrick 13-14, 18, 70, 164
Bumpers, Dale (Senator) 14
Bush, George Herbert Walker (President) 6-7, 13-14, 62, 67, 70
  Administration of 4, 6, 12, 14, 161, 164

Cambridge Arts Council 200
Carter, James (President) 57, 155
  Administration of 24, 124, 158
censorship 4, 6, 10, 11, 15, 30, 43, 45, 66, 67, 85, 157, 160, 180, 207, 210, 217, 221-222
CETA 19-20
Christian Action Network 18
Christian Broadcasting Network 2

Christian Coalition 18
Clinton, William Jefferson (President) 17
　Administration of 17-8, 38, 124

Coleman, E. Thomas (Representative) 6-7, 14
Congressional Arts Caucus 61, 63
controversial NEA grants/applications
　Artists Space 5-6, 161-162
　"Death Masks" 32
　Franklin Furnace 13
　Highways 13
　Institute of Contemporary Art 3, 5
　"Live Sex Acts" 12, 69
　"Piss Christ" 2
　Point of View 70
　"Poison" 69
　Portable Lower East Side 12
　"Queer City" 12, 69
　Scarlet O 13
　"Tongues Untied" 14, 69
　"Witnesses Against Our Vanishing" 5, 161
　see NEA Four
　see Mapplethorpe, Robert
　see Serrano, Andres
Coombs, Phillip 100
Corcoran Gallery of Art 3-4, 41, 73
Corporation for Public Broadcasting (CPB) 12, 69, 125
cultural democracy 33, 45-46, 101, 115, 194-195, 200, 207, 208, 216, 220-224
cultural diversity 9, 22, 29, 33, 38, 45, 123, 130, 158, 173, 193, 194, 210, 215-216, 219, 223-224
　see multiculturalism

dance 12, 54, 58-59, 63, 110, 115, 121, 125-126, 134-135, 137-138, 153, 159, 213
D'Amato, Alphonse (Senator) 2, 41
Delay, Tom (Representative) 64
design 19, 96, 122-126, 134, 151, 154, 199-202
Dannemeyer, William (Representative) 5
Donald, Barbara 112
Downey, Thomas (Representative) 63
Dukakis, Michael 62
Dutton, Frederic 100, 103

Eagle Forum 6
Eisenhower, Dwight D. (President) 91
　Administration of 51
　Commission on National Goals 51, 105
elitism 156, 172, 180-181, 183, 192, 194, 202, 220, 223

Federal Advisory Council on the Arts 51, 106-114
Federal Council for the Arts and Humanities 57, 63, 124, 140
Feltzenberg, Al 7, 162
film 14, 18, 54, 57, 69, 137, 151
Finley, Karen 7
Flanagan, Hallie 81, 85-87
Fleck, John 7
Ford, William (Representative) 170, 174
foundations and think tanks
　Exxon Foundation 159
　Heritage Foundation 158
　Rockefeller Foundation 152, 154, 159
　Twentieth Century Fund 18, 39, 44, 101, 106
Frohnmayer, John 5-7, 11, 13, 23, 45, 67-68, 70, 149
　as NEA, Chairman 147, 161-164
　see NEA, Chairman
Frost, Robert 98, 100
Fulbright, J. William (Senator) 97, 115

Garment, Leonard 7, 45, 53, 68, 152
Goldberg, Arthur 100, 104, 116
Golodner, Jack 110
Goodwin, Richard 111-112
government reports on arts, humanities and culture
　see August Heckscher
　see Independent Commission (1990)
　see NEA Reports and Studies
　see Presidential Task Force Arts and Humanities
government agencies and programs
　Department of Education (formerly U.S. Office of Education) 26, 125, 137, 151, 159, 216
　Department of Housing and Urban Dev. 157
　Department of Labor 26
　Department of State 96, 193
　Department of Transportation 200
　Department of Treasury 26, 77, 79, 92

government agencies and program (con't)
- General Services Administration (GSA) 125, 140, 210
- Government Accounting Office (GAO) 162
- Office of Management and Budget (OMB) 161
- United States Information Agency 125
- Urban Mass Transportation Admin. 200

Graham, Martha 65
Gunderson, Steven (Representative) 7

Hanks, Nancy 21, 23, 53-56, 149, 152, 164, 174, 176, 178, 181
- as Director, Special Projects, Nelson Rockefeller Fund 152
- as NEA Chairman 152-156
- *see* NEA, Chairman

Hansen, Julia Butler (Representative) 55
Heckscher, August 101-117
Helms, Jesse (Senator) 2, 4-6, 11, 41, 162, 207
Henry, Paul (Senator) 6
Hodsoll, Francis S.M. 23, 62, 64-65, 149, 163-164
- as NEA Chairman 157-161, 173, 179, 180, 189

Hopkins, Harry 80, 82, 84-85, 88
Hughes, Holly 7, 12, 76
Humphrey, Hubert (Senator) 97, 108-109

Independent Commission (1990) 5, 7-9, 22, 29, 30, 42, 45, 47, 68, 131, 218
Index of American Composers 89
Index of American Design 89
Individual Artists 18, 25, 53-54, 63-64, 71, 78, 109, 126-127, 131, 134, 147, 150-151, 154, 176-180, 184, 193-194, 214, 217-223
Institute for Museum Services (IMS) 64, 124, 176
intergovernmental arts activities
- Federal-State Assessment Task Force 57
- Local arts agencies 16, 20, 25, 62, 123, 126, 127, 132, 134, 139, 145, 159, 171, 176, 215, 217
- Regional Arts Agencies 15, 123, 217

State Arts Agencies 7, 20, 54-55, 57-58, 126-127, 132-133, 139, 145, 153, 163, 171, 175-176, 182-183, 217
International cultural exchange 35, 57, 96, 121
Isenberg, Max 100

Javits, Jacob (Senator) 63, 97, 108, 115, 170, 196-197
Johnson, Lyndon B. (President) 51, 112-113
- Administration of 52, 113

Kennedy Center for the Performing Arts 19, 23, 51, 55, 113
Kennedy, Edward (Senator) 4, 170
Kennedy, John F. (President) 97-117, 189
- Administration of 51, 98, 99
Keeney, Barnaby 113
Kearns, Carroll 102-103
Kline, Franz 98

Labor policies and the arts
- *see* CETA
- *see* WPA
Legal Issues
- Miller v California 67, 162
- Rust v Sullivan 10, 42
- Tashima decision 17
Library of Congress 101, 122, 125
Lin, Maya Yang 196, 198
Lindsay, John (Representative) 102, 108-109, 115
literature 54, 63, 95, 126, 137, 153
local arts agencies 16, 20, 25, 62, 123, 126-127, 132, 134, 139, 145, 159, 171, 176, 215, 217
Lowell, Robert 98

Mapplethorpe, Robert 3, 5, 7, 9, 11, 32, 44, 161, 180, 205, 208-209, 212, 225
media 21, 30, 35, 39, 40, 126-127, 137, 145, 191, 195
Metropolitan Opera 103
Mills, Robert 96
Miller, Arthur 98
Miller, Tim 7
Mondale, Walter 170
Morgenthau, Henry 79
Moynihan, Daniel P. (Senator) 100, 116
multiculturalism 24, 46, 163, 175, 213

museum 3, 15, 21, 32, 34, 54, 58-59, 115, 122, 124, 126, 135, 138, 153, 177, 216
music 18, 63, 81, 89, 103, 110, 121, 125-126, 137, 151, 153, 213

National Archives 125
National Art Education Research Center 159
National Assembly of Local Arts Agencies (NALAA) 16
National Assembly of State Arts Agencies (NASAA) 7, 134
National Campaign for Freedom of Expression (NCFE) 6, 11
National Cultural Alliance 25
National Endowment for the Arts (NEA)
  agency goals and purposes 22, 25-35, 153, 155, 156, 157, 176, 214-224
  authorizations 6-18, 23-40, 48, 52, 55-58, 65, 68-70, 71, 80, 144-149, 169-185, 198, 205-209, 213-222
  budget and appropriations 2-5, 11-18, 22-23, 37, 47, 52-72, 82, 86-87, 146, 151-155, 169-184, 212-224
  congressional oversight 9, 10, 13, 49, 53, 57, 60, 63, 163, 170, 183-185
  chairman 3-17, 23, 26, 30-33, 127-129, 134-135, 172-181
  roles and responsibilities 149-164, 207, 222-223
  grantmaking 2-37, 47-72, 172-176
    procedures 3, 5, 7, 22, 26, 30, 37, 54, 126-138, 193-195, 207, 222
    record 4-5, 10-12, 15, 31, 47, 65-78, 205-223
    standards 6, 8, 15, 17-19, 52, 171-180
National Council for the Arts 8-9, 13-16, 21, 26, 30, 57, 60, 65, 70, 128, 144, 159, 176, 207, 222
National Medal of Arts 145
  programs 2, 10, 18-24, 48, 57, 61, 70, 124-128, 133-139
  peer panels 3-22, 28, 30-33, 54, 65, 70, 129, 131, 159, 179, 207, 218-220
  reports and studies
    Annual Report 57, 127
    Peer Panel Study 22
    Toward Civilization 22
  staff and personnel 31
  see Controversial NEA

Grants/Applications
  see U.S. House of Representatives, appropriations and authorization
  see U.S. Senate, appropriations, authorization
National Endowment for the Humanities 64, 180, 213
National Foundation on the Arts and Humanities Act of 1965 and 1990 (also known as Public Law 89-209) 122, 125, 144
National Foundation for the Arts and Humanities 52, 55, 114, 165
National Gallery of Art 11-12, 26, 96
National Republican Congressional Committee (NRCC) 5
National Science Foundation 113, 189, 216
National Trust for Historic Preservation 125
NEA Four 7, 10, 15, 17, 32, 43
  see John Fleck, Karen Finley, Holly Hughes, Tim Miller
Newhouse, Nancy 112
New Deal 50, 52, 77-91, 96, 122, 191-202, 210, 212
  Emergency Relief Act of 1935 and 1939 79
  Federal Arts Projects (WPA) 80, 191
  Public Works Art Project (PWAP) 77
  Treasury Department, Section on Fine Arts 77, 80, 87, 89, 96, 192
New School for Social Research 8
Nixon, Richard (President) 97-98, 105, 152
  Administration of 7, 24, 164

obscenity and/or pornography 5-6, 18, 66-67, 162, 179, 180, 182-183, 205, 208-209, 212, 221
O'Donnell, Kenneth 112
O'Doherty, Brian 178
Opera America 54
Orr-Cahall, Christina 4
Oregon Arts Commission 161
other national cultural agencies and institutions
  see Federal Advisory Council on the Arts
  see Federal Council on Arts and Humanities
  see Institute for Museum Services

see John F. Kennedy Center for the Performing Arts
see Library of Congress
see National Archives
see National Gallery of Art
see President's Committee on the Arts and Humanities (PCAH)
see Smithsonian Institution

partnerships
  see foundations
  see intergovernmental
Peace Corps 111-112
Pell, Claiborne (Senator) 4, 21, 36, 55, 57, 60, 108, 116, 155, 170, 172, 178-183
People for the American Way 6, 11, 14, 43
Peyser, Peter (Representative) 170
populism 156, 180-181, 172, 217
President's Committee on the Arts and Humanities 124
Presidential Task Force Arts and Humanities 22, 61, 62, 131, 158
public art 78, 151, 172, 189-191, 200
public funding for the arts 1, 4-5, 7, 16, 83, 91, 122-123, 125, 152, 172, 175-180, 183-184, 190-191, 217-225
public interest 103-108, 116, 130, 145, 165, 181-182, 189-191, 199, 205-212

Quie, Albert (Representative) 174

Radice, Anne-Imelda 14-17, 44, 149, 164
Reagan, Ronald (President) 19, 40, 61-62, 138, 157, 158, 160, 164
  Administration of 2, 61
Regional Arts Agencies 123, 126, 132-134, 139, 150, 217
Regula, Ralph (Representative) 14
Reid, Ogden (Representative) 170, 174
Richmond, Fred (Representative) 61, 63
Robertson, Pat 2
Rockefeller, Nelson 116
Rohrabacher, Dana (Representative) 4
Rothko, Mark 98

Salinger, Pierre 100-101, 105, 116
Schlesinger, Arthur 100-101, 103, 105, 108-109, 112-113, 116
Serra, Richard 64, 196-200, 210

see arts controversies (non-NEA)
Serrano, Andres 2, 3, 5, 11, 32, 44, 161, 205, 212
Simon, Paul (Senator) 170
Smith, W. (Representative) 102
Smithsonian Institution 12, 101, 122
Sorensen, Ted 116
Southeast Center for Contemporary Arts 2
  see Andres Serrano
Southern, Hugh 3, 149, 161
Sprinkle, Annie 32
Stafford, Robert (Senator) 60, 170
Stegner, Wallace 15
State Arts Agencies 7, 20, 123, 126-127, 129, 145
Steinbeck, John 98
Stenholm, Charles (Representative) 4
Stevens, Roger L. 23, 56, 106, 113, 149-172
  as NEA Chairman 150-154
  see NEA, Chairman
Stevenson, Adlai 106
Straight, Michael 55, 155, 174, 177
symphony orchestras 54, 58, 61, 89, 110-111, 138

tax policy and the arts 3-5, 14, 82, 87, 96, 105, 107, 121-122, 130, 146, 161, 170, 172, 177, 181-182, 206, 213
theater 12, 15, 18, 54-55, 58, 83-85, 88, 106, 117, 121, 126, 135, 137, 153, 213
Thompson, Frank (Representative) 60, 63, 96, 97, 102, 108-109, 112, 115, 170, 177-178
Thompson, Helen 110
Traditional Values Coalition 6

U.S. House of Representatives
  appropriations 2, 4-5, 18, 82, 87, 130, 146, 170, 172, 182, 212-213
U.S. House of Representatives (con't)
  authorization 5-7, 11-12, 169-213, 216, 218
  Dies Committee 81, 84, 86
  Education and Labor Committee 102, 130, 169
  Interior Appropriations Subcommittee 2, 14, 58
  Subcommittee on Education, Arts, and Humanities 55, 155, 169-170, 183

Subcommittee on Select Education &
Post-Secondary Education 7, 55, 60,
169-170, 183
Subcommittee on Labor-Management
Relations 169
Un-American Activities Committee 93,
209
U.S. Senate
appointments and nominations 128,
145, 156, 158, 161
appropriations 170, 182
authorization 131, 169-170
Labor and Human Resources
Committee 169
Labor and Public Welfare Committee
29

Verveer, Melanne 14
Vietnam Veterans Memorial 52, 196-202
see Maya Yang Lin

Visual Arts 2, 18, 33, 61-63, 126, 134,
137, 151, 153, 176, 178, 190, 213

Washington, George (President) 189
Washington Project for the Arts 3
Weinberger, Casper 53
Western State Arts Foundation 161
Wildmon, Reverend Donald 2, 69, 207
Williams, Patrick (Representative) 6-7,
14, 42, 170, 173
Wilson, Woodrow (President) 114
Woodward, Ellen 86
Works Progress Administration (WPA)
79-91, 122, 173, 177, 191-196, 210

Yates, Sidney (Representative) 2, 4, 7,
14, 36, 57, 65

About the Book

Robert Mapplethorpe and Andres Serrano are notorious, as much because of NEA support of their work as for the work itself. This is one example of what can happen when politics meets culture, and it provides an appropriate lead-in for the issues explored in this book. As in other policy areas, cultural policies develop within a particular political context, evolve as a consequence of government action or inattention, and affect a variety of publics and interests.

America's Commitment to Culture discusses government support of culture as a public policy area. The book focuses on the rationales underlying public support for the arts and examines the development and practice of government as an arts patron. The contributors explore the inescapable politics accompanying public culture. Surveying the philosophical, economic, legal, and political underpinnings of cultural assistance, they articulate not only government's role in support of the arts, but also consider basic questions for future cultural policy.